SOPHOCLES: FOUR TRAGEDIES

SOPHOCLES
FOUR TRAGEDIES

Oedipus the King, Aias, Philoctetes,
Oedipus at Colonus

A NEW VERSE TRANSLATION BY
OLIVER TAPLIN

OXFORD
UNIVERSITY PRESS

OXFORD
UNIVERSITY PRESS

Great Clarendon Street, Oxford, OX2 6DP,
United Kingdom

Oxford University Press is a department of the University of Oxford.
It furthers the University's objective of excellence in research, scholarship,
and education by publishing worldwide. Oxford is a registered trade mark of
Oxford University Press in the UK and in certain other countries

Published in the United States of America by Oxford University Press
198 Madison Avenue, New York, NY 10016, United States of America

British Library Cataloguing in Publication Data
Data available

Library of Congress Control Number: 2015930645

ISBN 978-0-19-928623-2

Printed in Great Britain by
Clays Ltd, St Ives plc

for
Beaty and Charis
Jas and Silvia

FOREWORD

I HAVE harboured the ambition to compose a verse translation of Sophocles ever since I was a student, when my first love was Antigone. While *Antigone* waits impatiently to appear in a companion trio of "female" tragedies, this volume contains the four "male" tragedies. I have hugely enjoyed the challenge of finding a voice for this undertaking – a register that is not mundane, but also not overblown, and a metric which clearly differentiates speech and song. I only hope that it will prove as enjoyable to read as it was to write!

This is a complete and unadapted translation for the page (or e-page). I have become increasingly aware that, were I producing a version for the stage, I might mould it rather differently: the pre-awareness of a particular space and performers would interactively prompt shifts of dynamic and emphasis. At the same time, I like to think of readers sounding this published script out loud; and would be only too delighted for it to be put on in performance as it stands.

I am most grateful to Hilary O'Shea for commissioning the work in the first place, and to her and Judith Luna for helpful advice in the early stages. Also to Charlotte Loveridge who made it one her first tasks as Hilary's successor to read through the entire draft and offer perceptive comments. And I thank all those at OUP who have worked on the various stages of bringing the book to actuality.

I gladly take this opportunity to pay homage to the scholars and critics who have enriched my reading of Sophocles over the years, and four friends in particular: Colin Macleod, John Gould, Bernard Knox and Pat Easterling. Pat has kindly shown me substantial passages of her forthcoming commentary on *Oedipus at Colonus*; she also commented on a draft of my notes to the play. Her guidance has been, as ever, invaluable.

I dedicate this work to my wife and our daughter who have given me their unfailing encouragement and love and companionship. I add two friends with whom we have shared many delightful and delicious family occasions.

O.T.
2 January 2015

CONTENTS

INTRODUCTION:
SOPHOCLES AND GREEK
TRAGIC THEATRE

Sophocles and his Plays Set in their Times

ATHENS of the fifth century BC is enthroned secure at the core of the
ever-astonishing cultural achievements of Classical Greece. And
Sophocles is enthroned secure at the heart of that, the literary equivalent
of the Parthenon and its sculptures. Yet it would be a serious mistake
to suppose that his tragedies shine sparkling white against an azure
sky, serene, balanced, and freighted with grave wisdom. Sophocles'
plays are deeply disturbing and unpredictable, darkly unrelenting and
open-ended, constantly refusing to stand firm on any consistent kind of
redemptive justification of the ways of gods or of humans. And yet the
man who portrayed so starkly "the turbid ebb and flow of human misery", as Matthew Arnold well put it, was, to judge from what we know of
him, a sociable, prosperous citizen, not at all the tortured soul we might
expect (or even wish for?). But it is simplistic ideas about the relationship between creative artists and their work that should be adjusted.
Arguably it was because he was so firmly rooted in the world of his time
that Sophocles had the strength to take his audiences with him to the
verge of the abyss, and then to return them unharmed to everyday life.

What, then, was that world and that time? It is one of those strange
coincidences that the years of the great "golden" age of Greek tragic
theatre cover exactly the same span as Sophocles' long life; and that they
very nearly synchronize with the period that our calendar marks out as
the "fifth century BC". The first great tragedian, Aeschylus, is said to
have put on his first production in 499 BC, and it is clear that he and his
contemporaries were already producing fully fledged and serious tragedies in the 490s. Sophocles was born during that very decade. If, as I for
one believe, tragedy had suddenly burst on the cultural and poetic scene
at Athens shortly before then, this would mean that the whole enterprise
of Theatre and of Tragedy may have been born only some ten or twenty
years before our playwright.[1]

---

[1] While we know next to nothing for sure about the origin of theatre and of tragedy, it is
much more likely, in my opinion, to have been a sudden and brilliant invention rather than the
product of a long and gradual development. But this is, of course, a much-disputed subject.

Sophocles first put on tragedies in 468 (and won first prize at his first attempt, it is said). For the first dozen years of his career he was competing with the great Aeschylus at the height of his powers; for the next fifty years after that his chief rival was Euripides, who was some fifteen years younger. It would be a condescending mistake to suppose that all the other playwrights of the time were inferior second-raters, but these two were recognized in their own day as the greatest creative dramatists of the age. This was the very period which saw democratic Athens pass through its greatest cultural and economic flowering, and then go on to confront the toils of disease and war. Both Euripides and Sophocles died within a few months of each other, in 407 and 406 respectively (or possibly both in 406). So they did not live to see the Peloponnesian War end with the humiliating defeat of Athens by Sparta and her allies in 404.[2]

The years of Sophocles' maturity, say between about 460 and 432, were the heady years when Athens produced one of the most creative cultures known in human history. With an allowance of simplification, one might say that History, Philosophy, and indeed Comedy were all invented in this very time and place. The Parthenon was built, and many of the finest sculptures and paintings of ancient Greece radiated from this cultural hub. This one city—far the largest in the Greek world at the time, with a population of male citizens of about 30,000—housed, among others, Socrates, Phidias, Protagoras, Pericles, and Herodotus, (a personal friend of Sophocles). And the next generation, that growing up in Sophocles' later years, would include Plato, Thucydides, Alcibiades, and Aristophanes.

Within this prolific era Sophocles emerges as a central and congenial figure—rich, attractive, vigorous, sociable, as well as a great poet. Anecdotes clustered around his exploits, especially his love-life and his table-talk. In the prologue of Aristophanes' *Frogs*, which was put on soon after his death, the comic Dionysus delivers a kind of epitaph: "he was easy-going up here, and is easy-going down there." But Sophocles did also participate in the public life of the city. One year he was an official Treasurer, another (possibly more than once) he was one of the ten elected military Commanders; and late in life in 413 he was one of the ten "Councillors" convened after Athens had suffered military disaster in Sicily.

---

[2] This was not, however, the end of Athens, as it is often portrayed. Nor was it the Death of Tragedy (despite Nietzsche, among others). There was at least another century of creative activity in the theatre; but it was a "silver age" compared with the fifth century—and all too little survives from it.

A genial spirit, then, a famous lover (of both sexes), a good citizen, a model public figure. All this might not fit our preconceptions of the kind of person who should, by rights, produce disconcerting, soul-scouring tragedies. But, just as it took Athens at the crest of its strength and prosperity to create the whole genre of tragedy, it took a man of confidence and security to drive its portrayal of life so far into the dark territories of the human condition without flinching. It is as though he takes his audience by the hand to the verge of despair, and then keeps his feet so firmly planted in the stuff of human resilience that he can hold them back from falling into the black hole.

Such fierce material needed a kind of crucible to contain it. It could only become so harrowing and challenging once the society had produced an occasion to hold it without danger of corrosion. Whether the genesis of tragedy was long and gradual or, as I believe, a sudden invention, its stature as a major art-form in ancient Athens was undoubtedly indivisible from the inauguration of a major festival as the occasion for performances. And it is surely no coincidence that this was founded, or at least became centrally important, at the same time as the first establishment of a democratic constitution in 508 BC, a revolution which (to some extent at least) handed over power to the whole people. This festival, the Great Dionysia (also known as the City Dionysia) was open to all citizens and was held every spring in a large, open sanctuary of the god Dionysus beneath the Acropolis. It was quite possibly the first festival in ancient Greece to be devoted exclusively to poetry, without any admixture of athletics and other such events. There were also Rural Dionysia held in the villages throughout Attica; and serious theatrical performances, far from rudimentary or rustic, were put on at these also.[3]

All of Sophocles' plays were, so far as we know, created for first performance at the Great Dionysia. And right from the beginning they were (again, so far as we know) organized according to much the same programme as they continued to have during Sophocles' time.[4] A first day was given over to dithyrambs, a widespread pre-dramatic form of choral poetry; and then three days were devoted to tragedy, with one tragedian putting on his work each day. This took the form of three tragedies followed by a satyr-play, all performed by the same team of

---

[3] It is even possible that these pre-dated the City Dionysia, but there is no firm evidence for this.

[4] Comedy was added to the bill in the 480s. It does not seem, however, to have made its impact as a considerable art-form before the 440s or 430s.

actors and chorus.[5] These were, as with so many occasions in ancient Greece, mounted as a competition. Quite highly organized conventions controlled the recruitment, financing, and status of the fifteen members of the chorus, who had to be male Athenian citizens (there may have been twelve in early days). In Sophocles' day there were, separate from the chorus, three male actors (not necessarily Athenian), but in earlier times there had been only two. They took on all the individual roles between them, changing mask and costume as needed. The playwright himself was known as the *didaskalos*, the teacher, presumably because of his role in the development and rehearsal of the production.

The evidence seems firm that Sophocles composed between 120 and 130 plays over his long career. Supposing that these were all in sets of four for the Great Dionysia, he will have put on plays for about thirty-one annual festivals, in other words, for about half of all those held over the course of his adult life. And it is recorded that he won first prize on well over half of these occasions. Yet, of these many plays only seven tragedies have come down to us, and no complete satyr-plays.[6]

Most of his works seem to have survived intact until about AD 200 or 300, but after that only the seven which we have continued to be much copied. They were selected for primarily educational purposes. *Oedipus the King* and *Antigone* were always his most famous plays; and they presumably account for the selection of *Oedipus at Colonus* also as a kind of companion piece.[7] It should be emphasized, though, that these three plays were not originally conceived of as a trilogy, nor performed as one. *Aias* and *Electra* were also widely read and performed from early days. We cannot really say, however, why the other two, *Women of Trachis* and *Philoctetes*, were selected.

Scholars have not got very far with locating the seven surviving plays chronologically within Athenian history and Sophocles' career. The only two with firm dates are from near the end: *Philoctetes* was first put on in 409, and *Oedipus at Colonus* only after his death. There are anecdotes which date *Antigone* to 442, but, while that date is not in itself implausible, the stories are probably fictional. Otherwise, internal evidence of

---

[5] Satyr-plays, where the chorus always consisted of satyrs, those undisciplined followers of Dionysus, may have been introduced later than tragedy, but soon became a core component. The plays were set in the world of tragic myth, but outside the bounds of society and order, often entertainingly exploring origins for the institutions of the human world.

[6] We have several hundred fragments from the lost plays, but few are more than a line or two long. It so happens that the largest fragments by far, preserved on a papyrus, contain about half of a satyr-play, *Satyrs on the Track* (*Ichneutai*).

[7] It may also be relevant that Sophocles came from Colonus, a village close to Athens—see p. 212.

style and technique offer little help, except to indicate that *Electra* was relatively late, probably after 420. Scholarly studies suggest, but not firmly, that *Oedipus the King* is later than the other three earlier plays, and may well date from the 430s or 420s.[8] It is more likely than not that *Women of Trachis*, *Antigone*, and *Aias* were all first produced somewhere between 455 and 435, but this is far from sure.

Critics like to detect a progression in an artist's oeuvre, and tend to order works in a sequence from juvenilia to high maturity to "last things". But, apart from the two late works, which would have been readily dateable even without the external evidence, Sophocles generally denies us such progressions, whether naive or sophisticated.

So the four plays in this volume are not related by chronology. In fact, the main feature which they have in common is a central male character who is on stage for nearly all of the play—though *Aias* remains present in the last third of his play only as a dead body. Also all four have a male chorus, two of them consisting of local elders (the *Oedipus* plays), and two of loyal military companions. The other three plays (to appear in a companion volume) all have powerfully central female characters— Antigone, Deianeira, Electra—and two of them also have sympathetic female choruses. But this division of Sophocles' seven surviving plays into two groups is, it should be acknowledged, merely editorial.

Myth and Innovation

We simply take it for granted that Greek tragedies tell stories which are set back in the great "heroic" age, the world that had already supplied the tales of epic for hundreds of years before. But when the Athenians first developed their new dramatic art-form that was not the only possibility; they might, for example, have told stories of gods, or drawn from more recent historical times, the Iron Age rather than the Bronze Age.[9] Yet, from its earliest stages, tragedy settled on the old myths. This seems to have been almost a master-stroke of prescience, a kind of intuition that these would hold almost limitless potential for future development. This capacity is partly thanks to their combination of the realistic and

---

[8] Some scholars date *Oedipus the King* to the time of the terrible plague which devastated Athens in the years 430–427, on the grounds that the plague at the start of the play would then reflect the contemporary suffering. I am inclined to argue the contrary: that those are the very years that can be ruled out for the first performance, because the plague would have been too close to home, so to speak.

[9] Aeschylus' *Persians* of 472 is an example of this, but historical tragedy never became mainstream. Plays about Prometheus are the only known example of tragedies telling of immortals rather than humans.

the fantastic, so that they contain dynamic combinations of high nobility with family strife, of distance in social and political terms, yet topicality of places, cults, and institutions. But another important factor was surely that, if the new art-form was to set itself up as a serious rival to the traditional genres of epic and large-scale choral poetry, it was going to have to challenge them on their own ground. Tragedy's claim was to provide everything that they could offer plus the whole new and unmatchably vivid dimension of direct enactment. It even followed and capped epic poetry by taking on its two core story-clusters, namely the events surrounding the Trojan War and the dynastic struggles at Thebes.[10]

The tragic versions of these mythical narratives had another enormous advantage over epic and lyric versions, one that undoubtedly helped to eclipse them: the potential for invention. The epic poems, especially the *Iliad* and *Odyssey*, were frequently performed in the fifth century, but the words ("text" is a rather anachronistic term) were more or less fixed. Indeed, an agreed wording seems to have been essential for the coordination of competitions held between the performers of epic, the rhapsodes, while tragedy, by contrast, did not have any call to stick closely to previous versions. On the contrary, part of the excitement of the competition lay in finding new ways of manipulating the old stories. Variations, changes, and innovations were positively welcome, provided that they were plausible and purposeful.

So tragedy was constantly making use of earlier versions, but in order to depart from them as much as to follow them. Sophocles provides some good examples of this in practice. Thus, Aeschylus had already, before Sophocles, made a play about the humiliation and death of Aias (called *Thracian Women*). But his suicide there was described by an eyewitness: Sophocles goes to the extreme length of clearing the stage in order to enable a directly enacted suicide scene. Both Aeschylus and Euripides had previously dramatized the fetching of Philoctetes to Troy from Lemnos, but, while both had employed several more characters than Sophocles, neither of them introduced Neoptolemus. This is Sophocles' innovation, and it radically changes the whole dynamic of the play. The most extreme example of innovation in surviving Sophocles is probably *Antigone*: while he may not have invented Antigone herself from nothing, it is very probable that the whole story of her going to her death in order to bury her brother was Sophocles' own creation.

---

[10] Hesiod (early seventh century BC) says the Bronze Age of "demigod-heroes" was wiped out by these two great wars. A key turning-point in tragedy's challenge to epic must have been Aeschylus' *Achilles*-trilogy (from the 490s?), which refashioned the main sequence of the *Iliad* in three plays.

So it was part of the whole strength of tragedy that each play was *not* predictable, neither in its dramatic structure nor in detail of plot. The genre encouraged novelty, though nearly always deployed within the basic conventions of the art-form. So the familiar dogma that "they all knew the story already" is quite simply false: the audience never know what unforeseeable turns the dramatization was going to take. In keeping with this, the myths, while traditional in many ways, did not bring in tow any sort of inexorability or "Fate" intrinsically built into them. It is important that Sophocles was no less innovative, in narrative and in dramatic technique, than Euripides and his other rivals. He was nothing if not inventive.

Delivery, Performance, and Practicalities

The personnel and material resources of tragedy remained, so far as we can tell, pretty constant during the sixty-two years of Sophocles' productive career. So too did the basic formal structure and aural textures of the genre. Throughout there were within tragedies three main modes of vocal delivery: spoken iambics, sung choral lyric, and lyrics shared between chorus and actors.[11]

The plot, the action and argumentation of the story, was predominantly carried by the three actors, though with usually only two of them directly contributing at any one time. Their parts were nearly all delivered in the spoken metre, the iambic trimeter. This was used both for dialogues and for speeches of widely varying length, sometimes running to forty lines or more. The chorus also contributes occasionally to these spoken scenes, but was always limited to a few lines. For these spoken parts they were very probably represented collectively by the single voice of their leader.[12] This is in keeping with the way that the reasoned, argumentative matter of the drama is the territory of the individual characters, not of the chorus. In Sophocles the spoken iambic sections tend to take up about three-quarters of the entire play, as reckoned by the rather crude measure of the number of lines.

Every play incorporated a chorus, a feature which was of the very essence of the art-form. This was a group of singer-dancers whose role belonged within the created world of the play; their identity, whether male or female, was chosen by the playwright, though it was quite

---

[11] This topic will be more fully treated in the explanation of the metres and diction of the translation on pp. xxv–vi.

[12] While this is not totally certain, I have in the translation attributed all such spoken lines to the "chorus-leader".

common for them to be local inhabitants. The primary contribution of the chorus as a group took the form of dance-poems sung in lyric metres, and accompanied by a double-reed wind instrument, the *aulos*. These songs (or "odes") are interspliced with the sections of the play spoken by the actors. They are mostly arranged in stanza-pairs of some ten to fifteen lines, although there are also some stand-alone stanzas. They were all set in complex metres, every stanza-pair unique.[13]

The contribution of the chorus is developed through their role as involved witnesses; it is, in effect, to articulate a group response to the unfolding drama.[14] They are not tied down by the specific individuality and rationality that are intrinsic to the roles of the speaking actors. In a nutshell, the chorus always attempts, by means of its poetic and musical resources, to face what has happened, or may be about to happen. Collectively they do their best to make some sense of the events unfolding before them. They are never silenced or reduced to inarticulacy: on the contrary, they order their responses and thoughts into poetry, song, and dance. This highly crafted re-visioning of the events of the play adds a whole extra dimension to the texture of the dramatic matter, a scope that cannot be reached through the speech or person of a single character.

In addition to the spoken acts and the choral songs, there is a third distinct mode of expression, which may be covered by the loose term "lyric dialogue". These lyric dialogues involve the chorus and one (rarely two) of the actors singing in lyric stanzas, but contributing in widely varying proportions. And there are one or two (occasionally more) of them in every tragedy. Crucially, they are not as a rule positioned in between the spoken acts, as the odes are, but are an integrated part of the action of the play.[15] So they do not stand apart, like the purely choral songs, but are caught up in the main current of events. While they occur in a variety of circumstances, they all come at junctures of heightened emotional intensity, often, but not invariably, of distress. It is as though they break through the constraints of the measured and rational iambic

---

[13] On the difficulty of reaching any kind of metrical equivalence in translation, see pp. xxvi–xxvii. A batch of technical terms has accumulated around choral songs. The first entrance-song is conventionally called the "parodos", and each of the others is known as a "stasimon". We do not really know, however, what these terms signify. The same goes for the stanza-pairs being labelled as "strophe" and "antistrophe", and the stand-alone stanzas as "epodes".

[14] This paragraph is inevitably a personal statement. There has, of course, been endless discussion of the role of the chorus (not helped by a particularly vague couple of sentences in Aristotle's *Poetics*).

[15] They do, however, occasionally come in between the acts in later tragedies: this is to be found in *Oedipus at Colonus* and even more so in *Philoctetes*.

speech (and they do sometimes include some iambic lines within the lyric structure).

Finally, and less distinctively than these three modes, there are occasional passages of "recitative" metres (anapaests and trochaics) which are pitched somewhere in between iambic and lyric. These are usually delivered by the chorus-leader, and particularly accompany arrivals and departures. These intermediate types of delivery are typically used to signal a quickening pace as the final movement of the play approaches.

This, then, gives some idea of the sounds of tragedy. What of the material setting within which it was enacted and heard and seen? Ancient Greek theatres were invariably huge open-air viewing-places with room for thousands, rather than hundreds, of spectators ("viewing-place" is the meaning of the Greek word *theatron*). The actual performance space was a large flat area at the foot of a slope of raked seating (bleachers). All of Sophocles' plays were, so far as we know, composed for the Theatre of Dionysus at Athens, which made use of the slope beneath the south-east corner of the Acropolis.

It used to be given as a fact that the performance space (*orchestra*) was a circle, which was the standard form for theatres built later in the fourth century, such as the most famous example at Epidaurus. Many scholars now believe, however, that back in the fifth century the *orchestra* was rectangular. This is because it has been found that the stone seating at the front was constructed in straight segments; but since most of the seating in Sophocles' day was constructed in wood, it is not unexpected that the stone seating should be in similarly straight stretches. These would still be compatible with a circular *orchestra*, and I am inclined to favour this as providing both a more unified viewing focus and a better dance-space. It also used to be generally accepted that the audience-slope was large enough to seat some 15,000 spectators, a figure reached again by extrapolating from fourth-century auditoria. It now transpires that in the fifth century there were some houses halfway up the slope, which might indicate an audience of "only" about 6,000 (still a lot of people!). But it is not out of the question that some of the audience sat around and above the house-plots.

Whatever the truth of these disputed issues, the basic layout of the performance space, as it is incorporated into the fabric of the plays, is pretty clear and relatively uncontroversial. On the far side of the *orchestra* was the stage-building (*skene*) with a wide central door.[16] This most often

---

[16] The *skene* is very important for Aeschylus' *Oresteia* of 458 BC, but it is not agreed whether or not it existed before then.

represented a house or palace, although it so happens that this is the case in only one of the four plays in this volume, namely *Oedipus the King*. In *Philoctetes* it represents a cave, and in *Oedipus at Colonus* the way into the sacred grove—in both cases the doors will have been fixed open. In *Aias* there is, very unusually, a change of scene, so that for the first 814 lines the *skene* represents Aias' military quarters, while for the rest of the tragedy it is part of the wild, coastal landscape.

Both actors and chorus shared the *orchestra* space, without special differentiation. It may well be, however, that the actors tended to perform in the section further away from the audience. We also know from comic vase-paintings that in the theatres of the Greek West (south Italy and Sicily) there was standardly a wooden stage-platform of about 1 metre high, with steps going up to it. Since this feature is already there in the earliest paintings, from about 400 BC, it is possible there was also a stage like this in front of the *skene* at Athens. There is, however, no clear indication of this in any of our plays.

Scene-painting was being developed in the time of Sophocles, and was especially associated with techniques for representing perspective. It is not known, however, whether the same panels of scene-painting remained in place throughout each year's festival, or whether they were changed for each playwright, or, indeed, for each play. The variety of settings that we find in the plays could obviously make use of specific scene-painting that changed for each one, if it was available (and possibly for the change of scene in the middle of *Aias*). But, even without any play-specific painting, the signification of the location and background and of its entrance are clearly established within each play (with the partial exception of the later part of *Aias*).

There were also two pieces of theatrical machinery, which, to judge from allusions in contemporary comedy, were particularly associated with tragic theatre. One, the *ekkyklema* (the "roll-out"), was a wheeled platform which could be extruded from the central door: its core function was to make internal scenes visible on stage. Within the four plays in this volume it might have been employed to reveal the blinded Oedipus in *Oedipus the King* (see note on 1297ff.), and was surely used to reveal the tableau of Aias sitting among the shambles of slaughtered cattle (see note on 348–427). The other, the *mechane* (the "device"), was some kind of crane used to carry actors, especially those playing gods, through the air, so that they are to be imagined as flying.[17] This device is

---

[17] Divine epiphanies on the *mechane* are the so-called *theos apo mechanes* or *deus ex machina*. The *mechane* is very unlikely to have been used for Athena at the start of *Aias*—see note on 1.

especially associated with divine epiphanies at the end of tragedies, and its only possible use in these four plays is for Heracles towards the end of *Philoctetes*. But, while he is clearly higher up than the mortals, there is no allusion to his actually flying through the air.

To either side of the acting area were entrances, in effect roads, that were visible to the audience for at least several metres (known as *eisodoi* or *parodoi*). These did not have a rigidly fixed signification; but a clear sense of "topography" is still established internally within each play. Often these two directions were dramatically important, usually in significant opposition to each other; and Sophocles paid particular attention to this spatial dimension. Thus, in *Oedipus the King* one direction leads elsewhere within the city, while the other leads to various distant places—Delphi, Corinth, and the mountains. In *Oedipus at Colonus* one direction leads to the protection of Athens, the other to Thebes and the threats emanating from there. There is a particularly telling east–west alignment in *Aias*, sustained across the exceptional mid-play change of scene (see p. 83). The interesting exception is *Philoctetes*: one direction leads to the shore, where the ship that has come from Troy lies at anchor, but, because the play is set in an uninhabited part of the island, there is nowhere except wild terrain for the other *eisodos* to lead to. It will have been employed, if at all, only for Philoctetes' first entrance (see note on 219).

It is questionable whether there were any fixed structures within the *orchestra*. It is conventionally held that there was an altar of Dionysus, but this is far from certain. What is certain is that some plays, for example the opening scenes of *Oedipus the King*, call for a stage altar, but that may well have been a portable painted prop. This is probably also the case with the unhewn ledge of rock in *Oedipus at Colonus*; and the same would go for thrones, couches, and so on, which would be available when called for. These, like all the props and masks, were the responsibility of the *skeuopoios*, the "equipment-maker".

Masks and costumes, where appropriate, will have indicated gender, age, and social status. Special requirements, like Philoctetes' tatters or the blind-eyed masks of Oedipus and Teiresias, were exceptional. There were some conventional portable props: for example, kings carried a staff of authority, military men had swords, and so forth. But otherwise stage props were exploited only sparingly, and this would make them all the more imbued with potential significance. Sophocles made something of a speciality of significant stage-objects that carried power as symbols or tokens within the dramatic fabric. The sword in *Aias* and the bow in *Philoctetes* are the most obvious, but it is worth recalling also, for example, the discoloured bandages that bind Philoctetes' foot, the slaughtered cattle in *Aias*, and indeed the corpse of Aias himself.

The Qualities of Sophoclean Tragedy

What, in the end, is distinctive about Sophocles' kind of tragedy? Is there something uniquely Sophoclean in his world-view, his "philosophy", his whole burden? It has been a standard strategy for approaching such questions, already common in antiquity, to accentuate defining differences between the three great Greek tragedians, especially between Sophocles and Euripides. I am not, however, convinced of the validity of this comparative approach: the three seem to me to have far more in common than they have differentiating them.

Most of the ways in which it has been claimed that Sophocles is uniquely Sophoclean do not stand up to scrutiny. There seems, above all, to have been a desire for him to conform to some model of steadiness or solidity. In a much-quoted sonnet Matthew Arnold thanked Sophocles, "whose even-balanced soul . . . saw life steadily, and saw it whole". But the plays themselves are constantly unbalancing this claim with leaps and twists, both of plot and of ethical weighting. Arnold was nearer the mark when he wrote (in 'Dover Beach') of Sophocles' hearing "the turbid ebb and flow of human misery". And the turbid suffering of the human world is (so far as I can see) no more measured or just or explicable in Sophocles' plays than in any other great tragic literature. Nor are his plays, as has often been claimed, distinctively conservative or especially pious.[18] There is rather more truth to the branding of Sophocles as a "pessimist". Tragedy is not the place to go for optimism in the first place, but it may be true that Sophocles tends to offer less counterbalancing relief or consolation than most tragic drama. At the same time, his plays do not lead towards unqualified despair or resignation: on the contrary, they are in their own way strengthening.

What makes Sophocles great is not so much a life-view or "philosophy" as an intense and unflinching vision of the human world amidst its pain. It is not a matter of world-view so much as of atmospheric clarity, like on one of those days when you can see every detail of far-distant hills. That is to say that Sophocles' plays do what tragedy characteristically does, but with singularly stark power. "What tragedy characteristically

---

[18] The closing lines of *Women of Trachis* condemn the ways of gods to men as fiercely as any in literature. As E. M. Forster has an enlightened teacher put it in *The Longest Journey*: "Boys will regard Sophocles as a kind of enlightened bishop, and something tells me that they are wrong."

does" is an ambitious phrase. I would say that this was (to put it very simply and very briefly): to set up a complex and inextricable combination of strong emotion and challenging thought across a wide range of human experience, in order to reach towards making some kind of sense out of human suffering. The fusion of emotion and cognitive engagement produces form expressed in movement, poetry, and music.

The emotions aroused in Greek tragedy, and Sophocles in particular, go far beyond the cliché formulation of "pity and fear"—although pity is certainly central. Any full account would have to include grief, horror, indignation, disgust, affection, excitement, joy, elation, anguish, helplessness—all of them felt in anticipation and in the present and in retrospect.[19]

As for the range of issues on which Sophoclean tragedy provoked thought, an abbreviated list can do no more than to suggest their complexity and breadth. There are politics—in the sense of living in societies—power, persuasion, war, justice, revenge. There are the family, its bonds and conflicts, blood-kin, marriage, bereavement. There are the conflicts and interactions of male and female, public and interior, power and weakness, love and hate, hurtfulness and protectiveness. Emotions and their causes are thought about as well as felt—their rationality and irrationality, their justification and their harmfulness. Add to all that the workings of the mind, madness, how far motives are conscious, the benefits and dangers of rationality; responsibility, free will, determinism, the extent of choice, the attribution of blame. Tragedy further confronts the nature of truth, relativity, existence and seeming. And then there are the gods and the human sense of superhuman powers, whether they are malign or benign, whether the divine has any sense of justice, whether it can be understood or is essentially incomprehensible.

This amounts, all in all, to a scope that is nothing less than the meaning or meaninglessness of life, of grief, of death. But the best proof of these large claims—the eating of the pudding, so to speak—lies not in my lumbering formulations but in the huge variety of inspirations and provocations that have been brought to birth by later ages in response to Sophocles' seven surviving plays. Since there is no way of doing justice to any particular instances in this context, the point may be made by simply scattering a spread of names from the last 200 years, without specifying their very varied and even contradictory responses. Think of Hegel and Freud; think of Hölderlin, Yeats, Pound, Heaney,

---

[19] I am avoiding the concept of "catharsis", which is not as self-evidently of the essence as it is often taken to be.

Carson; von Hofmannsthal, Anouilh, Brecht, Fugard, Mueller, Rotimi, Dove; Mendelssohn, Reinhardt, Stravinsky, Cocteau, Graham, Guthrie, Pasolini, Jankso. A mixed bunch, to say the least! The point, though, is that Sophocles has meant so much, and has meant so many different things, to such different creative artists and thinkers, and in so many art-forms. He has offered them handles, threads, shapes to hold on to.

If I attempt, finally, to pick out two characteristics of Sophocles that have imparted to his plays such staying-power and such adaptability, it would be these. First, there is the brave, unflinching facing up to suffering, the engagement with "the human condition" in all its darker and more heart-rending aspects. No blinking, no evasion, no palliative. The creative form emerges with such power because there is no blurring or sideways glancing or postponement, no otherworldliness.

Secondly, in the face of this sombre fixity, Sophocles' plays are never reduced to inarticulacy or chaos or despair. They remain strong and engaged even amid the turbid ebb and flow; they find poetry and lyric and heat and light even in the most arctic conditions of human life. The most terrible possibilities are exposed and faced, and yet the response becomes absorbingly crafted words and movements and song. They "face the music" by turning the anguish into music. The sorrows are thus turned into a kind of benefit, and even beauty. Out of apparently meaningless suffering comes meaning and form. And so the viewer is strengthened for pressing on through the experiences of being alive.

THE PRIORITIES
OF THIS TRANSLATION

THESE plays of Sophocles were created primarily, maybe exclusively, to be performed. And, hand in hand with that, they are expressed in poetry, a poetry that was crafted to be delivered and heard in the theatre. This translation is in verse, and tries to do justice to both of those bedrock foundations: it is composed in a rhythmical language that aspires to be spoken and enacted; and the wording seeks to infuse musicality and colour into the dramatic texture as a whole. It has become almost a boast for British translators (though not so much for American colleagues) to declare that their translation 'does not pretend to be poetry . . . , does not poeticize . . .', and so forth. The underlying supposition is that plain prose keeps closer to the original Greek, and that unobtrusive modesty is somehow more faithful. It is my view that, on the contrary, such translations, by turning what is variegated into monochrome, become essentially alienated from their originals. For myself, I find it impossible to do justice to poetry by turning it into prose.

Joseph Brodsky wrote:[1] 'Translation is a search for an equivalent, not for a substitute . . . A translator should begin his work with a search for at least a metrical equivalent of the original form.' I strongly agree, and this means abandoning the safe pedestrian homogeneity that is the hallmark of so many modern translations. Poetry calls for poetry, or, at the very least, for verse.

There are, in fact, two quite different kinds of verse-form within Greek tragedy, and, in keeping with Brodsky's tenet, I have striven for two quite distinct measures in English.[2] About three-quarters of each play by Sophocles is set in the spoken metre of Greek drama, the iambic trimeter, a line of twelve syllables on an iambic base.[3] At first sight this may look remarkably similar to the ten-syllable line of English blank verse, but, in fact, 'short/long', is a very different dynamic from 'weak/strong'. Ancient Greek verse was not stress-based, as is English (and

---

[1] In a 1974 review of versions of Mandelstam.

[2] These metrical divisions, and the occasional third mode of 'recitative' metres, are explained on pp. xvi–xviii of the Introduction.

[3] This consisted of three blocks of four syllables in the grouping of "long or short/long/short/long". The long syllables could be broken into two shorts in places to make a total of thirteen or fourteen syllables in the line.

modern Greek), but was quantitative, made out of syllable-lengths. It
is not easy for us (Anglophones) to sense how the patterning of lengths
of syllables could provide form and musicality, but it is clear that that
is how it was. I have found, nonetheless, that the English iambic is (for
me) still the best metrical equivalent for the Greek.[4] I have set up a pulse
that is basically stressed iambic, but with no regular line-length, and
anything between four and fourteen syllables in a line. Quite frequently
ending a line with a weak syllable breaks up the metronomic regularity
of the iambic beat.

The remaining portions, a quarter or so, of the tragedies are nearly
all set in highly complex and patterned measures, conveniently labelled
as 'lyric'. Most of these were composed to be performed by the chorus
in unified song: they are the 'odes' which come in between the episodes
of the play's action.[5] There are also some lyrics which are shared in
a kind of "lyric dialogue" between actors and chorus, but so far as
metre and poetry are concerned they are on the whole like the songs,
not the spoken iambics. Most but not all of both these kinds of lyric are
arranged in pairs of metrically identical stanzas, presumably sung and
danced identically, even though they can be quite contrasting in tone
and matter.[6] Tellingly, no two stanza-patterns in the whole of surviving tragedy are completely the same; we have several hundred pairs
of stanzas, and every single pair is metrically unique. Complex verses
like this, made for setting to music, scarcely exist in English poetry,
so any metrical equivalent is going to have to be technically very different.[7] Most song-lyrics in English, from Elizabethan airs, to hymns,
to musicals, are organized in fairly short stanzas with clearly marked
rhythms. It is this that is generally what I have gone for in order to
achieve some kind of equivalence.[8] These verse-forms are much sim-
pler than the Greek measures, but they can at least aspire to musicality,

---

[4] I have generally tried to avoid runs of actual blank verse, because it brings such burdens
of association with Shakespeare, not to mention other great poets. I have, no doubt, fallen
into all too many echoes in any case.

[5] Further on the role and performance of the chorus, and on lyric dialogues, see the
Introduction, p. xvii.

[6] These are conventionally known as "strophe" and "antistrophe", but since these terms
mean little to us I prefer to speak simply of "pairs of stanzas".

[7] The matching of the long syllables of lyric to stressed syllables in English is even less
equivalent than with spoken iambics. It has been attempted, and has pedagogical value, but
it produces patterns of syllables that do not carry any recognizable musicality in English.

[8] I do not claim that my verse-forms and rhythms have any direct technical link with
Sophocles' original metrics. I have arrived at them in a rather intuitive way, usually by letting
some English phrases mill around in my mind until they form a ground-pattern on which
to build.

audibility, and accessibility, like the original. More often than not I have also exploited rhymes, or half-rhymes, or off-rhymes, of one kind or another. I have been encouraged by something of a return to rhyming and tight verse-forms in the poetry of our times.[9] And rhyme has been perennially used in popular song of all periods: tragic lyrics were, after all, the popular song of their day.

The dramatic poetry of Sophocles calls for verse in English in order to find any sort of metrical equivalent, but there is, of course, much more to it than that. Above all, what about "diction"? What kind of level and tone and crafting of language is called for to give some idea of the expressiveness of the Greek?

Again there is the basic division between the spoken iambics and the sung lyrics. Aristotle in his *Poetics* observes that the iambic metre is "particularly like speech". This is an important pointer; but, at the same time, it does not mean that the iambic parts are colloquial or naturalistically imitative of everyday talk. The diction of tragic iambics is constantly putting things in slightly unexpected, un-ordinary ways that heighten or sharpen its load of meaning. While many of the lines are made out of everyday words, they are not put together in everyday ways. This is particularly true of Sophocles.

There is also a scattering of higher-flown phrasing and vocabulary, and some word-forms that occur only in poetry. The Greek embraces both the colloquial and the poetical; it positively refuses a bland, unruffled diction. I try to reflect this unpredictability in my translation. While I do not want to produce incongruities which stick out like a sore thumb, I do seek variety of tone and level, and I do not hesitate to use phrases and vocabulary that may surprise.[10] It is a standard negative criticism of translations that they include turns of phrase that are either too low in diction or too high. But this easy complaint is not necessarily valid, because such variability is there in the original.

No one would dispute that the spoken parts of any translation of Greek tragedy should be "speakable". That claim usually, however, means no more than that they are evenly worded and avoid awkward phonetic turns of phrase. I aspire to something more than that. Plain, homogenous lines do not sustain attention: for Sophocles' spoken parts

---

[9] Including by some of the poets I most admire. I have been particularly influenced by Tony Harrison and Seamus Heaney in their versions of Greek tragedies, especially in their use of four-line stanzas—although I do not claim for a moment to be in their league.

[10] Robert Frost and Edward Thomas no doubt lurk at the back of my consciousness as I search for diction and phrasing that is plain language and yet with unpredictable turns and colouring.

to come alive in English some strangeness is needed, some twist, some grit. I hope that my verses will give people phrasings to be accentuated and relished out loud, something to "get their mouth around". I would encourage readers to say the words under their breath as they go along; or, even better, to gather in groups or classes or workshops and perform them out loud.

The sung lyrics are expressed in an appreciably more artful poetic register, and are even harder to capture in an English equivalent. They use a fair few rare and high-flown wordings, often put into quite twisted and artificial phrasings—they tend towards being "difficult". At the same time they still cohere as a challenging train of thought, and it would be a serious mistake to think of them as inaccessible to their Greek audiences. A long and strong tradition of choral lyric at religious and other ceremonial occasions meant that audiences were highly attuned to this kind of language and to its oblique thought-patterns. The lyrics were also undoubtedly audible: the long and expensive rehearsal periods had audibility and comprehensibility as high priorities. So I have attempted to find line-shapes and stanza-forms in English that allow the diction to be, to some extent, rich and strange, while at the same time restraining it from floating off towards the inflated or weird. My lyrics are considerably less challenging and less intricately crafted than the originals (and sometimes, to be frank, closer to doggerel than poetry), but it is some excuse that I have made accessibility and audibility into priorities.[11]

The other consideration to be always borne in mind is the fact that the lyrics of tragedy were originally set to music, and were sung and danced. So musicality, or rather "musicability", is something else to be worked into the mix so far as possible. I have translated in the hope that these versions of the lyrics might one day be set to music and sung. In any case, any translation which aspires to be read aloud should be aiming for some kind of responsive musicality.

As well as these matters of metre and diction, there is the further crucial requirement of performance and performability. Although this version has been made for publication, it still conveys, I hope, the lively theatricality of Sophocles. I have done my best to mould the words so that they are not just compatible with being acted out on stage, but so that they might be positively integrated, and indeed mutually enhancing,

---

[11] Seamus Heaney sent this advice to an American director of his *Cure at Troy*: "I'm devoted to the notion of each word being heard clearly by the audience. Bell-bing it into the ear, then carillon to your heart's content."

with embodiment as well as delivery. I have also, of course, followed the usual convention of adding stage-directions.[12]

Greek tragedies were all-embracing artworks. They inextricably combined poetry, music, dance, movement, speech, and spectacle. No translation can do justice to all of this ever-shifting multiformity, but there is, surely, some value in the attempt.

---

[12] Our Greek text includes none as such. For further explanation see p. xxxii.

NOTE ON THE
TEXT AND CONVENTIONS

THE manuscripts of Sophocles' plays were hand-copied for about a thousand years, and then neglected for much of the next nine hundred, before they were securely put in print at the end of the fifteenth century. It is not surprising that there is a scatter of miscopyings and errors in our few important medieval manuscripts. Nevertheless, the text is largely sound and agreed upon among scholars, and the places where a corrupt or disputed reading is serious enough to have a significant impact on a translation are fairly few and far between. I have generally followed the Oxford Classical Text, but have felt free to disagree with it; and I have raised what I regard as the most important textual questions in the notes to the lines in question.

The two kinds of possible corruption of the text that make the most impact on a translation are, in so far as they can be detected, omissions and additions. Editors maybe tend to be too ready to suppose that a line or lines have been lost in order to explain some minor problem, but it remains true that there are some places where this is the most likely explanation of something that has evidently gone wrong with the text as handed down to us. In those cases where I take this to be the best solution I have added some words of my own to give the gist of the missing words, and have put them between angled brackets (i.e. < . . . >).

Post-Sophoclean additions to the text, usually known as "interpolations", are a much more important matter. Their extent is much disputed, and some scholars believe they are widespread—perhaps 1 per cent or more of our texts—while others insist that there are very few, if any. I am one of those who believe that there are quite a lot, mostly just a line or two in length, scattered through our texts; and that the great majority of these are the work of actors, mostly in the fourth century. This is not at all an implausible scenario, because the plays went through a century and more of being widely performed professionally throughout the Greek world. And we know that the actors changed and adapted the texts, because the Athenians eventually attempted to establish an "authorized version".

The problem is that detecting these interpolations inevitably involves a high degree of subjectivity. The main clue is bound to be the adjudication of problems or anomalies in the text as it is transmitted.

But this method tends to imply that everything that is authentic Sophocles is perfect, and that everything that has been added is second-rate or incompetent. This is obviously a highly dubious business, but there is no avoiding the challenge. I have attempted to make up my own mind on such issues, and wherever I think there is a serious possibility of interpolation I have raised that in the notes to the passage in question. Where I believe that interpolation is highly probable (certainty is impossible), I have put square brackets (i.e. [. . .]) around the lines in question. I would encourage readers simply to jump over those lines.

The spelling of proper names poses a particular problem for any translator. It might seem at first glance that the names should simply be transliterated from the Greek. This would, of course, be closest to the original, but it is in practice over-alienating, because so many of the names have become familiar in adapted spellings. This is most obvious with place-names, such as Thebes for *Thebai*, Corinth for *Korinthos*, Troy for *Troia*, and so on. English has also traditionally used Latin spellings for other proper names. In many cases it would be easily acceptable if these were returned to their Greek spellings, for instance, Menelaos, Philoktetes, Olympos, and so on; the trouble is that there are others which would seem obtrusively strange, and some that might well strike most readers as outlandish. Two of the most obvious examples are Oidipous and Klytaimestra, long familiar as Oedipus and Clytemnestra. So I have (with some reluctance) taken the easy way out and used the standard Latin spellings in nearly all cases. I have, however, slipped in a few unobtrusive hybrids, like Heracles (Latin is *Hercules*, Greek *Herakles*); Iocasta (for Jocasta, Greek *Iokaste*); Teucros (Latin *Teucer*, Greek *Teukros*). There is one conspicuous exception where I have not been able to bring myself to use the familiar Latin/English spelling, and have used the Greek, however unfamiliar it may be at first: Aias. 'Ajax' is, to my mind, too far away from the much less consonantal Greek name (see p. 77, note 1).

There are some other recurrent features which pose particular problems for translators. One is insults and abuse: it is very hard to find equivalents across languages which carry the same kind of tone and level of aggression, not too crude, not too stilted. If only English still used "villain"! Another is interjections, places where characters utter sounds that are non-verbal: cries of pain or grief, but also of, for example, surprise, discovery, or joy. I do not at all go along with those who claim that these are somehow the origin or core of Greek tragedy, but they are there, and they need to be somehow conveyed in a translation.

Modern English is largely lacking in conventional interjections of grief ("alas!" and "ay me!" have become archaic); and equivalent interjections in Greek—such as *oimoi*, *papai*, *aiai*, *iou*, *e e*—do not generally have phonetic matches in English. Some translators resort to the solution of simply transliterating, but to my ear the resulting sounds are over-intrusively alien. In many places I have attempted to use one of the interjections or interjection-like phrases still recognized in English today, such as "ah" or "oh no!", but in others I have thought it better to replace the Greek interjection with a stage-direction, such as "(*cries of pain*)".

Finally there is the whole issue of what textual aids the translator should add to help the modern reader. The most prominent is stage-directions. I have followed the usual convention of including them in italics. It would be positively unfriendly to the reader not to do so; also it would discourage the awareness that this is a text made for performance. At the same time it needs to be stated bluntly that our Greek text has no explicit stage-directions as such. In other words all those included in this version are my own editorial additions. I have aimed to work out the directions of Sophocles' own first performance, and have envisaged them as set within the general space of the ancient Greek theatre, as briefly laid out on pp. xviii–xx above. I have applied the basic working assumption that when stage-action is important in a Greek tragedy it is clearly implied in the text. This thesis (which I have argued for in *Greek Tragedy in Action* and elsewhere) is not, however, above challenge. And even assuming it is justified, modern productions do not and should not (of course) regard themselves bound by it. This means that I have limited printed stage-directions to those which I feel are pretty securely justified (but have not included every minor indication that is evident from the wording). Needless to say, stage-directions can have a very significant bearing on interpretation. I have discussed the most significant, especially those that are open to serious dispute, in the notes.

I have broken with the usual editorial convention by adding scene headings and numbers for the spoken sections, and similar headings for choral songs and lyric dialogues. Most modern editions and translations have no such headings at all; those that do follow an arcane analysis into "prologue", "episode", "stasimon", "kommos" and "epilogue" (derived from a pedantic section of the *Poetics*, which is probably not even the work of Aristotle). These obscure more than clarify; the scene divisions added here may, I hope, help readers and performers to have a clearer idea of the play's construction. I should again emphasise,

though, that they are the product of my own structural analysis, and have no higher authority.

Finally the marginal line-numbers are another editorial addition. The numeration is that of the Greek text, as is uniform in modern editions, which is not by any means consistently matched by the number of the lines in the translation.

SELECT BIBLIOGRAPHY

THIS Bibliography is mainly restricted to accessible works in English, particularly those I have personally found most helpful.

Greek Tragedy in General

P. Easterling (ed.), *The Cambridge Companion to Greek Tragedy* (Cambridge, 1997).
J. Gregory (ed.), *A Companion to Greek Tragedy* (Malden, MA, 2005).
E. Hall, *Greek Tragedy: Suffering under the Sun* (Oxford, 2010).
R. Rehm, *Greek Tragic Theatre* (London, 1992).
R. Rutherford, *Greek Tragic Style* (Cambridge, 2012).
R. Scodel, *An Introduction to Greek Tragedy* (Cambridge, 2010).
O. Taplin, *Greek Tragedy in Action* (London, 1978).

Sophocles

TEXTS

R. Dawe (Teubner, Leipzig, 1975; 3rd. edn. 1996).
H. Lloyd-Jones and N. Wilson (Oxford Classical Texts, Oxford, 1990).
H. Lloyd-Jones (Loeb, Cambridge, Mass., 1994).

BOOKS (WITH CHAPTERS ON INDIVIDUAL PLAYS)

M. Blundell, *Helping Friends and Harming Enemies* (Cambridge, 1989).
F. Budelmann, *The Language of Sophocles* (Cambridge, 2000).
B. Knox, *The Heroic Temper* (Berkeley, 1964).
A. Markantonatos (ed.), *Brill's Companion to Sophocles* (Leiden, 2011).
J. Morwood, *The Tragedies of Sophocles* (Bristol, 2008).
S. Nooter, *When Heroes Sing: Sophocles and the Shifting Soundscape of Tragedy* (Cambridge, 2012).
K. Ormand (ed.), *A Companion to Sophocles* (Malden, MA, 2012).
K. Reinhardt, *Sophokles* (3rd. edn. Frankfurt a.M, 1947; English tr. Oxford, 1979).
D. Seale, *Vision and Stagecraft in Sophocles* (Chicago, 1982).
C. Segal, *Tragedy and Civilization: An Interpretation of Sophocles* (Cambridge, Mass., 1981).
R. Winnington-Ingram, *Sophocles: An Interpetation* (Cambridge, 1980).

OEDIPUS THE KING

Commentaries

R. Jebb (Cambridge 1893; reissued Bristol, 2006).
J. Rusten (Bryn Mawr, 1990).

Articles, etc.

E. R. Dodds, 'On Misunderstanding the *Oedipus Rex*' (1966), reprinted in *The Ancient Concept of Progress* (Oxford, 1973) and E. Segal (ed.), *Oxford Readings in Greek Tragedy* (Oxford, 1983).

B. Knox, *Oedipus at Thebes* (New Haven, 1957).

C. Segal, *Oedipus Tyrannus: Tragic Heroism and the Limits of Knowledge* (2nd. edn. New York, 2001).

J.-P. Vernant, 'Ambiguity and Reversal: On the Enigmatic Structure of *Oedipus Rex*' (1972), tr. in *Myth and Tragedy in Ancient Greece* (New York, 1988) and in E. Segal (ed.), *Oxford Readings in Greek Tragedy* (Oxford, 1983).

Reception

F. Macintosh, *Sophocles: Oedipus Tyrannus* (Cambridge, 2009).

AIAS

Commentaries

P. Finglass (Cambridge, 2011).

A. Garvie (Warminster, 1998).

R. Jebb (Cambridge 1896; reissued Bristol, 2006).

Articles, etc.

D. Cairns, 'Virtue and Vicissitude: The Paradoxes of the *Ajax*', in D. Cairns and V. Liapis (eds.), *Dionysalexandros. Essays . . . in Honour of A. Garvie* (Swansea, 2006).

P. Easterling, 'The Tragic Homer', *Bulletin of the Institute of Classical Studies*, 31 (1984).

A. Henrichs, 'The Tomb of Aias and the Prospect of Hero Cult in Sophocles", *Classical Antiquity*, 12 (1993).

J. Hesk, *Sophocles: Ajax* (London, 2003).

B. Knox, 'The *Ajax* of Sophocles' (1961), reprinted in *Word and Action* (Baltimore, 1979).

PHILOCTETES

Commentaries

R. Jebb (Cambridge 1894; reissued Bristol, 2004).

S. Schein (Cambridge, 2013).

R. Ussher (Warminster, 1990).

Articles, etc.

P. Easterling, '*Philoctetes* and Modern Criticism' (1978), reprinted in E. Segal (ed.), *Oxford Readings in Greek Tragedy* (Oxford, 1983).

H. Roisman, *Sophocles: Philoctetes* (London, 2005).

P. Rose, 'Sophocles' *Philoctetes* and the Teaching of the Sophists' (1976), reprinted in *Sons of the Gods, Children of Earth* (New York, 1992).

O. Taplin, 'The Mapping of Sophocles' *Philoctetes*', *Bulletin of the Institute of Classical Studies*, 34 (1987).

Reception

O. Mandel, *Philoctetes and the Fall of Troy* (Nebraska, 1981).

OEDIPUS AT COLONUS

Commentaries

M. W. Blundell (Newburyport, Mass., 1990).
R. Jebb (Cambridge 1900; reissued Bristol, 2004).

Articles, etc.

P. Burian, 'Suppliant and Saviour: Oedipus at Colonus', *Phoenix*, 28 (1974).
P. Easterling, 'Oedipus and Polyneices', *Proceedings of Cambridge Philological Society*, 13 (1967).
P. Easterling, 'The Death of Oedipus and What Happened Next', in D. Cairns and V. Liapis (eds.), *Dionysalexandros. Essays . . . in Honour of A. Garvie* (Swansea, 2006).
L. Edmunds, *Theatrical Space and Historical Place in Sophocles' 'Oedipus at Colonus'* (Lanham, Md., 1996).
A. Kelly, *Sophocles: Oedipus at Colonus* (London, 2009).

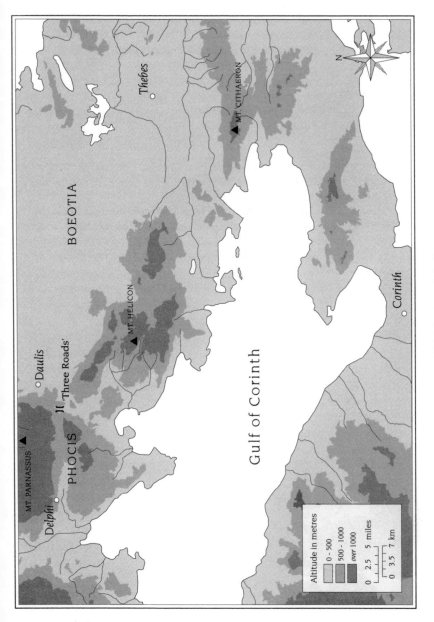

MAP 1 The life-story of Oedipus

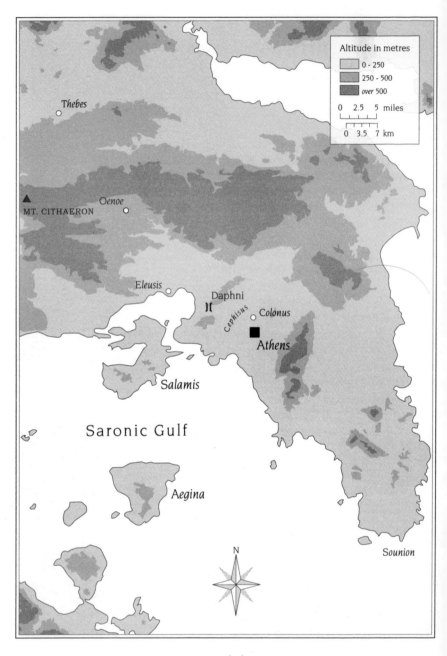

Altitude in metres

0 - 250
250 - 500
over 500

0   2.5   5 miles
0   3.5   7 km

Thebes

MT. CITHAERON   Oenoe

Eleusis   Daphni   *Cephisus*   Colonus
                                   Athens

Salamis

Saronic Gulf

Aegina

N

Sounion

MAP 2 Attica

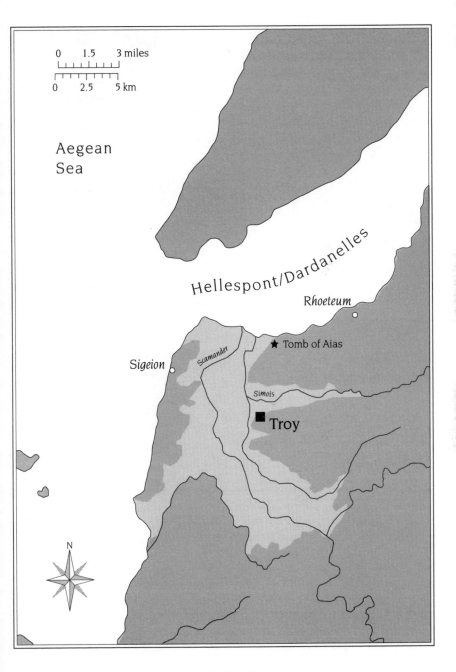

MAP 3 Troad

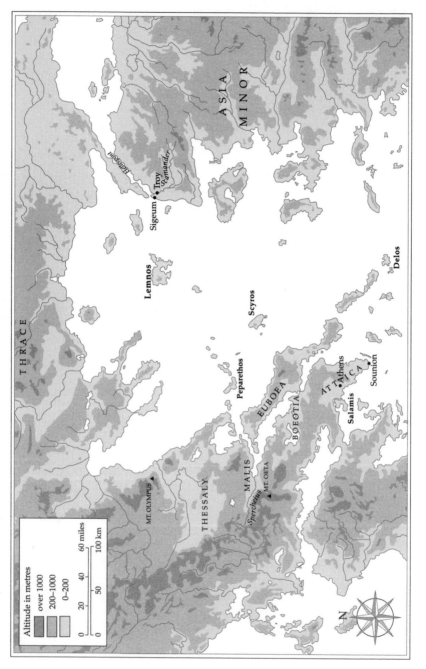

MAP 4 Northern Aegean and Southern Thessaly

OEDIPUS
THE KING

INTRODUCTION TO
OEDIPUS THE KING

Note on the title: in Greek the play's title is *Oidipous Tyrannos*, which in Latin becomes *Oedipus Rex*. "*Tyrannos*" was very probably a subtitle, not going back to Sophocles, added to distinguish this play from his second *Oedipus*, subtitled "*epi Kolono*", "*at Colonus*". Whenever the soubriquet *Tyrannos* dates from, it does not carry the pejorative connotations of "tyrant". While the Greek word did collect a more and more negative usage during the fifth and fourth centuries this depended on context, and in *OT* [the conventional abbreviation] the word is used of Oedipus several times without any censorious associations—it simply means "sole ruler".[1]

Archetypal Tragic Fall

From soon after its first performance *OT* came to be regarded as an archetypal Greek Tragedy. Oedipus' abrupt and total transition from prosperity to disaster epitomizes the tragic fall. He starts the play at the height of honour, power, and fame: he ends it broken, polluted, and powerless. The Messenger sums this up (1282–5):

> Their old prosperity in days gone by was truly there:
> but now, through this one day, there is instead
> lament, disaster, death, disgrace,
> and every ill that has a name—

But the play's extraordinary resilience rests not just on the pattern of the reversal of fortune, but on the how and the why. What does its drama exemplify about the human condition? Over the centuries there have been so many different shots at answers that, while showing how each age brings its own priorities to bear on the artistic creations of the past, they do also reflect the multiform richness of the ancient Greek work.

For Aristotle in his *Poetics*, written about 100 years after the play—and still the most influential treatise on tragedy ever written—its supremacy lay in the way that the handling of the plot aroused the proper

---

[1] The prominent use of the word by the chorus at line 873 is problematic because it does seem condemnatory, at least at first sight—see note.

tragic response (*catharsis*) in those who saw or read it. For Aristotle's Renaissance interpreters it resided rather in the fatal flaw (*hamartia*) of the great ruler, and its consequences: the play becomes a moral story of power, guilt, and punishment. For German Idealism the fascination came from the confrontation between the heroic individual and the constraints of the inevitable: the human will is seen locked in conflict with the higher powers, with Fate. Freud, who coined the term "Oedipus complex" in 1910, detected clues to subconscious sexual desires of all men; according to him, Sophocles divined the riddle of the subconscious and its disturbing secrets. At much the same time the early twentieth-century "ritualists" detected a Christ-like scapegoat pattern; the hero-figure has to be humiliated and expelled in order to save the society as a whole. Then mid-twentieth-century critics, most notably Bernard Knox, under the influence of Existentialism, singled out the individual will set against the pressures of mundane conformity; magnificent self-destruction is better than petty compromise. More recently, ideas about the relativity of values and cultural determinism have promoted socio-political contextualization, setting the aristocratic hero in tension with the anti-individualism of democracy. To these I would add an interpretation, explored on pp. 9–11 below, that *OT* is a gripping dramatization of the way that all humans have necessarily to construct their own life-stories, and how there is always a possibility that they might be terribly mistaken.

Each of these very various viewpoints contains some insight, even though some may claim more validity than others. This very multiformity is relevant to the play's retention of an archetypal tragic power that is still effective. Oedipus himself comes across as paradigmatic because, as all the various interpretations would agree, he is a kind of Everyman. The utter reversal of his life could happen to any man or woman. It is emblematic of this that the place where three roads meet, where Oedipus killed his father, is a specific locality on the "Sacred Way" to Delphi, the route taken by all Athenians and many others (see note on 733–4). As they go past the junction, they might well think, "There, but for good Fortune, go I". That same haunting thought lurks in the mind of anyone who sees or reads this disturbing yet still exciting play.

This setting-up of Oedipus as a kind of model is already inherent in the tragedy itself, almost a premonition of its own future canonical status. In his very first speech he refers to himself as "I, Oedipus, whose fame is known to all the world" (8); near the end he demands to be sent away to "this mountain which is famed as mine—my own Cithaeron" (1451–2). It is implicit in these phrases that he should be recognized, not only within the Thebes of the play but throughout the whole world, as some kind of pattern of the hero and his fall. This stature comes out most clearly in the great choral song that is sung in response to Oedipus' realization of the whole terrible truth about his life-story (1189–96):

> Who can add up, after all,
> happiness in total
> reaching more than seeming,
> and decline from seeming?
> With your fate before me,
> paradigm before me,
> yours, Oedipus, I boast
> nothing human blest.

The Greek word translated here as "paradigm" is *paradeigma*: Oedipus is the model of the fragility of human good fortune.

Tracing and Explaining the Past

While Oedipus himself may exemplify the tragic fall, his play is in several ways *un*typical of Greek tragedy. To begin with, no other tragedy is so obsessed with reconstructing the past. Most are set at the time of the catastrophic turn of events, whereas in *OT* the events have already happened long before. The play is made around their discovery. It is permeated with the language of finding, exposing, throwing light, revealing. The plot is driven by Oedipus' quest to unveil knowledge: first to find out who is the person who killed the former king, Laius,[2] and hence caused the plague; and then, arising out of that and displacing it, the search for his own parentage. So the revelations are disclosed by working backwards from the known world of Thebes, to his killing of Laius, to his childhood, to the journey he made as a baby, and finally back to the house and bed of his parents.

This search for knowledge is even reflected in his name. Traditionally this was derived from *oid-*, meaning "swelling", and *pous*, meaning "foot", a reference to the mutilation of his feet as a baby. This is alluded to at line 1036, but in the play itself there is a more prominent connection made with a different set of *oid-* words meaning "know" and with *pou* meaning "where".[3] Oedipus has to find out and know where he really is.

His life-story *seems* to have been a series of random events and choices which have generally turned out very well; he seems to be, as he puts

---

[2] For the proper pronunciation of this name with three syllables see note on 103.

[3] See esp. 413–15, 924–6.

it, "born the child of Fortune in her generosity" (1080–1). But it turns out that, on the contrary, his journey since birth has taken a very particular shape: his life has been a circle, or, more accurately, an irregular circuit. It began and ended in the same place: the womb of Iocasta. As the chorus express it, with a touch of slightly macabre fascination, " you have made the voyage twice / into one engrossing harbour" (1207–8). And the beginning and completion of his life-route both passed through the very place where the play is set, the space in front of the royal palace at Thebes. He was carried out across here as a two–day–old baby; and he returned triumphantly across that space to become the husband of the queen who lives there in the palace.

Although the whole story is set back in mythical times, the places that it links together were still very real places at the time of its first performance in Athens, and are still much the same even today (see Map 1). So from Thebes, near the southern edge of the plain of Boeotia, the baby was handed to a trusted shepherd to be disposed of "on a track-less mountainside" (719)—this was Cithaeron, only some 15 km to the south of Thebes. And from there he was taken by another shepherd to his home-city of Corinth, some 50 km away across harsh terrain (see note on 1026 ff.). As Oedipus tells at lines 774 ff., he grew up there until, on his own initiative, he went to consult the oracle of Apollo at Delphi. On receiving the terrifying oracle about killing his father and sleeping with his mother, he sets off over land until he reaches the place where three cart-tracks meet, a location that is precisely pinpointed—see the note on 733–4. After his fatal meeting there with the old man, who is in fact his father, Oedipus continued on the mountain road to Boeotia, and so to Thebes. Here he defeats the Sphinx, and as a reward, marries the widow of the recently murdered king.

While there is this compelling shape to Oedipus' life-story, that does not necessarily mean that is all the work of higher powers imposing their will on helpless human pawns. There are, however, features of Sophocles' fashioning of the myth that have encouraged a widespread notion that Greek tragedy, and *OT* in particular, is all about Fate with a capital F. To put it simply (too simply to do justice to some of the highly metaphysical discussions), this approach maintains that everything is predetermined, either by the gods or by other inscrutable powers; and the point of the tragedy lies in watching the struggling humans act out what has to be. Oedipus is then seen as the supreme exemplar of this cosmic condition: he is a great man, who heroically defies his fate, and refuses to be crushed by it—even though he can still never avoid it in the end.

It is true that the oracle given to Laius has predicted Oedipus' deeds of patricide and incest before he is even born; and the prediction is reiterated when he consults the oracle himself. But, quite apart from the possible fallibility of oracles, or their possible non-literal meaning, this is far from predetermination in any sense that bears on the actual acting out of the tragedy. Fate is not an agent, and does not intervene to make things happen. Conversely, humans in tragedy are not seen as puppets or some kind of "automata" acting out the determinations of higher powers.[4] They are portrayed as free agents, making their own decisions and choices, working out their own destinies, as best they can. Laius and Iocasta choose to expose the baby; the shepherd chooses to spare it ("I did it out of pity, master", 1178). It was of Oedipus' own volition that he went to Delphi, that he did not give way before the old man where three roads meet, that he faced the Sphinx, became king of Thebes . . . And so forth. None of the characters behaves like a puppet, or someone who is not in control of their own decisions and actions.[5]

Humans live their own lives, then, with only rare interventions or interferences from outside superhuman powers. And yet they always (of course) end up doing what the gods have determined, or the oracles have foretold, or the curses have called down. And in tragedy—unlike mundane reality—oracles, seers, dreams, curses, and suchlike always prove to be valid. So it creates a world in which it makes sense to say that human affairs are "double-determined" or "overdetermined"; that while the two (or more) causations interact to some extent, one does not subsume the other(s).

The gods are not what *make* the humans act as they do. Fate is a way of seeing things in the long term, a perspective that the gods have all along. The gods have decided or know what will happen in advance. So with the passing of time they can watch things fall into place; they sometimes give hints and glimpses to humans through oracles, omens, and so on. Meanwhile humans have to get on with their lives, and make decisions as best they can, trying to take into account any hints they may have received from the gods. But it is only with *hindsight*, after it has all happened, that humans can see how things have fallen into place; how, if seen from certain angles, events have made patterns. Thus, once the truth has been exposed, Oedipus can say, "Apollo, friends, Apollo / it was made my fate grow / ill, so ill" (1329–30). But he has still lived his own life, and, even at this terrible moment, he insists that it was his

---

[4] Except when they are specifically maddened or possessed—the exception that proves the rule.

[5] The nearest to an exception is two phrases in the messenger's account of Oedipus' behaviour inside the palace after discovering the truth—see note on 1258–61.

own decision to blind himself—he was not being controlled by any other power: "but my own hand, / no other, struck and made me blind."

With hindsight, once everything has fallen into place, this may be seen as a kind of shape; but, as the events were being enacted, there was no malign manipulation at work. The agents acted in completely human and understandable ways. Only when the whole truth has been pieced together does it appear instead to be a horrible nexus of "Fate".

Justice? Misfortune?

Granted that the humans make their own decisions, and are not manipulated by higher powers, then that surely entails that they are entitled to credit where credit is due, and that they have to take responsibility and blame for the things they do wrong. That is indeed, in my view, the general state of affairs in Greek tragedy. Does that mean, then, that *OT* is a story of a downfall that is deserved, even maybe an exemplary enactment of divine justice?

This kind of moralizing explanation has been widely embraced as a way of palliating the grim downward trajectory of the play. It has been supposed, especially in the early modern period, that Aristotle's term *hamartia* authorized this view; and, whether or not Aristotle meant his term to be moralizing (or rather, signifying a morally neutral though still disastrous mistake), the crime-and-punishment pattern of storytelling has inevitably been a powerful influence. So *OT* has been claimed to exemplify how '*hybris*' precedes a fall.[6] Some justify this by asserting that Oedipus has committed a damning crime, such as killing the old man he met at the three-roads, or recklessly defying the prediction of the oracle. Others have claimed that he has a fatal flaw, such as haughty pride, or tyrannical hunger for power,[7] or even a wilful failure to recognize the obvious. And this, they claim, justifies the gods in bringing him down, imparting to the tragedy a satisfying shape and meaning.

Oedipus is, granted, not wholly innocent. He has killed strangers, even if arguably in self-defence. And he is undeniably hasty in becoming suspicious and angry. Most notably, he furiously and falsely accuses both Tiresias and Creon of conspiring against his rule. But this is surely

---

[6] The word *hybris* is never used directly of Oedipus in the play, although it does occur in the prominent but difficult choral passage at line 873—see note. Modern scholarship interprets *hybris* as meaning, not reckless defiance of divine power, but something more like high-handed behaviour aimed at arbitrarily humiliating others, human or divine.

[7] It would a mistake to seize on the word *tyrannos*, which is used of Oedipus several times—see the preliminary note on the title above.

not enough to explain or justify his downfall. His strong and passionate temperament, and his insecurity in his power, are both characteristics that are essential for making the whole story convincing: it takes
a man of this sort to have achieved what he has. As Creon says when he
delivers a shrewd parting-shot, "you are oppressive when you go too far
in anger" (673–4). This is true, but it does not amount to *hybris* in any
sense of the word; and it is not "crime" enough to deserve the "punishment". Oedipus is not innocent, but he is not presented by Sophocles as
guilty of any outstandingly heinous fault. It is not his faults that give the
tragedy its momentum.

There are some more far-fetched theories of how Oedipus is culpable.
It has been claimed, for example, that his crime is stupidity, because he
should have put two and two together long before, and thus avoided
at least some of the disasters. And there have been "conspiracy" theories that say that he has known the truth of the situation all along,
either consciously, in which case he has unscrupulously concealed it, or
unconsciously, in a state of denial. But all such constructs are built on
a "who–done-it?" approach which puts the pieces of evidence together
in a completely different way and different order from the play itself.
Sophocles has skilfully constructed the sequence and the human
responses in such a way as to make it entirely convincing that Oedipus
does not see the truth sooner.

If, then, the tragedy is not driven by Fate or the gods, and if it is not
a story of crime and punishment either, what do Oedipus' quest and
its consequences exemplify? The answer to this is (in my view) that he
epitomizes the random vulnerability of human fortune, the fragility of
the assumptions that make life prosper. The play does this by bringing
out how humans (universally or almost universally, it may be claimed)
necessarily construct life-stories for themselves, and how there is
always the possibility that that story—our own story—may be terribly
mistaken. There are innumerable features of any individual's situation
which constantly have to be taken on trust in order to get on with life—
foundations, "givens", to do with place and time and relationships and
social contexts. People could not daily distrust these "givens" and still
get on with the business of living.

Yet not all of the elements of any particular person's story are invul-
nerable certainties. Most, if asked to enumerate the basic "givens" of
their life-story, would begin with who their parents were, where they
grew up, how they moved towards their present place and way of life,
who are their most trusted nearest-and-dearest. Oedipus exemplifies
this when he has to give an account of his past at lines 774 ff. From his

more recent past certain fixtures are taken for granted from the start of the play: he arrived in Thebes as a stranger, he overcame the Sphinx, he became the husband of Iocasta, he enjoys great power and respect in the city, and so forth. For most people, for nearly all the time, "facts" like these are facts and remain secure, undisturbed.

At the same time, everyone knows on some level that some features of our individual life-stories are vulnerable, that they may unfortunately turn wrong on us. The assumption of good health might, to take the least uncommon example, turn out to be unjustified. Or one's trust in someone close may be betrayed. Occasionally people even discover that a certain family relation is not actually genetic kin, or that the usual story about some member of the family is a fabrication. We are, at some level of consciousness, braced for single eventualities like these, traumatic though it would still be to discover any such unsuspected turn.

But it is very difficult for anyone to contemplate the possibility, however remote, that their own life-story is fundamentally mistaken from top to bottom, that it is a house of cards. If this were to be suggested, the first and quite rational response would be for the person to attempt to show that the challenge to their assumptions is mistaken. This is what we see Oedipus doing in *OT*. And, given the "dramatic irony" of knowing better than he does, we, the audience, watch with a growing sense of ominous anticipation. Oedipus rejects Tiresias as a corrupt fraud (wrong, but not unthinkable); Creon must be implicated; the insult about his father is imputed to drunkenness; Laius was, allegedly, killed by a gang, so not by him . . . Once the old Corinthian has added the startling new information about his parentage, Oedipus jumps to the conclusion that he is low-born; Iocasta's distress is put down to her snobbery about his pedigree. By the time that the old slave of Laius arrives, Oedipus has only a fragile membrane of evasions stretched between him and the truth. But he still stands by this while the facts press ever more heavily against it: as a baby he came from Thebes . . . but was not the shepherd's own child . . . from the house of Laius . . . from the hands of Iocasta . . . because of the prophesies . . . . The final pieces in the reconstruction of his history break the membrane; or, to use another metaphor, they pull out the cards that have been holding up the whole edifice. The realization of the truth is not gradual: suddenly, in one terrible moment, Oedipus sees that his secure life-story has been totally and utterly mistaken, and that there is another, quite different set of explanations for everything that he has founded his life upon.

Fortunately such radical overturning of basic life-assumptions is rarely demanded from anybody. But it remains a remote possibility; and some people do have to face drastic, even if not such total, revisions of how they see the whole course of their life. Oedipus is the extreme example, made more extreme by being a man of great fortune and power and prosperity. His own self-assessment is thus diametrically wrong (1080–3):

> . . . I regard myself as born
> the child of Fortune in her generosity,
> and I shall never be demeaned by that.
> She is my mother; and the Months, my brothers,
> have delineated me as humble, then as great.

He is indeed the child of Fortune, as we all are, but in his case it is an ungenerous Fortune; and the passage of time marks him out as high and then as low, not the other way round.

The Puzzle of the Ending

There remains an as-yet unresolved dispute about significance of the conclusion of the play, and even about whether we have Sophocles' original ending or a later tampering. There is a worrying cluster of textual and dramaturgical problems in the last 100 lines of our play,[8] but it is not these that are cause for concern so much as the contradiction of a whole series of pointers to a different final dispensation. These crop up first in three prophetic riddles posed by Tiresias, riddles that are not fully resolved, or, rather, are frustrated. First he predicts that (417–18):

> . . . the fearful-footed curse
> from mother and from father shall
> with double spike expel you from this land.

He goes on to specify Mount Cithaeron as Oedipus' eventual destination (420–1):

> There is no anchorage,
> no hollow of Cithaeron's mountainside
> that shall not resonate in echo to your cry . . .

And thirdly in his last speech he makes predictions about the person whom Oedipus is searching for (454–6):

> From someone who has sight he shall turn blind,
> from someone rich become a beggar,

---

[8] The main problems are listed in the note on 1416 ff.

and then he'll make his way towards an alien land
by probing for his footsteps with a stick.[9]

Between them these seem to call for the "solution" that, when he has found out the truth, Oedipus will go into exile, and that he will make his way to the mountain.

In the closing scene Oedipus repeatedly urges that he should be thrown out of Thebes—see lines 1291–2, 1340–2, 1410–12, and 1436–7. And the destination of Cithaeron is specifically urged by Oedipus himself when he tells Creon (1449–54):

> . . . you should not ever make
> this city of my fathers have to harbour me alive in it.
> No, let me go and live up in the mountains,
> there, this mountain which is famed as mine—
> my own Cithaeron—
> the place my mother and my father, when alive,
> had designated as my proper tomb:
> so then I'll die as they had meant to do away with me.

At this stage, less than a hundred lines before the end, the audience is clearly being led to expect that this is how the play will conclude: the blind man will make his lonely way off to the trackless mountain where he had been taken to die when two days old. There would be a certain "poetic justice" to this; and there might also be a suggestion of the scapegoat ritual.[10] It is obvious that there would be a certain cathartic satisfaction if the play were to end this way.

But *OT*, as we have it, definitely does not satisfy these expectations. Instead Creon says that the oracle must be consulted again before anything is done (1436–45, reiterated at 1517–19); although Delphi has already pronounced on the guilty man, he insists on double-checking. In keeping with this, it is explicit that Oedipus is taken back inside the palace at the very end (1429, 1515, 1521).[11] Some scholars believe that there is so much that is unsatisfactory in the closing scene that the relevant lines are not authentic Sophocles, and that his original play did indeed end with Oedipus making his way to Cithaeron. This is undeniably a drastic theory, which would change the whole burden of the play's conclusion, but it is not patently false, and for myself I do not think it is out of the question.

---

[9] It may be worth noting, though, that in the final scene there is no sign that Oedipus has a stick. On the contrary, he needs both arms free to embrace his daughters.

[10] This kind of ritual (the *pharmakos*) was not as prominent in Greek cult as in Judaic, but it was not unknown.

[11] The consequential stage-directions are discussed in the note on 1523–4.

Assuming, though, that our text is sound, and that Sophocles' play did indeed end with Oedipus being taken inside, then what is the point of arousing the expectation that he will be sent off into the wilderness, only to frustrate this purgative impetus? It must, it seems, be to emphasize the powerlessness of Oedipus, and his lack of understanding of the way that everything has changed. He still thinks he knows what is best, and he still wants to have his way, but he is overruled. As Creon says in his closing lines (1522–3):

> Useless wanting to remain all-powerful,
> since the power that you wielded
> has not followed with you all your life through.

It would be a harrowing enough prospect if Oedipus were to set off alone into exile, but having to stay trapped in the polluted house at Thebes is arguably even worse. And it might be maintained that this is truer to the grim realities of the human condition. We cannot simply walk out on misfortune and put it behind us; we have to go on living with it. We are trapped inside the house of our life.

Whichever was Sophocles' ending, Oedipus remains one of great archetypes for bringing us face to face with the tragic aspect of the human condition. It is not for nothing that the play has come to be seen as paradigmatic.

OEDIPUS THE KING

LIST OF CHARACTERS

OEDIPUS, king of Thebes, believed to have been born at Corinth

OLD PRIEST OF ZEUS

CREON, brother of Iocasta

TIRESIAS, blind old seer of Thebes

IOCASTA, wife of Oedipus, widow of the previous king, Laius

OLD CORINTHIAN, former hireling shepherd (sometimes known as 'Messenger')

OLD SLAVE OF LAIUS, personal servant and shepherd to the former king (sometimes known as 'Shepherd')

MESSENGER, a member of the Theban royal household

TWO LITTLE DAUGHTERS OF OEDIPUS (not named)

CHORUS of loyal elders of Thebes

Place: before the royal palace at Thebes.

Oedipus enters from the palace doors. Children and young people, accompanied by an old priest, come on from the 'city' side, and sit around the altar in front of the palace, holding leafy branches with woollen wreaths tied round them.

OEDIPUS

My children, youngest generation
from this ancient land of Thebes,°
why have you hurried here with suppliant branches?°
Why is the city thick with incense smoke,
and chants of Paean° mixed with cries of pain?
I thought it would be wrong
to find this out through other sources,
so I've come to hear you for myself—
I, Oedipus, whose fame is known to all the world.
It's proper you, old man, should act as spokesman for them: 10
is it fear that brings you here like this? Or need?
It is my wish to offer every help I can—
I'd have to be impervious not to melt
with pity seeing such a gathering.

PRIEST

Great Oedipus, commander of our land,
you see us here, all ages, on your altar steps:
some still too little to fly far;
some bowed with age, like me, the priest of Zeus;
and these here chosen from among the young.
Yet others are assembled with their garlands
in the centre of the town before the double temple   20
of Athena and the mantic altar of Apollo.°
You see this for yourself:
our city's foundering, and can no longer
keep its head above the bloody surf of death.
The buds that should bear fruit become diseased,
our grazing cattle-flocks become diseased;
our women's labour-pains produce still-births.
Detested Plague, the god who lights the fever-fires,
has pounced upon our town,

and drains the homes of Thebes to empty husks.
Dark Hades is enriched, a profiteer in groans and tears.° 30
We, old and young, are suppliants here,
because we value you, not as the equal of the gods,
but as a man outstanding in the tos and fros of human life,
and in exchanges with the higher powers.
You once arrived in Thebes, and freed us
from the dues exacted by that cruel singing lynx.°
Despite no clues from us, without instruction,
but, it is believed, with backing from a god,
you set us straight upon our feet.
So now, all-powerful Oedipus, we all 40
submit ourselves into your hands as suppliants;
we beg of you to find some safety-shield for us.
Perhaps you've heard some message from a god,
or man? (Those people with experience
I find most skilled at gathering advice.)
Do something, best of men, raise up our land once more;
do something, but be careful too.
This country calls you 'saviour' now,
because you showed effectiveness back then:
don't make our record of your rule a time
when we were lifted up, but only to collapse once more. 50
No, plant our country firm to stand unshakeably.
You brought good luck with you before:
now be that man again.
If you are going to go on ruling in this land, as now,
it's preferable to have that power with people
round about than with an emptiness.
[A city's like a ship: if it's unmanned, no crew to people it,
then it is nothing but a hulk.]°

OEDIPUS

My pitiable children, yes,
I know full well what longing has impelled you here;
I know how you're all sick at heart. 60
And yet not one of you knows sickness
that can equal mine—for each of you is suffering singly
for himself alone, whereas my heart aches
for our land as well as you and me.
So you are not awakening me from idle sleep:
I've wept so many tears;

and I've explored the many tracks
my thoughts have taken me along.
And after all my searching I have found
one single remedy—and that I've set in action:
I've sent off Creon, brother of my wife, to Delphi°   70
to inquire from great Apollo's oracle
what I should do or speak to make this city safe.
But when I calculate the days, I'm worried
that he has been gone for longer than the usual time.
But when he does return, I would be in the wrong
if I do not enact whatever is directed by the god.

SCENE 2

Creon is seen approaching from the 'abroad' side.

PRIEST

And timely fitting with your words, these people signal here
that Creon is approaching now.

OEDIPUS

Apollo, may he bring with him reviving fortune,
light that's like a gleaming eye.   80

PRIEST

His news is surely good, since otherwise
his head would not be garlanded with laurel-leaves.

OEDIPUS

Now he's in earshot and we soon shall know.
My kinsman, Creon, say:
what message do you bring us from the god?

CREON

It's good—for even our ordeals
may prove a benefit, I say, if all ends well.

OEDIPUS

The message, though? From what you say,
I cannot tell if I should be encouraged or alarmed.   90

CREON

If you would like to hear before this crowd,
then I'm prepared to speak. . . or shall we go inside?

OEDIPUS

Speak out in front of everyone:
I feel more grief for these poor people than for my own life.

CREON

Then I declare that this is what I gathered from the god:
Apollo tells us clearly that there is miasma here,
pollution inbred in this very land;
and that we have to drive it out,
not let it thrive incurable.

OEDIPUS

What kind of cleansing? What is it that's occurred?

CREON

It's blood which blasts this land:
and so we must eject the guilt,   100
or else repay the death by further death.

OEDIPUS

Who is the man whose fate the oracle proclaims?

CREON

The ruler of this land, my lord, was Laius,°
before you came and took the reins in hand.

OEDIPUS

I know of him by hearing—but never saw him face to face.

CREON

He met with violent death—
and now the oracle speaks clear:
we must exact revenge upon his murderers.

OEDIPUS

But where on earth might they be now?
Where can we find the faded tracks
left from a crime committed long ago?

CREON

Here in this land, it said.
There is a chance of catching what is looked for: 110
while what is disregarded will escape.

OEDIPUS

Was Laius at home, or in the countryside,
or in another land, when he was murdered?

CREON

He said that he was going on a pilgrimage,
but never came back home again.

OEDIPUS

And was there no report of what occurred?
no fellow-traveller with evidence that might give help?

CREON

No, all of them were killed—except for one.
He ran away in fright, and said he only saw
one thing for sure, and nothing more.

OEDIPUS

And what was that?
One clue might lead to many more,   120
if we could get a slender prompt from which to start.

CREON

He said that bandits came on them;
and that the king was killed not by one man
but by the violence of many hands.°

OEDIPUS

But how could any bandit have been bold enough,
unless incited by some payment made from here?°

CREON

Yes, we thought that. But after Laius was dead,
no one was there to help us in those troubled times.

OEDIPUS

But when your king had met his end so violently,
what could have held you back from finding out?

CREON

That riddle-singing Sphinx made us   130
abandon what remained obscure,
and concentrate on what lay in our path.

OEDIPUS (*making an announcement*)

Back from the first beginnings I shall beam a light once more.
For rightly has Apollo turned attention
to this matter of the murdered man—and you as well.
So you shall see me justly join in fighting hard
to win full vengeance for this land and for the god.
I'll act as best I can, not as for some remote

acquaintance, but for my own self,
to banish this miasma from our air.
His unknown killer might well want
to make a similar attack on me,   140
and so I'm acting for myself as well as him.
Now quickly, children, stand up from these steps,
and take your suppliant boughs.
And someone call a meeting of the Theban people here,
to make it known that I shall leave no stone unturned.

An attendant goes off towards the city.

We'll either shine as fortunate, thanks to the god—
or else we sink.

PRIEST
Let us be going, children, for this man's proclamation
is the thing we came here for.
And may Apollo, sender of this oracle,
come to our rescue, and bring ending to this plague.   150

°*The Priest and young people depart towards the city;*
Oedipus goes back inside the palace, while Creon goes off in the 'city' direction.
The Chorus of Theban elders enters from the city.

CHORAL ENTRANCE SONG

CHORUS
°What are you, message from golden Delphi
to glorious Thebes, newly arrived?
What have you told us, Delian Paean?
I shake with fear, I'm terrified.
Is this oracle something strange to us,
or renewed by the turning year?
Speak to me, child of hope the golden,
immortal voice, and let me hear.

°First I summon you, deathless Athena;
and Artemis, whose circle-throne
protects the city; and you, Apollo.   160
Appear all three together, come,
triple-protectors! As before you drove
away the flame that hurt my home,
when ruin was rushing over my city:

so now bring help again, now come.

Numberless the pains I bear,
all our land is sick;
and my mind can find no spear 170
to drive this plague back.
There are no fruitful grains
growing from the earth;
and women's fierce labour-pains
bring no child to birth.
You can see life after life
fly like birds that soar,
faster than fire's spreading breath
to Death's western shore.

Numberless, my city's dying,
bodies on the earth, 180
plague-ridden children lying
uncared for in death.
Wives, mothers, grandmothers
group at every shrine;
there and here, the grieving gathers,
moaning full of pain.
Hymns and paean chime discordant
with despairing cries.
Come from Zeus, come, golden daughter,
show us your bright eyes.

°Ares, war god, god of death, 190
flays me with his fiery breath;
even without shield of bronze,
screaming he attacks and burns.
May he turn about his step
off to the Atlantic deep,
or off to the Thracian Sea's
inhospitable rough shores.
Anything surviving night
dawning day can set to right.
Zeus, lord of the lightning blaze, 200
blast him with your thunder blows.

°Arrows from your golden bow
with perfect aim, Apollo, draw;
rescue, stand in front of us,

with your sister Artemis,
blazing torches in her hands.
°Come too, god with hair in braids
of gold and wine-stained face,
our Dionysus, matching pace   210
with your bacchant women; blaze
with pitch-pine torches, dash
Ares, fatal fever-god,
spurned by every other god.

                          SCENE 3

Oedipus enters from the palace.

OEDIPUS
   °At prayer.
   And for these things you pray for,
   if you heed my words in full, and take my treatment
   for this scourge, you should get help,
   and reach a lifting of these troubles.
   I make this declaration as one
   who's foreign to this story, foreign also to those deeds—   220
   had I a close connection, I could not
   myself progress with an impartial search.
   But since it's only later I've become
   a citizen° among the citizens, I make
   this proclamation to you Thebans one and all.
   I say that any one of you who knows
   whose hand it was killed Laius, the son of Labdacus,
   that man must tell the truth in full to me.
   Or else, if any man confess of his free will
   that he's the one, he need not fear the consequence:
   because he takes the guilt upon himself,
   he shall not suffer any pain
   beyond departing without hurt in exile from this land.
   Or else, if anyone has knowledge of a person
   from another place who is the murderer,   230
   then let him not remain in silence—
   I have my rewards, and he shall earn my gratitude.

But if you hold your tongue, or if someone, through fearing
for a kinsman or themselves, rejects this my decree,
then hear from me what I shall do:
I hereby formally declare
that no one whatsoever in this land,
where I am holder of the royal power,
shall give protection to the guilty one,
nor speak to him, nor join with him
in making prayers or sacrifice, or any sacred rite.   240
All must expel him from their homes,
because that person spreads miasma fouling us,
as has been newly made apparent
by the holy Delphic Oracle to me.
So now you see what kind of man I am,
a fellow-fighter for the god and for the murdered man.
°[I pray the guilty party, whether it's a single man
who has escaped detection, or someone with accomplices,
may that man miserably wear away his wretched days.
What's more, I pray that if he be a member
of my household, and with me complicit, then   250
may I be subject to those curses
I have just called down on them.]
I do command you to fulfil all this,
both for my sake, and for the god,
and for this failing land, infertile, god-accursed.
For even had the issue not been prompted by the god,
it was not right for you to leave it undischarged like that;
after a noble man, your king, had been cut down,
you should have sought the matter out.
But now I hold the power he held before,
and have in common the same bed and wife as him,   260
and would have shared in children from one womb—
had he not been unfortunate, in that disaster struck him down—
for all these reasons I shall face the fight on his behalf,
as if it were for my own father.
I shall go to any length to catch the guilty murderer
of Laius, the son of Labdacus, the son of Polydorus,
son of Cadmus, king before, son of Agenor long ago.°
And as for any who do not comply, I pray the gods
make sure their farmlands offer up no fruit,
their wives no children from the womb;   270

but may they waste beneath this plague or even worse.
You other Thebans, though, who give approval
to these things, may Justice be your champion.
and all the gods forever favour you.

CHORUS-LEADER

I can declare, my lord, and under sanction of your curse,
I did not murder him;
nor can I point my finger at the man who did.
But since Apollo prompted this inquiry,
it's for him to name the murderer.

OEDIPUS

You may be right—but there's no human   280
who can force the gods against their will.

CHORUS-LEADER

May I suggest what strikes me as the second way?

OEDIPUS

If there's a third, don't hesitate to tell me it.

CHORUS-LEADER

I know the man whose vision is the closest
to the lord Apollo, and that's the lord Tiresias.
One who referred this quest to him
might gain the clearest view.

OEDIPUS

I've not been slow in acting upon this as well:
I've followed Creon's word, and sent for him already,
twice—it is surprising he's not here by now.

CHORUS-LEADER

The other stories are mere rumours, indistinct with time.   290

OEDIPUS

What stories? For I have to follow every lead.

CHORUS-LEADER

It was reported he was murdered by some wayfarers.

OEDIPUS

I've heard that too, but no one's seen the one who did the deed.

CHORUS-LEADER

If he knows any trace of fear, he'll not hold back
once he has heard the power of your curse.

OEDIPUS
  Someone who's not afraid to do
  will have no dread of words.

CHORUS-LEADER
  Well, here's the one to test him out:
  the sacred prophet's being led here now.
  He is the one and only living man
  who has innate the sense of truth.

SCENE 4

Tiresias approaches slowly, led by a young slave.

OEDIPUS
  °Tiresias, you who encompass all things with your mind,   300
  those suitable for teaching and things mystic,
  both heavenly and earthbound worlds,
  although your eyes can't see,
  you know the way this city is afflicted.
  You are the only shield and rescue we can find, my lord.
  In case you have not heard this news,
  Apollo has replied to us when we enquired,
  that there is only one solution for this plague:
  we must unmask the murderers of Laius for sure,
  and either sentence them to death,
  or else expel them exiled from this land.
  So please do not withhold what means you have,
  a message from your birds, or any other route of prophecy,   310
  to clear yourself, our city, me as well—
  to clear away the whole miasma from the murdered man.
  We are in your hands,
  and it's the finest kind of service
  for a man to use his powers as best he can.

TIRESIAS
  Ah, ah. . . It can be terrible to know
  what brings no benefit to him who knows it—
  I was well aware of this but had forgotten,
  for otherwise I never would have ventured here.

OEDIPUS

 What's this? You're so reluctant in approaching.

TIRESIAS

 Send me back home again.
 Take my advice—you'll find it's easiest   320
 for you to bear your burden, and for me to carry mine.

OEDIPUS

 Your words are not acceptable, and, by refusing to respond,
 you are disloyal to Thebes, the land that bred you.

TIRESIAS

 Because I see your questing thought° is off the mark;
 I would avoid the same mistake. . .

OEDIPUS

 If you have knowledge, do not turn your back—
 we all of us as suppliants beg of you.

TIRESIAS

 Because you all are ignorant.
 I shall not open up my troubles, not to speak of yours.

OEDIPUS

 You're saying that, though knowing, you'll not speak?   330
 You mean to leave us all betrayed? Destroy your city too?

TIRESIAS

 I shall not further hurt myself nor you.
 You question me for nothing, since you shall not learn from me.

OEDIPUS

 Despicable! You'd stir bad temper in a lump of stone.
 Are you refusing to tell anything?
 you mean to stand beyond our reach, intransigent?

TIRESIAS

 You criticize my temperament,
 yet fail to see your own, which shares your life with you;°
 and you find fault with me instead.

OEDIPUS

 Yes, who would not be moved to angry temper
 hearing words like these, an insult to your city?   340

TIRESIAS

 Events will turn out as they will,
 no matter if I cover them with silence.

OEDIPUS

What will turn out. . .
that's surely what you should be telling me?

TIRESIAS

I shall explain no more.
Feel free to rage at that as fiercely as you like.

OEDIPUS

All right! You've angered me so deeply
that I'll not suppress what I suspect.
It's my belief you helped to hatch the plot,
and did the deed—except for actual killing with your hands.
Had you the power of sight, I would have said
that you alone had done this thing.

TIRESIAS

Is that the truth? Then I tell you:
stand by your own decree that you proclaimed,   350
and from this day do not address these men, nor me—
because you are the foul pollutant in this land

OEDIPUS

You have the gall to stir this slander?
You can't believe you'll get away with this!

TIRESIAS

I have escaped already.
I sustain the truth to be my strength.

OEDIPUS

Who did you learn this from? Not from your craft, I think.

TIRESIAS

I learned from you:
you pressed words out from me against my will.

OEDIPUS

What words? Repeat them to make sure I understand.

TIRESIAS

Did you not understand before? Is this a test?   360

OEDIPUS

Not so I fully understood. Repeat again.

TIRESIAS

I say you are his murderer—the one you seek.

OEDIPUS

Redoubled insults! You shall regret these words.

TIRESIAS

Then shall I tell you something to enrage you even more?

OEDIPUS

Say anything you want—it will be wasted breath.

TIRESIAS

I say that, unaware of it, you're living
in a state of shame with those you hold most close;
and you can't fathom how the place you're at is bad.

OEDIPUS

You shall not get away with saying things like this.

TIRESIAS

I shall, if there is strength in truth.

OEDIPUS

There is, with one exception: you.   370
You have no part in this
because your ears and brain are just as blind as are your eyes.

TIRESIAS

Poor fool, you cast all this abuse at me,
and yet that same abuse will soon
be aimed at you by every person here.

OEDIPUS

Your life is passed in one long night;
and so you have no power to damage me,
or anyone with eyes that see the light.

TIRESIAS

It is your fate to fall, but not by any power of mine.
Apollo is enough, and shall accomplish what he will.

OEDIPUS

°Creon! Are these inventions his idea, or yours?

TIRESIAS

Creon presents no threat to you: you do yourself.

OEDIPUS

So: wealth and kingship and ambitious plans   380
for ever-higher steps in life's ascent,
see how resentment gets stored up for you!
To take control over this rule of mine—

a gift unsought, donated by the city—
it's for this that trusty Creon, friend right from the start,
has been devising moves behind my back
and hungering to throw me out.
For this he has deployed this old trick-spinning conjuror,
this door-to-door spell-casting quack,
who has his eye on profit only,
while at his proper craft he's blind.
How can you claim to have clear powers of prophecy?   390
Back when the singing-spinner bitch was here,
how come you had no key to free these citizens?
It's true the riddle wasn't just for anybody's guess,
it needed some prophetic skill.
But you displayed no special wisdom
from the birds or from the gods.
But then along I come, know-nothing Oedipus:
I put a stop to her and got the answer
using just my wits, not learning from the birds.
And I'm the man you're trying to eject,
imagining that you yourself will stand beside the throne
as Creon's right-hand man.   400
But you and your conspirator will both regret
attempting to scapegoat like this.
If you did not appear so old,
you would pay dear for harbouring such thoughts.

CHORUS–LEADER
It seems to us observers this man's words and yours
were spoken, Oedipus, in anger.
But what we need is not outbursts like these,
but thoughts on how we might best solve Apollo's oracle.

TIRESIAS
You may be king,
but I still have an equal right to make reply.
I also have this power because I am no slave   410
to serve your beck and call: I am Apollo's.
So do not write me down in Creon's list.
And since you have insulted me as blind, now listen:
°you have your sight, yet do not see the truth
of how the place you're at is bad, or where you live,
or who they are you share your home with.

Do you know what people you are from?
You little realize you're an enemy to your own kin
below the earth and here above.
One day the fearful-footed curse
from mother and from father shall
with double spike expel you from this land.
You see things focused now, but then you shall see dark.
°There is no anchorage,   420
no hollow of Cithaeron's mountainside,
that shall not resonate in echo to your cry,
once you have learned about your marriage-song,
and what a treacherous harbour-home
you entered in full sail, thinking your voyage fair.
And there's a further crowd of horrors, which you'll find
enough to crush° you, and your children too.
Now, after that, go spread your smears
all over Creon and my words.
There is no human who shall be
more harshly ground to dust than you.

OEDIPUS

I cannot bear to listen any more to this man's raving.
To hell with you—best turn back round,   430
and hurry far off from this house.

TIRESIAS

I never would have come, not I, had you not called for me.

OEDIPUS

And if I'd known you'd talk such lunacy,
I never would have brought you near my home.

TIRESIAS

That's how I seem to you, a ranting lunatic:
your parents, though, who gave you life,
they thought me sane enough.

OEDIPUS

What parents? Stop! Who were the ones who gave me life?

TIRESIAS

This very day shall give you life,
and shall unmake you too.

OEDIPUS

Your words are all enigmas, too obscure.

TIRESIAS

Aren't you the best enigma-solver here? 440

OEDIPUS

Yes, mock at me, but that is where you'll find me great.

TIRESIAS

It was that very stroke of fortune that undid you.

OEDIPUS

I was the saving of this city—that's enough for me.

TIRESIAS

I'm going, then. . . My boy, take me away from here.

OEDIPUS

Yes, have him take you.
You're nothing but a nuisance here.
Once you've moved on, you'll give us no more grief.

TIRESIAS

°I'll go then once I've had my say.
I do not fear to face your frown,
since there's no way that you can blot me out.
I tell you then:
this man you have been searching for 450
with curses and decrees, the murderer of Laius,
he is right here.
Though said to be an immigrant,
he shall be shown to be a true-born Theban—
yet he'll take no pleasure in that turnabout.
From someone who has sight he shall turn blind,
from someone rich become a beggar,
and then he'll make his way towards an alien land
by probing for his footsteps with a stick.
°And he shall be revealed
as brother and as father
to the children that he has at home;
as son and husband
to the woman who once gave him birth;
as fellow-sower and as killer 460
to the father who begot him.
Now go inside and work that out.
And if you can then prove me false,

feel free to say there is no insight
in my power of prophesy.

Tiresias is led off towards the city; Oedipus goes indoors without speaking.

CHORAL SONG

CHORUS
°Who has the chanting crag of Delphi's
shrine denounced as fouled
with such unspeakable pollution,
hands covered in blood?
Now is the time he should be running
far off to escape,
more strongly than the storm-winds' horses,
to evade the swoop
of Zeus' own son armed with his lightning-
fires and thunder-peals,   470
along with Death's unerring demons,
vengeful at his heels.

From Parnassus' snowy brightness
word has freshly shone:
pursue like hunters, track the traces
of the unknown man.
He must be ranging through the forest
wilds and caverns, sole,
alone and bellowing in anguish,
like some mountain bull.
He flees from Earth's primordial navel   480
and its prophesies;
but they for ever swarm around him
like tormenting flies.

°How shaken I am by the things I hear,
dreadfully shaken by the subtle seer.
To accept or deny, I cannot say—
hope lifts ignorance flying away.
Not now, not ever before have I heard
of any enmity or deadly feud
between the royal line of Labdacus
and Oedipus, the son of Polybus.°   490
There's no good reason to subject to test

Oedipus' high repute, standing as best;
no reason to drag him into the dock
to answer for a murder shrouded in dark.

Great Zeus and Apollo may understand
all human things, but among mere mankind,
whether a prophet should be ranked before
men like me for truth, I can't gauge for sure.   500
Unless I see these accusations shown
as proved, I'll not join those who do him down.
In full view the feathered girl confronted
him, and he stayed firm, wise and undaunted.
He stood the test, the city judged him kind: 510
he'll never be found evil by my mind.

SCENE 5

Enter Creon from the city direction.

CREON

I hear, my fellow-citizens, that Oedipus our king
has been attacking me with serious accusations.
I cannot let this go unchecked.
If it's believed I've done him wrong in word or deed
at such a crucial time, I have no wish to live for long,
not with such slanders pinned on me.
The harm this does is not confined, it goes far wide,   520
if I'm to be to be denounced as treacherous
by you and friends throughout this land.

CHORUS-LEADER

He said such things, but maybe they were spurred
by anger rather than by balanced thought.

CREON

But was it claimed in public that the seer had been suborned
through plots of mine to speak a pack of lies?

CHORUS-LEADER

Yes, claimed, but I don't know with how much thought.

CREON

And was this accusation made with steady look,

emerging from a mind in full control?

CHORUS-LEADER

I can't be sure. It's not my place to scrutinize   530
the actions of my king. But here he comes outside himself.

Enter Oedipus.

OEDIPUS

Well, well, it's you! What are you doing here?
How dare you come before my palace doors
with such barefaced effrontery,
when you're so clearly out to murder me,
so blatantly to steal my throne?
Good god, just answer this:
did you regard me as a coward or fool
when you embarked upon this scheme?
Or else perhaps you thought that if you sidled up on me
by stealth, then I would blithely notice nothing,
and would not defend myself.
It is a foolish undertaking to attempt to seize
a throne without a good supply of gold and friends—   540
you'd need a mass of troops and funds for that.

CREON

I tell you this: you should now listen
to my counter-speech, and only then make up your mind.

OEDIPUS

You're skilled at speaking,
but I'm bad at listening. . . to you at least,
because I've found in you my deadly enemy.

CREON

Now first you should hear what I say to that.

OEDIPUS

Don't tell me that you're not corrupt.

CREON

If you consider mindless stubbornness
a thing of value, you're not thinking straight.   550

OEDIPUS

If you consider you can harm your kin,
and go scot-free, then you're not sensible.

CREON
> I grant you that the sentiment is just;
> but tell me how you think I've done you wrong.

OEDIPUS
> Was it your advice, or was it not,
> that I should send off for that sanctimonious seer?

CREON
> It was, and I still stand by that advice.

OEDIPUS
> How long a time has passed since Laius. . .

CREON
> Since he did what? I cannot follow you.

OEDIPUS
> . . . has been gone, vanished, fatally struck down.   560

CREON
> It would amount to many, many years.

OEDIPUS
> Was this man active as a prophet in those days?

CREON
> He was: a wise one, honoured then no less than now.

OEDIPUS
> Did he refer to me at all back at that time?

CREON
> No—not at least when I was standing near.

OEDIPUS
> Did you not mount a search to find the murderer?

CREON
> We did, of course—but not a thing emerged.

OEDIPUS
> How come, then, that this sage did not speak out?

CREON
> I've no idea. And when I do not know, I hold my tongue.

OEDIPUS
> Yet this you know, and could admit, were you my friend. . .   570

CREON
> What's that? For if I know it, then I'll not refuse.

OEDIPUS

. . . that had he not conspired with you, he never
would have talked of me as murderer of Laius,

CREON

Well, you're the one to know if that is what he said.
But now it's fair for me to question you, as you have me.

OEDIPUS

Go on then, question: I shall not be proved a murderer.

CREON

Well then: you're married to my sister, yes?

OEDIPUS

Yes, there is no denying that.

CREON

And do you give her equal power as ruler here?

OEDIPUS

Whatever she may ask from me she gets.   580

CREON

And am I not a third, and equal to the two of you?

OEDIPUS

And that is why you've proved a treacherous friend.

CREON

Not if you see things as I do: so just consider this.
Do you think anyone would rather be a ruler
dogged by fear than sleep secure,
if they could still wield no less power?
Well, I for one have no desire to be a king
in preference to living like a king;
no, nor would anyone with any sense.
Now, as things are, I can have anything I wish from you,   590
yet free of fear: while if I were to rule,
I'd have to do all sorts of things against my will.
So how could monarchy be more desirable for me
than influence and power without the pain?
I'm not so far misguided as to hanker
after anything but honours that bring benefits.
As things are now, all people wish me well;
for now all welcome me with warmth;
and now if anyone desires something from you,

they come and seek me out,
since I am sure to be the key to their success.
How could I give up this to grasp those other aims?
[A mind that has good sense would not become corrupt.]°   600
I am no lover of that frame of mind,
nor could I act with someone else that way.
To make a test of this, go and enquire at Delphi:
see if I've relayed the oracle with honesty.
And if you then discover I've been plotting
with the soothsayer, put me to death
by double vote—my own as well as yours.
But don't condemn me by your own unproven guess
and nothing else. It is not right to judge
the bad as good on whim, nor good as bad.   610
To cast aside a sterling friend is equal
to rejecting your own cherished life.
You shall know this for sure in time,
since time alone reveals the man who's truly just,
while one short day's enough to show who's bad.

CHORUS-LEADER
  His words sound good to cautious ears, my lord:
  those who make hasty judgements are not safe.

OEDIPUS
  But when a secret plotter's making rapid moves,
  I must be quick to countermove in turn.
  If I just sit and wait here patiently,   620
  then he'll achieve his aims
  while mine are lost and gone.

CREON
  So what is it you want? To send me into exile?

OEDIPUS
  No, no, it is your death, not just exile.

CREON
  °Now you have shown how deep resentment goes.
  You won't relent, or trust in me at all?

<OEDIPUS
  I know a traitor when I see one.>

CREON
  Because you are not thinking for the best.

OEDIPUS
What's best for me, I am.

CREON
But you should think of me no less.

OEDIPUS
But you're corrupt.

CREON
Suppose you're wrong?

OEDIPUS
Rule has to be maintained.

CREON
But not by someone who misrules.

OEDIPUS
Thebes, hear him, Thebes!

CREON
My city too, not only yours.   630

CHORUS-LEADER
Stop this, my lords: I see the queen, Iocasta,
coming here outside—and in good time time:
you should resolve this quarrel with her help.

Enter Iocasta from the house.

IOCASTA
Stop! Why have you embarked
upon this war of words, you foolish men?
Have you no shame, that, though our land is sick like this,
you start upon some private feud?
(*to Oedipus*) You go inside.
And, Creon, go to your own home as well.
Don't make a mighty storm out of some petty pain.

CREON
Sister, your husband Oedipus is making
fearsome threats against me:
to thrust me into banishment, or else put me to death.   640

OEDIPUS
That's true: because, dear wife, I've caught him
scheming ways to do me vicious harm.

CREON (*solemnly*)
    May I live damned and die accursed,
    if I have done these things you charge me with.

IOCASTA
    I beg you, by the gods, believe him, Oedipus.
    Above all else respect the oath he swears upon the gods,
    then me and these men present here.

°LYRIC DIALOGUE

CHORUS
    Think, agree and give your word
    willingly I beg you, lord.   650

OEDIPUS
    What d'you want me to retract?

CHORUS
    Please treat this man with respect,
    never proved a fool before,
    now strong through the oath he's sworn.

OEDIPUS
    Do you know what you request?

CHORUS
    I know.

OEDIPUS
    Say what you suggest.

CHORUS
    Do not damn with unclear proof
    a friend who stands under oath.

OEDIPUS
    Be well aware that by your asking this
    you're also asking for my death or exile from this land.

CHORUS
    By the god who looks upon   660
    the other gods, the sacred Sun,
    may I without god or friend
    die, if that is in my mind.
    When the city is so hurt,
    yet more troubles tear my heart,

adding from you two this pain
onto those already known.

OEDIPUS

All right then, let him go—
though this means certain death for me,
or else forced exile stripped of rights.   670
My pity has been stirred by your appeal, not by his case.
He still shall have my hate wherever he may go.

CREON

You give way sullenly, and with ill grace—
just as you are oppressive when you go too far in anger.
Natures such as yours quite rightly cause themselves most grief.

OEDIPUS

Just go away, and let me be.

CREON

I'm on my way. You stay unthinking,
and it's to these men I owe my life.

Exit Creon towards the city.

CHORUS

Why, my lady, do you pause
before taking him indoors?

IOCASTA

Tell me first what has occurred.   680

CHORUS

This misunderstanding flared
from their words; and, though not right,
bitter language can still bite.

IOCASTA

Was this quarrel on both sides?

CHORUS

Yes, both.

IOCASTA

What were their words?

CHORUS

That's enough, enough—it's best
for our land if you desist.

OEDIPUS

You see, though meaning well, how you have gone too far
with soothing and with taking off my edge.

CHORUS

Lord, I'd be a blatant fool,   690
crazy with no sense at all,
if I turned my back on you,
you who steered my country through,
as it rode a sea of pain.
Now please guide us straight again.

SCENE 6

IOCASTA

Please let me know as well, my lord,
what matter has provoked so fierce a fury in your heart.

OEDIPUS

I shall tell, seeing that I hold you, wife,
more highly than these men.   700
It's Creon; he has laid such plots against my life.

IOCASTA

As clearly as you can, explain just how
this quarrel was provoked.

OEDIPUS

He says I was the murderer of Laius.

IOCASTA

He claims to know this?
Or taking it from someone else?

OEDIPUS

He sent along a crooked prophet-man to speak for him,
so that he keeps his own mouth free from blame.

IOCASTA

Then you can free yourself from those concerns.
Just listen as I shall convince you there is no one human
knows the science of prophecy.
And here's my pithy proof of this.   710
One day an oracle was brought to Laius—
I don't say from Apollo, but his ministers—

which said it was his fate to be killed
by a son who would be given birth by me and him.
Yet he, as is reported, was cut down by foreign bandits
where three wagon-tracks converge.°
As for the child, when it was less than three days old,
he fixed its ankle-joints,
and put it into someone else's hands
to cast out on a trackless mountainside.
And so Apollo never brought those things to pass: 720
that boy was not his father's murderer,
and Laius did not incur that dreadful fate
at his son's hand, as he so feared.
Yet that is what the fortune-telling prophecies
had mapped out in advance.
So you should pay them no attention, none.
For when a god requires some course,
then he will easily reveal it for himself.

OEDIPUS
Something you said just now
has set my mind in turmoil, wife,
and sent it on a wandering way.

IOCASTA
What worry is it makes you flinch and speak like this?

OEDIPUS
Did I not hear you say that Laius was murdered
where three wagon-tracks converge?   730

IOCASTA
That's how it was reported, and that is still the word.

OEDIPUS
What is the region where this deed took place?

IOCASTA
°The country is called Phocis:
there the track from Thebes divides,
one way to Delphi, while the other comes from Daulia.

OEDIPUS
And how much time has passed since this event?

IOCASTA
It was announced in Thebes not long before the time
when you emerged as ruler here.

OEDIPUS

Oh Zeus, what are you set on doing with my life?

IOCASTA

What is this, Oedipus, so pressing on your mind?

OEDIPUS

Don't ask me. First describe what Laius looked like;   740
what stage of life he'd reached.

IOCASTA

Well, he was tall; his hair was newly sprinkled grey;
and not dissimilar to you in build.

OEDIPUS

O this is terrible! I think I've put myself, all unaware,
beneath a dreadful curse,

IOCASTA

What do you mean, my lord? I feel afraid to look at you.

OEDIPUS

I have a creeping fear the prophet can see clear.
You would make things firmer with one answer more.

IOCASTA

I'm frightened, but I'll answer anything you ask.

OEDIPUS

Did he go in a simple style,   750
or like a head of state with lots of bodyguards?

IOCASTA

The group was five in all, with one a herald;
and there was just a single wagon carrying Laius.

OEDIPUS

O god, this is too clear!
But who reported all these details at the time?

IOCASTA

A slave, the one man to survive and come back home.

OEDIPUS

Is he by chance inside the house right now?

IOCASTA

°I know he's not, since after he returned,
and saw you in control, upon the death of Laius,
he grasped my hand and begged to be sent off   760
to where the sheep-flocks have their grazing grounds,

so he might be as far away from any sight
of Thebes as he could be.
And I agreed to send him there: he was deserving,
for a slave, of even greater gratitude than this.

OEDIPUS

Could he be quickly fetched back here?

IOCASTA

It's possible. But what makes you ask?

OEDIPUS

I am afraid I may have said too much aloud,
and that is why I want to see him now.

IOCASTA

Then he shall come.
But surely I as well should rightly know, my lord,
what weighs so anxiously upon your mind.   770

OEDIPUS

I shall not keep you in the dark,
not now that my forebodings have advanced so far,
for there is no one with more right than you
to know what trials I'm going through.
My father's name was Polybus, the lord of Corinth,
my mother Dorian Merope.°
I grew up honoured there as first among the citizens,
until a quirk of fortune struck—something surprising,
yet not worth all the trouble spent on it.
There was this man at dinner who had drunk too much,
and flushed with wine he called out
that I was not my father's true-born son.°   780
Although provoked, I just restrained myself that day,
but on the next I went and put the issue
to my father and my mother: they were furious
against the man who had let slip the insult.
I was glad of their assurances—and yet. . .
this kept on needling me, and spreading.
So without my father and my mother knowing,
I sailed secretly to Delphi.°
Apollo sent me off dissatisfied
upon the matter that I went there for:
instead he uttered loud and clear   790
foul and unbearable predictions.

He said that I was bound to make love
with my mother, and exhibit progeny
that people could not bear to look upon;
and I would be the killer
of the father who begot me.
°On hearing this, I turned my back upon
the land of Corinth; and I used the stars
to steer well clear of that direction, somewhere
where I could be sure I'd never see
the shameful horrors of my evil oracle fulfilled.
And as I journeyed on, my path came to that region
where you say this king of yours was killed.
Now, wife, I'll tell you all the truth.   800
As I approached this three-road place,
a herald came towards me with a man
upon a horse-drawn cart, as you described.
The man in front, with the old man's encouragement,
began to use brute force to shove me off the road.
I aimed a blow in anger at the one who hustled me.
And then the old man kept a watch
as I was passing by the cart,
and brought the double spike-ends of his goad
right down upon my head.
He more than paid for that.   810
I struck him sharply with my stick;°
and knocked down by this hand of mine,
he toppled headlong from the wagon.
I killed them, every man.
But if that stranger there was linked with Laius at all,
then who can be more wretched
than this man before you here?
What human more detested by the gods?
No citizen's permitted to receive me in their house,
no one can speak a word of greeting,
but must drive me from their homes.
What's more, this curse was laid upon me
by none other than myself.   820
And I pollute the dead man's marriage-bed
by my embracing of his wife
with these same hands° as he was murdered by.
Am I not evil, utterly unholy?

I who must be exiled from this land,
and yet in exile never see my family,
nor take one step upon my fatherland—
since otherwise I'm bound to go to bed
with my own mother, and to kill old Polybus,
the father who begot and raised me up.
Someone who reckoned this would be cruel treatment
by a god would have it right.
By the great inviolate powers, I pray
I never, never look upon that day.   830
May I be blotted out from humankind,
before I see so foul a stigma branded on my life.

CHORUS-LEADER

This makes us anxious, lord, yet keep up hope,
until you've heard the eyewitness.

OEDIPUS

Yes, that remains my thread of hope:
to wait with patience for the shepherd-man to come.

IOCASTA

And when he has appeared, what is it that you want of him?

OEDIPUS

I'll tell you what: if he turns out to say the same as you,
I shall have then escaped disaster's grip.   840

IOCASTA

What was it that you heard me say especially?

OEDIPUS

°You said he witnessed that it was a band of robbers
killed him: if he sticks by that number—robbers—
I was not the murderer.
There is no way that one can ever equal many.
If, on the other hand, he says it was a solitary man,
the balance of this action clearly tips me down.

IOCASTA

Well, that is certainly the story as it was reported then;
and he can not retract that back,
since all the city heard, not me alone.   850
And even if he does diverge from what he said before,
it's still impossible for him to make

the death of Laius confirm the oracle.
Apollo said that he was bound to meet his death
killed by my son: yet that poor infant
never murdered him, but it died first.
So as for prophecies, I never more shall peer
this way or that because of them.

OEDIPUS

You speak good sense. Yet all the same
send someone off to fetch that labourer without fail.   860

IOCASTA

I'll have him fetched at once.
But now let's go indoors—I want to do whatever is your wish.

Oedipus and Iocasta go inside.

°CHORAL SONG

CHORUS

I pray to keep in step with me
a life of holy purity;
may all my words and actions have
their stamp in steps that pace above,
in laws begotten in high aether,
laws with Olympus° as their father.
No mortal nature gave them birth;   870
oblivion cannot deal them death.
In them the god is bold,
and never can grow old.

°Proud arrogance begets bad kings,
proud arrogance crammed with bad things,
untimely and without advantage,
first climbs up to the highest roof-ledge,
but then. . . inevitable fall,
so steep that feet are bound to fail.
Yet that wrestling which serves my land   880
I pray the god do not unbind.
I shall forever hold
to god as my strong shield.

If in word or deed someone's high and mighty,
treads the path of pride, taking Justice lightly,

scornful of the gods, then may fate take vengeance,
dealing just deserts for this self-indulgence.
If he grasps ill gain, embraces impiousness,   890
then he touches the untouchable in madness.
No one can defend his life when that happens;
no one can avoid the gods' angry weapons.
So, if such misdeeds earn praise as meritorious,
why should I dance and sing in the sacred chorus?°

°If these signposts don't point with any reason
on the way to truth, teaching every person,
I'll no more revere Earth's unsullied navel,
nor approach Abai, nor Olympia's temple.   900
O all-powerful Zeus, if that name be proper,
don't let this elude your eternal power.
Those prophetic sayings, telling what was fated
for Laius decay, fade obliterated.
Nowhere Apollo's rights flourish brightly glowing;
darkness follows close—and religion's going.   910

SCENE 7

Enter Iocasta with sacred symbols.

IOCASTA
    I thought it for the best, good gentlemen,
    to pay a visit to our temples
    with these wreaths and frankincense in hand.
    For Oedipus is too much tortured
    by all sorts of fleeting pains,
    and does not gauge new thoughts
    by past experience, as should a thinking man.
    He's prey to anyone who plays on fear,
    and my advice no longer carries weight with him.
    Apollo, you are closest to our house,°
    so first I turn to you as suppliant with these prayers: 920
    please find for us a purge without impurity.
    At present, we're alarmed to see him,
    as the helmsman of our ship, so thunderstruck by fear.

°*Enter the Old Corinthian from the 'abroad' direction.*

OLD CORINTHIAN
Could you kindly tell me, strangers, where
the house is of King Oedipus? Say where.
Or better still the man himself—do you know where?°

CHORUS-LEADER
This, stranger, is his house, but he's indoors.
This lady is his wife and mother to his family.

OLD CORINTHIAN
May his lady-wife, then, prosper happy,
and with happy ones around her.   930

IOCASTA
And I wish you the same for these kind words, old stranger.
But go on: what is it that you want,
and what is it you have to tell us?

OLD CORINTHIAN
Happy news, my lady, for your household and your husband.

IOCASTA
What may that be? And who have you come from?

OLD CORINTHIAN
I'm from Corinth, and the news I'm bringing
will be pleasing—that's for certain—
yet you may feel sorrow also.

IOCASTA
What's this? How can it have this double power?

OLD CORINTHIAN
First, the people there intend to make him ruler
of the land of Corinth—that is what they're saying.   940

IOCASTA
How come? Does ancient Polybus no longer rule?

OLD CORINTHIAN
No because he's dead and buried.

IOCASTA
What's this you say, old man? That Polybus is dead?

OLD CORINTHIAN
Death deserves me if it's not the truth I tell you.

IOCASTA

(*to servant*) Quick, go and tell this to your master.
So, you oracles sent by the gods, see where you stand!
For ages Oedipus has steered clear of that man,
for fear that he would kill him:
and yet now he's died by random chance,
not by his hand at all.

Enter Oedipus from the palace.

OEDIPUS

Well, dearest wife Iocasta, why have you
called me here outside the house?   950

IOCASTA

First hear the news from this old man. Then ask
where all those solemn god-sent oracles have gone.

OEDIPUS

Who is this man, and what has he to say to me?

IOCASTA

He's come from Corinth to report your father
is no longer: Polybus. . . he's dead.

OEDIPUS

What is this, stranger? Give your news yourself.

OLD CORINTHIAN

If you want to hear my message plainly,
then be certain he is dead, departed.

OEDIPUS

Was this by treachery? Or did some illness take him?   960

OLD CORINTHIAN

Just a little shift of balance
sends old bodies to their rest.

OEDIPUS

It was from illness, then, he died, poor man.

OLD CORINTHIAN

Yes, and all the many years he'd measured in his lifetime.

OEDIPUS

Well, well, dear wife!
So why should any man consult the mantic Pythian shrine,
or hearken to the birds which screech above our heads?
On their authority I was supposed to kill my father;

yet he's dead and laid beneath the earth,
while I stayed here, my blade at home untouched—
unless perhaps he gave up life from missing me:
that way he would have died because of me.°   970
In any case, old Polybus is resting down in Hades' realm,
and he has swept away these oracles of ours
along with him, completely valueless.

IOCASTA
And is that not what I've been telling you?

OEDIPUS
You have; but I've been led astray by fear.

IOCASTA
Well then, stop treating things like this so seriously.

OEDIPUS
But I must surely live in fear of making love. . .
in my own mother's bed.

IOCASTA
°Why should we humans live in fear
when fortune has control of us,
and there's no knowing anything
with certain foresight? It is best to live
and let things be, so far as we are able to.
That's why you should not be afraid about   980
this union with your mother.
Just think how many men have gone to bed
together with their mothers in their dreams.
The man who wastes no time on matters such as these
can weather life most easily.

OEDIPUS
All your advice would be quite right,
were not my mother still alive.
While she draws breath, I'm bound,
however sensible your words, to live in dread.

IOCASTA
At least your father's death shines as an eye of comfort.

OEDIPUS
A great one, yes: but I am still in dread of her who lives.

OLD CORINTHIAN (*breaking in*)
May I ask who is this woman you are so afraid about?

OEDIPUS

   It's Merope, old stranger, wife of Polybus.   990

OLD CORINTHIAN

   What about her makes you fearful?

OEDIPUS

   There was a dreadful, god-directed prophecy.

OLD CORINTHIAN

   May another person hear it—or is it forbidden?

OEDIPUS

   You may of course: Apollo told me once
   that I was bound to sleep with my own mother,
   and to shed my father's blood with my own hands.
   And that is why I have been keeping
   Corinth at a distance for so long.
   Meanwhile I've prospered: yet. . .
   how sweet it is to look into one's parents' eyes.

OLD CORINTHIAN

   And it is in fear of that you've stayed away from there?   1000

OEDIPUS

   Yes, that, and not to be my father's murderer.

OLD CORINTHIAN

   Since I've come in goodwill, I should surely
   free your lordship from this terror?

OEDIPUS

   If you could, I would reward you handsomely

OLD CORINTHIAN

   That is chiefly why I came here:
   so that once you're home I might be well rewarded.

OEDIPUS

   But all the same I'll never ever venture near my parents.

OLD CORINTHIAN

   Son, it's clear you have no notion what you're doing.

OEDIPUS

   Why? Tell me what you mean, old man.

OLD CORINTHIAN

   It's because of them you're steering clear of home?   1010

OEDIPUS
That's right: for fear Apollo turns out to be true.

OLD CORINTHIAN
Meaning you would take pollution from your parents?

OEDIPUS
Precisely, old man. That's my constant dread.

OLD CORINTHIAN
Don't you realize that your fears are based on nothing?

OEDIPUS
How can that be, as long as I'm the offspring of those parents?

OLD CORINTHIAN
Because Polybus was not your blood-kin.

OEDIPUS
What did you say? Polybus was not my parent?

OLD CORINTHIAN
Not a fraction more than I am—equally indeed.

OEDIPUS
How can my father be the equal of a nobody?

OLD CORINTHIAN
Since that man did not beget you, nor me neither.   1020

OEDIPUS
What was the reason, then, he called me 'son'?

OLD CORINTHIAN
You were once a present to him,
taken from these hands of mine.°

OEDIPUS
If he'd received me from another's hands,
how could he then have cherished me so much?

OLD CORINTHIAN
He had long been childless, and that moved him.

OEDIPUS
And when you gave me, had you bought me?
or just come upon me?

OLD CORINTHIAN
It was in the forest glens of Mount Cithaeron° that I found you.

OEDIPUS
Why were you travelling in those parts?

OLD CORINTHIAN

I was looking after flocks for summer pasture.

OEDIPUS

You mean you were a vagrant shepherd hired for pay?

OLD CORINTHIAN

True, my son, and yet you—you I rescued at that crisis.   1030

OEDIPUS

Why? What was wrong when first you took me up?

OLD CORINTHIAN

Well, your ankle-joints could tell that story.

OEDIPUS

Ah, why bring up that old affliction?

OLD CORINTHIAN

I released you from the clamps that pinned your feet together.

OEDIPUS

Humiliation I've derived from infancy.

OLD CORINTHIAN

Yes, you take your name from that misfortune.°

OEDIPUS

For god's sake, did my mother or my father
do this thing to me? Speak out.

OLD CORINTHIAN

I've no notion. But the man who gave you must know better.

OEDIPUS

You mean you took me from another,
and you didn't come on me by chance?

OLD CORINTHIAN

No, it was another shepherd passed you to me.   1040

OEDIPUS

Who was he? Can you say precisely who?

OLD CORINTHIAN

I believe that he was called the slave of Laius.°

OEDIPUS

The man who used to be the ruler of this country here?

OLD CORINTHIAN

That's it—he was shepherd to that very man.

OEDIPUS

And is he still alive for me to see him?

OLD CORINTHIAN (*towards Chorus*)

It's you locals who should know the answer best to that.

OEDIPUS

Does anyone among you people present
know the shepherd that he means?
you may have seen him working in the fields or here in town?
Declare it, since the moment's come
for all these things to be revealed.   1050

CHORUS-LEADER

I think he is none other than the peasant
you were keen to see before.
But it's Iocasta here should know this best.

OEDIPUS (*turns to Iocasta*)

Dear wife, you know that man we summoned recently:
is he the one this man is speaking of?

IOCASTA

It doesn't matter who he means.
Pay no attention to it.
Disregard his words as empty air,
don't give these things a second thought.

OEDIPUS

That is impossible:
when I have got such clues as these,
I must reveal my origins.

IOCASTA

No, by the gods, if you have any care for your own life,   1060
do not pry into this.
My suffering's enough.

OEDIPUS

Take heart. For even if my mother is revealed
to be a slave, three generations slave,
you'll never be exposed as lowly born.°

IOCASTA

Please listen to me, all the same. . .
I beg of you, do not do this.

OEDIPUS

>There is no way that you'll dissuade me:
>I have got to find these matters out for sure.

IOCASTA

>I'm only thinking of your good with this advice.

OEDIPUS

>This thinking of my good has been annoying me.

IOCASTA

>Poor man, I only hope
>you never find out who you are.

OEDIPUS

>Go, fetch that shepherd for me, someone.
>Leave her to glory in her high-class pedigree.   1070

IOCASTA

>Ah sorrow, man of sorrow!
>That's the only title I can give to you.
>And nothing other ever.

Iocasta rushes off into the palace.

CHORUS–LEADER

>Why ever should your wife have rushed away
>in such a wild distress?
>I fear dark things will break out from her silence.

OEDIPUS

>Well let them break—and come what will!
>My seed-bed: still I need to see it clear, however humble.
>She has superior ideas, as women do,
>and may well be ashamed at my low family.
>°But I regard myself as born   1080
>the child of Fortune, in her generosity;
>and I shall never be demeaned by that.
>She is my mother; and the Months, my brothers,
>have delineated me as humble,
>then as great. With such a pedigree
>I never shall turn out as other than I am:°
>and never rest till I've discovered my true blood.

Oedipus and the Old Corinthian remain on stage.

CHORAL SONG

CHORUS
　°If I trust my intuition
　as a prophet, it is certain
　you shall host new celebration,
　O Cithaeron, Theban mountain.
　There tomorrow, mother-nurse,
　native to our Oedipus,　　　　　　　　　　　　1090
　by the full moon's radiance
　all night we shall sing and dance,
　since you cherished our young prince.
　Apollo, may you find this pleasing,
　to you, healing-god, we sing.

　°Oedipus, who was your mother,
　who? A nymph who lives for ever,
　mounted by the great god Pan,　　　　　　　　1100
　mountain-god, bore you his son?
　Or a bedmate of Apollo's,
　lover of the upland meadows?
　Or of Hermes? Or of bacchic
　Dionysus, mountain antic,
　who received you as a present,
　from a nymph with sparkling eye,°
　his favourite company for play?

SCENE 8

The Old Slave of Laius° slowly approaches from the 'away' direction.

OEDIPUS
　I would conjecture, gentlemen,
　although I've never had to do with him,　　　　1110
　that this must be the shepherd we've been seeking for.
　For, look, he matches this man here in length of years;
　also I know these servants bringing him are men of mine.
　But you can tell this better than I can,
　because you've seen the man before.

CHORUS-LEADER
  That's him for sure, I recognize him.
  He enjoyed the special trust of Laius, although a herdsman.

OEDIPUS
  Stranger from Corinth, I shall ask you first:
  is this the man in question?   1120

OLD CORINTHIAN
  There he stands before your eyes, sir.

OEDIPUS (*to the old Theban*)
  Hey you, old man, here, look me in the face
  and answer everything I ask you.
  Did you once belong to Laius?

OLD SLAVE OF LAIUS
  That's right. I was his slave—not purchased,
  born and bred within the household.

OEDIPUS
  What kind of work? How did you use your time?

OLD SLAVE OF LAIUS
  Most of my life I've spent in tending flocks.

OEDIPUS
  And in what regions have you mostly herded them?

OLD SLAVE OF LAIUS
  There was Cithaeron and the highlands thereabouts.

OEDIPUS
  And did you ever know this man from there?

OLD SLAVE OF LAIUS
  Know doing what? What man d'you mean?

OEDIPUS
  This man who's standing here.
  Have you encountered him?   1130

OLD SLAVE OF LAIUS
  Not such that I could say from memory.

OLD CORINTHIAN
  That is not surprising, master.
  But it should be easy to remind him clearly.
  Surely he'll remember how we, up around Cithaeron,
  used to pass the time together,
  three years in succession, six months spring to autumn,

him with double flock, and me with single.
Then with winter coming, I would drive
my creatures to their home-pens;
and he would drive his to the folds of Laius.
(*to the old slave*) Did it used to be just as I say, or not?   1140

OLD SLAVE OF LAIUS
Yes, that's all true—although it was long, long ago.

OLD CORINTHIAN
Tell me, then, do you remember giving me
a little boy to foster and bring up as mine?

OLD SLAVE OF LAIUS
What's that? What makes you ask me that?

OLD CORINTHIAN (*indicating Oedipus*)
This is him, my old friend:
he is the man who was that little babe.°

OLD SLAVE OF LAIUS (*fiercely*)
To hell with you! I tell you, hold your tongue

OEDIPUS
No, no don't threaten him, old man:
it's your words call for threats far more than his.

OLD SLAVE OF LAIUS
Why, mighty lord? What have I done that's wrong?

OEDIPUS
Not answering the question
this man asked about the child.   1150

OLD SLAVE OF LAIUS
Because he does not realize what he's saying. . .
he's interfering over nothing.

OEDIPUS
If you won't speak obligingly:
you'll speak when you're in pain° all right.

OLD SLAVE OF LAIUS
No, by the gods, don't hurt me, an old man.

OEDIPUS (*to his attendants*)
Quick, one of you tie back his arms.

OLD SLAVE OF LAIUS
Why, why? What is it that you want to know?

OEDIPUS
    First, did you give this man the child he asked about?

OLD SLAVE OF LAIUS
    I did give him—if only I had died that day!

OEDIPUS
    You will die now, if you don't tell the honest truth.

OLD SLAVE OF LAIUS
    Far worse than that, if I *do* speak.

OEDIPUS (*threatening punishment*)
    It would appear the man is trying to delay.   1160

OLD SLAVE OF LAIUS
    No, no, I'm not. I've said I handed him the child.

OEDIPUS
    Where did you get it from?
    From your own home, or someone else's?

OLD SLAVE OF LAIUS
    No, not my own: I had the child from someone.

OEDIPUS
    A citizen? Which one? Out of which house?

OLD SLAVE OF LAIUS
    No, by the gods, good master, no, don't ask me more.

OEDIPUS
    It's death for you, if I am made to question you again.

OLD SLAVE OF LAIUS
    All right: the child came from the house of Laius.

OEDIPUS
    Was it a slave, or was it one from his own kin?

OLD SLAVE OF LAIUS
    Ay me, I'm on the verge of speaking the obscene truth. . .

OEDIPUS
    And I of hearing it: yet hear it out I must.   1170

OLD SLAVE OF LAIUS
    The boy was called his own.
    But she inside could best
    tell you the facts, your wife. . .°

OEDIPUS
    Was she the one who gave it you?

OLD SLAVE OF LAIUS
Her, yes, my lord.

OEDIPUS
What was her reason?

OLD SLAVE OF LAIUS
So that I would do away with it.

OEDIPUS
Her own child?

OLD SLAVE OF LAIUS
She was afraid of deadly prophesies.

OEDIPUS
What?

OLD SLAVE OF LAIUS
That he would shed his parents' blood.

OEDIPUS
Then why, why hand it on to this old man?

OLD SLAVE OF LAIUS
I did it out of pity, master.
I supposed that he would take the child
off to another land, to where he came from.
But he preserved it for the very worst: 1180
because if you are who he says,
then you were surely born to sorrow.

OEDIPUS (*with a terrible cry*)
It all has come out clear.
Now, light of day, may this be my last sight of you.
I am the man who's been exposed
as born from those I should not,
coupled with those I should not,
killing those I never should have killed.

Exit Oedipus into the palace; Corinthian and Old Slave unobtrusively depart.

CHORAL SONG

CHORUS

°Human generations,
in my calculations
your whole life-sum, worked out,
comes to nothing, naught.
Who can add up, after all,
happiness in total   1190
reaching more than seeming,
and decline from seeming?
With your fate before me,
paradigm before me,
yours, Oedipus, I boast
nothing human blest.

Your arrow-shot, so certain,
won you happy fortune;
you brought down the maiden
of the clutching talon;
stopped her riddling power,   1200
shielding as a tower
death-blows from my city.
So we called you mighty
king, and heaped upon you
all the highest honours,
and you ruled supreme
in this great Theban realm.

Now, though, what a different story!
Who is housed with wilder grief,
who sunk in deeper misery,
with reversal of his life?
All-too-famous Oedipus,
°you have made the voyage twice
into one engrossing harbour—
as a child you grew there,
then you plunged in as a husband,°   1210
coming back as groom there.
How could they, your father's furrows,
mauled in marriage by your plough,
how endure so long in sorrow,

never crying out aloud?

Time all-seeing has uncovered
and, despite you, lit on you,
exposed that the selfsame mother
bore you and your children too,
wretched son of Laius.
Oedipus incestuous,
judged your union no union.
How I wish I'd never met you,
never set my eyes upon
yours; as I now lament you,
from my mouth keen sorrow spilling.   1220
I tell you the bitter truth:
you gave back my breath for living,
and you've closed my eyes in death.

SCENE 9

Enter Messenger from the palace.

MESSENGER
You elders, most respected in this land, what acts
you shall be hearing of, what acts be seeing;
how great the grief you are to feel,
if you still care about this royal house of Thebes!
I don't believe the mighty river Danube or the Dnieper°
could wash this house to make it clean:
so foul the horrors that it hides,
and that it shall soon open to the light,
deliberate not passive harm.   1230
And self-inflicted wounds are those
that give us sharpest pain.

CHORUS–LEADER
The things we knew before were quite enough
for heavy grief. What more have you to tell?

MESSENGER
The most immediate news to speak and learn
is that our queen Iocasta's dead.

CHORUS-LEADER
   Poor soul—what caused her death?

MESSENGER
   She brought it on herself.
   You're spared the worst of what was done,
   because you were not there to see,
   but I shall still recall as best I can,
   so you may know of that poor lady's sufferings.   1240
   Once she had come in frantic through the doors,
   she rushed straight to her chamber with its marriage-bed,
   her fingers twisted in her hair.
   Once there she shut the doors,
   and called aloud on Laius, long gone,
   remembering his seed from time gone by,
   which had produced his death as fruit,
   while leaving her to bring to birth
   a misbegotten crop from his own son.
   She cried for her old bed of love,
   where she had doubly mis-conceived,
   a husband by a husband,
   and then children by her child.   1250
   Just how she met her death I cannot tell,
   since with loud shouting Oedipus broke in;
   and so we did not see her passion to the end,
   but turned our eyes upon his moving round instead.
   He paced about, and called on us to find a sword for him,
   and asked where was that wife who was no wife,
   but mother-soil that had produced a double crop,
   himself and then his children too.
   And as he raged some power showed him the way—
   it wasn't one of us, the people standing by.
   He howled a dreadful howl, and then,
   as though he had some guide,°   1260
   he hurled himself against the double doors,
   and forced the panels from their frames,
   and plunged into the room.°
   And there we spied the woman hanging
   with her neck noosed in a twisting cloth.
   He saw, and with an awful roar, released the knot.
   Once she was laid upon the ground,
   what happened next was horrible to see.

For he extracted the long golden pins
which fixed her robes; and then he lifted them
and stabbed them in the sockets of his eyes.   1270
And as he did, he cried that they should see no more
the sort of evils he had suffered and had done,
but that in future they should stare in darkness
at the ones that they should not have seen,
and fail to know those that he'd longed for.
With chants like these, he raised the pins
and stabbed his eyes again and yet again,
and made the bloody jelly soak his cheeks,
and kept on spattering the drops of blood
until a livid shower had fallen thick as hail.°
So from the pair has broken out these horrors,   1280
both the man and woman inextricably.
Their old prosperity in days gone by was truly there:
but now, through this one day, there is instead
lament, disaster, death, disgrace,
and every ill that has a name—
they are not missing one.

CHORUS–LEADER
How is the wretched man now?
Any easing of his pain?

MESSENGER
He's calls for someone who will open wide the doors,
and show to all the citizens of Thebes
the man who killed his father, and who made his mother. . .
but the words he used are too obscene for me to say.
He wants to cast himself from out this land,   1290
and not remain a curse laid by himself upon this house.
But he lacks strength, and needs support
from someone who will guide him:
the burden of his torment is intolerable.
And he shall show all this to you as well.
Look now, the gates are being opened:
soon you shall be watchers of a spectacle°
that even one who loathes it must yet pity.

Messenger unobtrusively goes.

SCENE 10

°*Oedipus emerges from the doorway, his eyes stabbed out and blood running down his cheeks; he is without any guide.*

CHORUS-LEADER

What terrible suffering for humans to see,
far the most terrible I've ever known.
What is the madness that's grappled with you?　　　　1300
What is the god that has fastened on you
with longer than long leap clawing your life?
Sorrow, I cannot bear even to see you,
although there is much I'm longing to ask,
much to discover, and much to observe—
such are the shivers you quicken in me.

OEDIPUS

Ah ah, I am sorrow!
Where upon earth am I carried?
Where in air does my voice flutter?　　　　1310
Such a distance, my demon, you've darted!

CHORUS-LEADER

To somewhere dread, not to be heard, not to be spied.

OEDIPUS

Black, black
overshadowing my dark mind,
unbearable, bestial, no fair wind.
Agony yet again, again
the spike of these spasms and my unkind
memories both stab me deep with pain.

CHORUS-LEADER

It is no wonder that amid such sufferings
you double grief and double your lament.　　　　1320

OEDIPUS (*recognizing the Chorus*)

You, you
still remaining with me, loyal friend,
and staying to care for me, though blind.
I sense your presence from the sound;
clearly I recognize your voice,
even with darkness on my eyes.

CHORUS-LEADER
It's such a dreadful deed: how could you bring yourself
to blot your eyes? Which god incited you?

OEDIPUS
°Apollo, friends, Apollo
it was made my fate grow   1330
ill, so ill. But my own hand,
no other, struck and made me blind.
Why should I see when nothing sight
can show could offer me delight?

CHORUS-LEADER
These things were as you say.

OEDIPUS
What can I watch, or what love?
or what greeting can still move
delight? Take me from these lands,
take me, all disaster, friends,   1340
the man through and through accursed,
hated by the gods the most.

CHORUS-LEADER
Your fortune and your state of mind are dark indeed.
I wish I'd never ever crossed your path.

OEDIPUS
Curse him, whoever he may be,
who loosed harsh fetters and set free   1350
my feet; saved me from fateful
death, yet did me no favour.
Dead I would not have brought pain
on me and those I call my own.

CHORUS-LEADER
I too would wish the same.

OEDIPUS
And then I would not ever
have come to kill my father,
not have been called the bridegroom
of her that I was born from.
But now I am the fruit accursed   1360
of him who sowed my life first.

If there is sin primeval,
Oedipus has that evil.

CHORUS-LEADER

I cannot say I think you well advised:
better dead than still alive and blind.

OEDIPUS

Don't try to preach to me that what I've done
was not done for the best; and stop advising me.   1370
I cannot think I ever could have looked with seeing eyes
upon my father down in Hades,°
nor upon my wretched mother,
since I have so much offended both of them
that hanging would not be enough.
Or was the sight of my own children,
misbegotten as they were,
a prospect to be longed for?
Not ever with these eyes of mine, no, never.
Nor ever see this city, its great walls and sacred images,
from which I have excluded my own self,
[though raised to be the greatest man in Thebes,]°   1380
by telling everyone to keep at bay the man accursed,
now marked out as unholy by the gods—
and of the blood of Laius.
When I have coated such a stain upon myself,
was I to look upon these things with open eyes?
No, not at all. If only there had been a way
to block the flow of hearing, I'd have made
my wretched body all encased
[both blind and hearing nothing.
For it's sweet to live with mind beyond the reach of pain.]°   1390
°O Mount Cithaeron,
why accept me in your arms?
why not hold on and kill me there and then,
so that I never would have shown the world
where I was born from?
O Polybus and Corinth,
old ancestral home by name,
you bred me with a skin so beautiful,
an abscess underneath,
since now I'm found to be

infection from infected blood.
O you three roads, and secretive ravine,
and thicket with that narrow place
where three ways meet,
who drank my blood spilt by my hands,
blood of my father's blood, 1400
do you remember still
the acts that I committed there?
And then what I went on to do, once I'd come here?
°O wedding, joining, making love,
you first engendered me, and then, once born,
emitted that same seed;
and so you brought to light
fathers who were brothers,
children who had sibling blood,
and brides who were both wives and mothers—
along with all the other acts
which are the most repugnant for humanity.
But it's not right to put in words
what's wrong to act in deeds:
so now at once, I beg you, throw me out somewhere, 1410
or kill me off, or hide me° deep beneath
the ocean waves, where you'll not see me ever more.
Come on, feel free to touch this wretched man.
Believe me, don't be frightened,
for no one else of humankind is fit to bear
my tainted burden but myself.

°SCENE 11

Creon approaches from the city direction.

CHORUS–LEADER
But here comes Creon at the proper time to deal
with what you're asking for, in action or with planning.
He's the only person left to guard our country in your place.

OEDIPUS
Ah, what on earth am I to say to him?

How can I to hope to gain his trust,   1420
now it's emerged that I so clearly did him wrong before?

CREON

I have not come to ridicule you, Oedipus,
nor censure you for any wrongs now past.
°<Yet I am shocked to find you wandering outside like this;
and, you loyal elders, should not be allowing him.>
But even if you've lost your sense of shame
in front of mortal men, at least respect
the blaze of mighty Sun that nurtures all;
do not expose a blight to be like this uncovered,
a thing that neither earth nor holy rain nor light
could find acceptable.
Accompany him inside the house immediately,
for piety requires that only family   1430
should see and hear the troubles of their own.

OEDIPUS

Since you have stretched so far beyond my expectations,
and, best of men, have come to me, the worst,
please do this for me—it is for you I ask and not myself.

CREON

What is this that you so desire of me?

OEDIPUS

To cast me out beyond this land as soon as possible,
to somewhere where there'll be
no human to encounter me.

CREON

I would for sure have done this, but I wanted first
to know for certain from the god what should be done.

OEDIPUS

But his whole message was made clear: 1440
the father-killer, the abomination that I am,
should be destroyed.

CREON

Yes, that was said; but we are now at such a pass,
it's better to make doubly sure what should be done.

OEDIPUS

So you'll consult about a man as abject as I am?

CREON
   Yes, and this time you'll have to trust the god.

OEDIPUS
   I ask from you, then, that you follow these instructions:
   first, the woman in the house,
   give her the funeral you wish,
   for you should rightly lay to rest your own.
   But as for me, you should not ever make
   this city of my fathers have to harbour me alive in it.   1450
   °No, let me go and live up in the mountains,
   there, this mountain which is famed as mine—
   my own Cithaeron—
   the place my mother and my father, when alive,
   had designated as my proper tomb:
   so then I'll die as they had meant to do away with me.
   And yet of this I'm sure: that no disease
   or any other cause could cut me down,
   because I never would have been preserved from death,
   except to face some fearsome doom.°
   So much for my own destiny—let it go where it will.
   As for my children, Creon, you need not go
   to trouble for the males°—they're men,
   and never shall lack livelihood, wherever they may be.   1460
   °But for my girls, my two poor, pitiable daughters
   (whose dinner-table never has been set
   in separation from myself, and who have shared
   in everything that I have put my hands to),°
   I charge you take good care of them.
   Please first allow me just to touch them with my hands,
   and to lament our miseries.
   Do this, my lord; do this, true noble man.
   If I could only feel them in my arms,
   then I might sense that they were mine,
   as when I used to have my sight.   1470

The two little daughters of Oedipus approach, weeping.

   But what is this? I think that I can hear them—can't I?—
   my two dear ones shedding bitter tears.
   Can Creon have felt pity and have had
   my darling girls fetched here for me?
   Can I be right?

CREON

>You are. I have arranged for this because I knew
>what great delight they'd bring you now,
>as you have always felt for them.

OEDIPUS

>I thank you from my heart, and hope that on your way
>god will protect you better far than me.
>My children, where are you?   1480

The girls go to Oedipus, who takes them in his arms.

>Come here, this way towards my arms,
>your brother's arms, which now have taken on
>the function of this kind of seeing
>from your father's eyes which used to shine so bright—
>the man who, all unlooking and unasking,
>has turned out to be the ploughman°
>who grew harvest in the field that he was grown from.
>I weep for you, although I cannot look on you,
>as I reflect how bitter your whole life will be,
>the kind of life that people will impose upon you.
>What city gatherings will you attend,
>what festivals, without returning home   1490
>in tears instead of heartened by the spectacle?
>And once you have arrived at readiness for marriage,
>who will he be, the man who'll gamble on the danger
>of incurring all those slurs and insults
>that will damage both his children and him too?
>What horror is there absent?
>Your father was the killer of his father;
>then he ploughed and sowed the mother
>from whom he himself had grown from seed;
>then got you from the source that gave him birth.
>Such are the taunts that will be thrown at you—
>who then shall marry you?   1500
>There can be no one, girls, but you are bound
>to wither barren as unmarried maids.
>Son of Menoeceus, as you are the only father left
>for these two girls—now we their parents
>have both been erased—
>do not stand idly by while they, your kin,

go wandering poor and husbandless;
don't bring them down to my low depths.
Take pity on them, seeing how they are so young,
and stripped of everything except what you can do for them.
Show your agreement, noble lord,
by reaching out your hand and touching me.   1510

Creon does so.°

For you, my daughters, were you old enough
to understand, I would give much advice.
But now, instead, just hope and pray for this:
that you may live wherever best you can,
and may enjoy a better life
than me, the father who begot you.

CREON
°That is long enough for weeping; time to go inside the palace.

OEDIPUS
I have got to, though it's far from welcome.

CREON
All things have their proper moment.

OEDIPUS
Let me tell you my conditions?

CREON
Speak, and then I'll know them.

OEDIPUS
That you cast me from this country.

CREON
That's the god's gift you're demanding.

OEDIPUS
But it's clear the gods detest me.

CREON
If that's so, you'll soon obtain it.

OEDIPUS
So you are agreeing?

CREON
When I'm short of knowledge, I don't idly chatter.   1520

OEDIPUS
Hurry me away then.

CREON
　Go, then;

Disengaging the girls from his embrace.

　time for parting with your daughters.

OEDIPUS
　No, no, do not take them from me.

CREON
　Useless wanting to remain all-powerful,
　since the power that you wielded
　has not followed with you all your life through.

°*An attendant leads Oedipus off indoors;*
exit Creon, taking the two girls with him, in the direction of the city.

CHORUS–LEADER
　°Look at this, my fellow-Thebans, this is Oedipus before you;
　he who solved the famous riddle, he who was so forceful,
　widely envied for his fortune;
　what a howling tempest of disaster he has voyaged into.
　Think of this, and call no human being happy,
　not while they're still waiting for that final sunset,
　not until they've run their course and passed the
　finish–post without disaster.   1530

AIAS

INTRODUCTION TO
AIAS

Iliad, *Hector, Troy*

Aias[1] does not at all conform to the stereotype of a Greek tragedy. It is not set at a royal palace, but in a theatre of war; it centres on a great heroic figure, but he has been utterly humiliated before the play begins. He is dead before the tragedy is two-thirds through, and his body lies there on stage for the rest. Yet *Aias* is recognized as a powerful study of human greatness and its hazards, explored with some great poetry and unpredictable dramatic turns.

The tragedy is structured in three parts. In the first, lines 1–645, we see and hear how Aias' violent vengefulness has been thwarted by the goddess Athena, so that he is irremediably brought low. Throughout the third part, lines 866–1420, his dead body lies on stage, while there is prolonged dispute over whether he should be further humiliated or to some degree restored. The much shorter middle section, round which the play is pivoted, gives some explanation for the anger of Athena, reported from the seer Calchas, and on either side of that there is an extraordinary solo speech. In the first of these (646–92) Aias, in the presence of his dependants, dwells on the topics of time and change, and seems to be saying that he has changed his mind and decided not to kill himself. The others are misled, and this has become known as 'the deception speech', one of the most discussed problems of interpretation in all of Sophocles. In the second 'suicide' speech (815–65) Aias, on stage by himself, prepares for death, and ends by throwing himself onto his fixed sword. This is highly exceptional dramatic technique; and it culminates with the exceptional on-stage death, witnessed by the audience.[2] It is a plausible guess that the solo death scene was the core of Sophocles' conception, and that he built the rest of the play round that.

Aias was one of the great figures of the epic tales of the Trojan War,

[1] The Greek form of the name, pronounced something like "eye-ass". The association of his name with the cry of grief, "aiai", at 430–2 brings out how distant the Greek name is from the English form of his Latin name, Ajax, with the *j* and *x* both alien consonants.

[2] We know that in an earlier tragedy by Aeschylus, *Thracian Women*, Aias' suicide was, in accordance with the usual convention, narrated in a messenger speech. For discussion of the much-disputed staging of the suicide see relevant notes.

and his self-inflicted death was much portrayed in poetry and art before Sophocles. While the *Iliad* is in significant respects the prototype of tragic drama, not many tragedies directly overlap with it;[3] and the story of Aias' suicide, consequent on the award of Achilles' armour to Odysseus, is never directly anticipated in the *Iliad* itself. The central events of *Aias* were narrated in minor, so-called "cyclic", epics that covered matters at Troy after the end of the *Iliad*. Nonetheless, *Aias* is probably the most pervasively Iliadic of all the tragedies we have, and the figure of the proud, physically huge, stalwart warrior, second only to Achilles, is very much as in Homer. Two of his main Iliadic exploits are directly recalled by Teucros at lines 1272–87 (see notes). Teucros also emphasizes an important Iliadic feature: that the other leading Greek warriors are not at Troy as subordinates of Agamemnon and Menelaus, but as autonomous allies who are doing them a favour (1197 ff.).

The Homeric figure who hovers behind *Aias*—even more than Achilles—is the Trojan Hector. At the same time as being remembered as Aias' greatest enemy, there is a kind of affinity between these two noble "losers". The speech of pleading by Tecmessa, Aias' war-wife, at 485 ff. is suffused with echoes of Andromache's pleas to Hector in *Iliad* 6. And Aias' agonized weighing of alternative courses of action at 457 ff., with its firm conclusion on what the noble man should do, chimes with Hector's deliberations *in Iliad* 6 and 22. But the greatest emphasis is laid on the sword, the gift of Hector to Aias after their inconclusive single combat, as narrated in *Iliad* 7.[4] Aias dwells on its inauspicious provenance both at 661–5 and at the start of his final suicide speech at 815 ff.:

> It was a gift from Hector, my worst enemy,
> the man most hated in my sight;
> and here it stands firm fixed
> in hostile Trojan soil. . .

He then goes on, though, to speak of the sword killing him cleanly in a way that will be "most kindly". The impossibility of the clear, absolute delineation of friendship and enmity is indeed one of the leading themes of the play. The rock of enmity is veined with streaks of affinity.

Something similar to the ambivalent affinity with Hector can be seen in Aias' relationship with the land and landscape of Troy. The Greeks have spent nine long years on "hostile Trojan soil"; the seasoned soldiers

---

[3] Not of those that survive, at least. Aeschylus composed an Achilles-trilogy that evidently followed the narrative structure of the *Iliad* quite closely. The surviving anonymous play *Rhesus* (traditionally attributed to Euripides) overlaps to some extent with *Iliad* 10.

[4] When Teucros draws the sword from Aias' body, he tells (in a departure from the *Iliad*) how his gift of a belt had played a reciprocal role in Hector's death; see 1028–35.

of the chorus complain of the hardships of being so long on campaign in their last song at 1185–91 and 1199–1210. Yet, when Aias in the first rush of his grief sings that he has been too long at Troy (412 ff.), he calls on

> Tracks lapped by waves,
> and sea-formed coast caves,
> thickets by the brine,
>
> . . .
>
> you nearby flow
> of Scamander's streams,
> kindly to the Greeks. . .

He has grown appreciative of the alien place where he has spent long years—and where he will lie in death. It is to those places along the shore that he sets off, avowedly to purify himself, but in truth to kill himself (see 654–5). And as he nears the end of his final farewell to this world above he is careful to include (862–3)

> . . . all you springs and rivers here, and Trojan plain
> I say farewell, my nourishers.

What has happened is that the enemy land has become in some ways his benefactor, and he has developed an ambivalent affection towards it. And this is, in the end, the place where he will be buried, and where he will have his 'sepulchre, memorial / for mortals evermore' (1166–7).

Aias' tomb is given a further allusive yet important connection with the Hector of the *Iliad*. At *Iliad* 24.797, just eight lines before the end of the epic, the Trojans set the ashes of Hector in a "hollow grave-trench", the only occurrence of this phrase in Homer. At *Aias* 1165 the chorus advise Teucros to find a "hollow grave-trench"—exactly the same words—for the body of Aias; and the same phrase is repeated by Teucros at 1403, very near the end of the play. Hector, the defeated hero of the *Iliad*, is honoured finally with a tomb that will be celebrated by future generations: so too, with a kind of parallelism, is the fallen Aias. There is even a suggestion of the site of a future hero-cult (see further below).

Changeability, Deception, and Insight

Quite apart from any question of cult, Aias is regarded as an exemplar of the "hero" in a more modern sense, "the Sophoclean hero". This is the great individual, best portrayed by Bernard Knox, who stands fixed, resolute, uncompromising, regardless of whatever tragedy may ensue. Achilles in the *Iliad* is the prototype.

One of the immutable precepts of this kind of hero is claimed to be:

"love your friends and harm your enemies". That is all very well, but any narrative of any depth is liable to come up against the issue of: "how do I determine who is my friend and my enemy, and what happens if they change?" Achilles himself epitomizes this when, at *Iliad* 9.611–15, he tells his old mentor Phoenix to stop making a case in favour of Agamemnon, "for fear you become hateful to me who love you". So a reversal of friendship and enmity is not unthinkable, even to Achilles. Such changeability is crucial to this tragedy, not only because Aias has become the implacable enemy of his former allies, but because Odysseus' willingness to shift is crucial for the fate of Aias' body and the whole conclusion of the play.

When Agamemnon urges Odysseus to extract every ounce of revenge on the dead man, he contradicts him: "I hated him so long as it was right to hate" (1347); and he recognizes the converse: 'It's true that many present friends may later turn to sour" (1359). It would, however, be an oversimplification to suppose that the wily Odysseus has reached an entirely new kind of flexibility, anathema to the old breed of the "Achillean hero". Aias himself has anticipated this attitude in the course of his "deception speech" (678–83):

> For I have newly come to realize
> an enemy should only earn our enmity
> so far as fits one who may yet become a friend;
> and I shall only give a friend support
> so much as suits one who may not remain a friend for good.
> The truth is, comradeship turns out for most
> to be a faithless anchorage.

Those critics who are determined that Aias must stand above this kind of "decadent" compromising attitude hold that, even as he articulates these sentiments as applicable to others, he is exempting himself and his immutable world-view from them. This must be conveyed, they claim, by his delivering the lines in a contemptuous or sarcastic tone. The objection to this interpretation is that Aias has just spent the previous eight lines (669–77) expounding, in words of powerful poetry, how the whole cosmos and natural world (the seasons, sleeping and waking, and so on) have to follow sequences of changeability. So there has to be something more going on in this speech than sardonic self-exemption from its contemplation of time and change.

This leads (inexorably!) to a consideration of the much-debated—and no doubt irresolvable—issues of "the deception speech". It should, first, be recognized as clear that Aias intends all along to kill himself; the only change is that he has decided to go along the shore to the more isolated "meadow washing-places" (654–5) rather than carrying out the act in the domestic setting of his quarters. Secondly, there is no doubt that both Tecmessa and the chorus are misled, and that they believe themselves to have been deceived. But it is out of the question that that is the sole, or even the main, purpose of the speech. Putting Tecmessa and the chorus off his track could have been much more simply achieved; and that is deeply inadequate as the primary explanation of a highly wrought and poetic sequence of thought that begins (646–8):

> Long and incalculable Time
> grows everything from dark into the light,
> and covers all that has appeared once more.
> So nothing is unthinkable. . . .

What gives the speech much of its enigmatic quality is that very little in it is downright false; that nearly everything can be understood simultaneously both at a literal—and misleading—level, and at a more searching, generalizing level that is not false, and which even conveys a degree of truth. Aias concludes (690–2):

> I'm going on the path I have to tread.
> Do as I say, and soon perhaps you'll find
> that, even if I am for now unfortunate,
> I shall have been kept safe.

And this will turn out, in due course, to be in a real sense true: in the end his body will be honourably buried, and his wife and son and the dependent chorus will be protected from danger. There is a level on which Aias is no more exempt from the universal laws of changeability than are night and day. He will not have been preserved from death by suicide, but his honour and the secure future of his dependents will have been restored, "kept safe". In this way there is a sense that Aias' lines are attempting to convey some larger truth about shifting cosmic forces, a level of meaning deeper than the immediate issue.

Sophocles has, it seems, taken on an impossibly difficult challenge in attempting to make an entire speech of nearly fifty lines false on one level, while being at the same time true, or at least prescient, on another. An interpretation along these lines does, at least, go some way towards explaining the expansiveness and the poetic richness of this magnificent speech. It also lifts Aias above the level of rigid mean-mindedness that characterizes both Agamemnon and Menelaus: their vision can reach no further than the short-term gratification of their revenge. As for Odysseus, while it is impossible for Aias' personal antipathy to be cancelled out, as is recognized by Teucros' courteous refusal of his help with the burial, there is, at a more universal level, a degree of mutual insight shared between them.

Downfall and Restoration

Why is Aias brought down so low? Does he deserve such a heavy and gruesome fall? On a plain human level the answer might be yes, because he intended to slaughter the leaders of his own allies, and to do so by stealth. He did, indeed, kill the keepers of the captured livestock as well as the animals themselves. But in the play itself the emphasis of explanation is not weighted towards this homicide.

The prologue establishes the centrality of Athena to his fate; and, once his madness is gone, Aias and his friends all take it as given that it is the wrath of the goddess that has brought about his downfall. In the first half of the play there is no explanation of why she is angry, beyond the warning lesson she draws for Odysseus (127–30):

> . . . be careful not to speak
> with arrogance towards the gods,
> or take on airs because you are superior to others
> in your strength or hoards of wealth.

Nothing more explicit is revealed until after Aias has departed at the end of his "deception speech". It is then that Teucros' servant reports what the seer Calchas said in explanation (758–61):

> Those men whose presence builds up to excess
> . . . are then brought crashing down
> through harsh misfortunes planted by the gods—
> whoever is begotten as a human, and yet fails
> to keep his thoughts within the human scale.

Calchas then goes on to narrate two instances in the past when Aias had spoken in an above-human way, the second addressed directly to Athena herself, when he insisted that he could do well enough by himself without the help of the gods. The two occasions do not seem so very terrible in themselves, but the point clearly is that they are symptomatic of a mind that "fails to keep thoughts within the human scale".[5] Aias' mind, like his body, aspires to be superhuman. That is why Athena is so determined to bring him down. And, so far as a god is concerned, that is reason enough.

---

[5] This same phrase is repeated by Calchas in 761 and 777.

Athena is not, however, one of the series of gods invoked in Aias' final suicide speech; and after his death the only direct allusion to her is Tecmessa's complaint that she destroyed Aias to gratify her favourite, Odysseus (952–6). Calchas had told Teucros that Athena's wrath would last for this one day only (756–7); and it makes good sense if the fading out of this motif is linked to the significance of Aias' eventual burial.

Clearly the final procession off-stage at the end of the play signifies that Aias is no longer reduced to a state of total dishonour and humiliation; respect for his greatness is restored. There is a yet further dimension to this burial: the subdued implication that Aias' tomb will in future be the site of hero-cult—that is to say, that the dead hero will be given sacred honours as a powerful kind of demigod.[6] Huge grave-mounds marked (and still mark) the profile of the landscape around Troy; and they were already a "touristic" site when visited by Xerxes, the king of Persia, in 480 BC. One of these mounds was held to be the tomb of Aias, and it is very likely to have been well known in the time of Sophocles, although the first specifically attested visit to it was by Alexander the Great a century or more later.

We cannot be sure when the hero-cult of Aias near Troy first began, but it is likely to have been before the fifth century. In any case, the cult was located in later antiquity at a tumulus on the headland at the eastern edge of the Trojan plain, a short distance up the Dardanelles from their entrance, where the coast becomes more hilly (see Map 3).[7] This site was known as "Rhoiteion" (Latin "Rhoeteum"), after a nearby township, but this name does not occur in Sophocles' text. The play does, however, indicate that the burial is to be further east along the shore from the Greek camp, which was traditionally held to have been on the flat shore by the mouth of the river Scamander. Aias' quarters were at the eastern end of the camp (see note on 4); when he goes off along the shore by himself at 692, this must be further in the easterly direction. And the final funeral procession will have departed yet further away from the camp. This tallies well with the location of Rhoeteum.

There is also one striking passage in the play that seems to point towards a future hero-cult. At 1171 ff. Teucros sets up a living "tableau" in which Tecmessa and her son Eurysaces sit touching the body of Aias, as though they were suppliants taking asylum at a sacred place (see note

---

[6] On hero-cult, which is particularly important in *Oedipus at Colonus*, see further pp. 212–3.

[7] The conspicuous mound that is still to be seen (*In Tepe*) dates from Roman times; but there was a story (found in Pausanias) that the original tomb was washed away, and that it contained a gigantic human skeleton. The third-century BC poet Euphorion implies that the location was ancient by using the phrase "one story told by bards relates . . .".

on 1171–81). And just before this the chorus, urging Teucros to find a suitable grave, had used a striking phrase (lines 1166–7):

> where he'll take possession
> of his musty sepulchre, memorial
> for mortals evermore.

This "memorial evermore" surely evokes the notion of a future hero-cult.

Athens—and Beyond

The issue of the posthumous status and power of Aias will have been of special interest at Athens. On the establishment of the first democracy in 508 BC, the organizer, Cleisthenes, set up ten "tribes", each named after a hero (in the cult sense), and one of those was Aiantis. Herodotus explains that these "eponymous" heroes were native to Athens, except for Aias, "whom he added, although foreign, because he was a neighbour and ally" (5.66). The point is that Aias came from Salamis, the large island close to the coast of Attica and of the next city to the west, Megara, and that Salamis had become annexed to Athens only in the sixth century. The close connection of Salamis to Athens is worked into the play.[8] In his suicide speech Aias begins his last farewell (859–61):

> O daylight, and you sacred soil
> of my own Salamis, bedrock of my ancestral hearth;
> and glorious Athens, with your race akin to mine. . .

And in the very last words that the chorus sing in the play, they are fearful whether they will ever get home (1216–22):

> I only wish I was by that
> wooded cape, sailing on past
> sea-beaten Sounion's headland,
> to greet sacred Athens at last.

This infiltration of an Athenian interest may also help to explain the emphasis in the play on the young boy Eurysaces, especially in two scenes, where Aias wishes a good future for him, bequeathing him his shield (545–77), and secondly, where Teucros sets him beside his father's corpse (1168 ff., cf. 1409–11). Eurysaces also had a hero-cult at Athens in his own right, and it is quite possible that this existed even before any mythical connection was made between him and Aias. It is notable that Aias emphasises his "legitimacy" as the child of a war-captured mother

---

[8] The chorus are also genealogically connected with Athens by Tecmessa at 202 (see note).

in his farewell speech to the boy (545 ff.).[9] So Sophocles' *Aias* does contain a thread of Athenian connection, and it may be that Athena's wrath lasts only for the one day of the tragedy because he will after death have a beneficial connection with "sacred Athens", the city which was so closely associated with the goddess.

It would be a distortion, however, to claim this "nationalist" aspect as the essential point of the play. The core of the play lies, rather, in the portrayal of this fascinating and terrifying figure of a man, a man who both physically and mentally pushes against the upward limit of the human scale. He is too great, too close to being like a god. And so he has to fall. But the expression of his fall is magnificent: the lyrics of his despair, the speech to his son, his final farewell to this world of light, and, perhaps above all, the enigmatic meditation on time and change in the 'deception speech'. Cumulatively these build to make him one of the greatest individuals of all Greek tragedy. It is undeniable that the last third of the play, while his huge body lies there on stage, cannot recapture that sublime level of expression, but it does still show a diminished world attempting to assess his stature, and to accommodate his spirit.

---

[9] Teucros is also the son of such a union, and the question of his status is given attention at 1012–16, 1226–30, and especially 1288–1307.

AIAS

LIST OF CHARACTERS

ATHENA, goddess, daughter of Zeus

ODYSSEUS, one of the leading Greek warriors, from Ithaca

AIAS, one of the leading Greek warriors, from Salamis

TECMESSA, a captured Phrygian princess, in effect Aias' wife

EURYSACES, infant son of Aias and Tecmessa

TEUCROS' MAN, often known as 'Messenger'

TEUCROS, Aias' half-brother

MENELAUS, one of the two Sons of Atreus, who have assembled the Greek expedition to Troy

AGAMEMNON, Menelaus' elder brother

CHORUS of Salaminian sailor-soldiers, who have come to Troy in the service of Aias

Place: before the quarters of Aias in the Greek shore-camp at Troy; later changing to further along the shore.

Odysseus comes on warily from the side of the main camp, stooped down try-
ing to make out footprints. Athena follows, watching.°

ATHENA
  I am for ever catching you, Odysseus,
  sniffing out some move to make against your enemies:
  and so I find you now outside the camp of Aias,
  where he's stationed at the fringes of the fleet.°
  I've watched you scouring and comparing tracks
  to trace that man's fresh-printed movements,
  and determine whether he's inside or not.
  Good work! Your trail has brought you to your prey,
  like some keen Spartan hound upon the scent:
  your man has just now gone inside,
  his brow and deadly sword-hand drenched with sweat.   10
  So there's no need to peer inside his gates.
  But tell me why you're going to such pains,
  then you can find out more from one who knows.

ODYSSEUS
  How readily I recognize your voice,
  Athena, closest of the gods to me.
  And even if you are invisible,
  I hear your sounds and grasp them in my mind
  as though the trumpet's brazen mouth° had sounded out.
  Yes, you are right: I'm prowling round to catch an enemy,
  Aias, bearer of the famous shield:°
  he is the one, no other, I've been tracking down.   20
  I'll tell you why: this very night he's done a thing
  which makes no sense—that's if the deed is really his,
  because we're floundering with nothing known for sure.
  And I have volunteered to bear this task of finding out.
  We have discovered all our captured flocks°
  hacked down and mangled, and their guards as well.
  Now everyone is pinning blame for this on him.
  There is a witness saw him all alone
  and pounding on his way across the plain   30
  with dripping sword in hand. He detailed this report to me,

and I am off upon the track at once.
Some traces I can follow well, but others have me baffled,
and I can't detect who's where.
You've joined me at the perfect time;
I shall be guided by your touch
from now on, as I have been in the past.

ATHENA
I was aware of this, Odysseus,
and set out in advance to be your guardian,
and a ready helper with your hunt.

ODYSSEUS
Dear mistress, are my efforts closing on the mark?

ATHENA
This is the very man who did those deeds.

ODYSSEUS
But why should he unleash such aimless violence?   40

ATHENA
It was Achilles' armour° made him full of anger.

ODYSSEUS
Yet why this onslaught on the flocks?

ATHENA
He thought he was discolouring his hands
with *your* life-blood.

ODYSSEUS
What? He meant to strike against the Greeks?

ATHENA
And would have done, if I had not been vigilant.

ODYSSEUS
What made him confident enough to dare this thing?

ATHENA
He moved against you in the night, by stealth, alone.

ODYSSEUS
Did he succeed in getting near his goal?

ATHENA
Right to the doorway of the twin command.°

ODYSSEUS
What held his hand in check when he was thirsty for our blood?   50

ATHENA

    I did. I held him off by casting on his eyes
    mistaken fantasies, malignant raptures;
    and I diverted him against the flocks of spoils,
    not yet shared out, still under herdsmen's watch.
    There he attacked the animals,
    and, cleaving all around him, butchered them.
    One moment he believed he had
    the Sons of Atreus, and was killing them,
    then turned on now one leader, now the next.
    Meanwhile I spurred him as he ranged in his delusions,
    driving him to fall into the fatal net.   60
    Then when he'd had enough of this pursuit,
    he roped together all the herds and cattle left alive,
    and drove them here back home, as though
    he had caught humans, not mere animals with horns.
    And now he's got them all tied up indoors
    and is tormenting them.
    I'll show this mad affliction right before your eyes,
    so you can then report to all the Greeks.
    No, stay. Take heart and face the man,
    and don't expect disaster;
    I shall turn askew the focus of his eyes,
    so that he won't perceive you face to face.   70

Calling out to Aias.

    Hey there! I'm calling you—
    the man who's shackling prisoners—
    I mean you, Aias. Kindly come on here outside.

ODYSSEUS

    Whatever are you at, Athena?
    No, don't call him here outside.

ATHENA

    Stay quiet; don't show yourself a coward.

ODYSSEUS

    For gods' sake, don't! Just let him stay inside.

ATHENA

    To stop what happening?
    Was this man not a man before?

ODYSSEUS

    Yes, and a mortal enemy to this one—and still is.

ATHENA

    So laughter at your enemies is not the sweetest sort?

ODYSSEUS

    Well, I am happy if he stays indoors.   80

ATHENA

    Are you afraid to see a man who's clearly mad?

ODYSSEUS

    If he were sane, I wouldn't flinch in fear from him.

ATHENA

    But he won't even see you standing near.

ODYSSEUS

    How can that be, if he still has his sight?

ATHENA

    I shall obscure his eyes although they see.

ODYSSEUS

    Well, I suppose a god can manage anything.

ATHENA

    Then stand there quietly as you are.

ODYSSEUS

    I'll stay. . . but I would rather be elsewhere!

SCENE 2

ATHENA (*calling again*)

    Hey you, Aias, I call to you again!

    Why do you rate your ally at so little worth?   90

AIAS (*appears in the doorway*)

    Greetings, Athena, greetings, child of Zeus,

    what a comrade you have been to me!

    I shall adorn you with pure golden trophies

    as a thank-you for this haul.

ATHENA

    That is good. But tell me: have you well and truly

    dipped your blade in blood of Greeks?

AIAS
    I can boast that—I won't deny that claim.

ATHENA
    And have you really made your hands all bloody°
    with the gore of Atreus' Sons?

AIAS
    So that they'll never more dishonour Aias.

ATHENA
    The men are dead, I gather from your words.

AIAS
    They are. Now let them try and take my armour!   100

ATHENA
    And what about Odysseus? How go things with him?
    Or has he managed to escape?

AIAS
    You're asking where that filthy vermin is?

ATHENA
    Odysseus, yes, your stumbling-block.

AIAS
    He, mistress, sits inside, my choicest prisoner—
    I don't want him to die just yet.

ATHENA
    Before you do what? What do you want more from him?

AIAS
    After I've bound him to the building's centre-post. . .

ATHENA
    How will you then humiliate the wretch?

AIAS
    . . . I'll lash° his back to crimson. . . then he dies.   110

ATHENA
    Don't torture the poor man so cruelly.

AIAS
    I bid you all the best in every way, Athena,
    but for this. He has to pay this very penalty.

ATHENA
    Well, since you take such great delight in this, set to,
    and don't spare anything from what you have in mind.

AIAS

    Then back to work!
    And this I have to say to you:
    stand always by my side, so good an ally.

Aias goes back inside.

ATHENA

    °You see, Odysseus, how the power of the gods is great.
    Could there be any man who had more foresight?
    any better apt to fit the action to the time?   120

ODYSSEUS

    None that I know.
    I pity him, poor fellow, even though my enemy:
    to see him clamped tight with catastrophe.
    In this I'm thinking not so much of him, more for myself:
    it makes me see that we who live and breathe
    are nothing more than phantoms,
    or insubstantial shadowings.

ATHENA

    In view of this, be careful not to speak
    with arrogance towards the gods,
    or take on airs because you are superior to others
    in your strength or hoards of wealth.   130
    A single day can tip the scales of human fortune
    down, and lift them up again.
    The gods befriend the sensible,
    and they detest those who do wrong.

°*Athena and Odysseus depart. The Chorus of Aias' loyal troops enter from
the direction of the camp.*

°CHORAL ENTRY RECITATIVE, FOLLOWED BY SONG

CHORUS

        Aias, son of Telamon,
        lord of bedrock in the sea,
        wave-surrounded Salamis,°
        when your fortune's prosperous,

I am happy by your side.
But when Zeus' thunder strikes,
or pernicious slandering
from the Greeks envelops you,
then I shiver terrified,
like a pigeon's fluttering eye. 140
Just so, after this last night,
allegations trouble us,
rumours meaning our disgrace:
that you breached the grazing-grounds,
killed the captured animals,
common booty of the Greeks,
hacked them with your gleaming blade.
That's the story, whispering,
that Odysseus has contrived,
passing it to everyone;
and persuades them, since, of you,
such a tale's believable. 150
Each who hears more gladly gloats
with spite at your calamities.
If one shoots at someone great,
then the arrow cannot miss:
if they told such tales of me,
they would not be credited.
Envy creeps up behind power.
Yet the small without the great
make a weak wall of defence;
little stones are fitted best
in between the boulder rocks, 160
great supported on the small.
It's impossible to teach
foolish men to understand.
Fools like this are chattering;
and we have no strength to keep
them off without your presence, lord.
Once they have escaped your gaze,
they then chirp like flocks of birds.
If you suddenly appeared, 170
they would cower in silent hush,
frightened by the eagle's power.

Which god pushed you into your attacks
on the people's cattle herds and flocks?
Could it be Artemis° hit you hard
for some triumph you did not reward,
cheated out of trophies owed to her,
or not thanked for hunting of her deer?
Did bronze Ares,° ally in some fight,   180
feel insulted, and punish this slight
by devising trickery in the night?

Never if sane would you go so wide
off mark as to massacre the herd;
stroke of god must have glanced a blow.
Zeus, Apollo, keep these slurs at bay.
If those two high kings and bastard brat
of low Sisyphus° spread round about
slanders falsely, don't, lord, hide your face;   190
don't stay like this in your shore-side place
any longer, gathering more disgrace.

Stir yourself, stand upright,
you have stayed too long time,
keeping out from the fight,
sending sparks, blazing harm,
flaring up to the skies.
While your proud enemies
fan the flames of their lies
all through the windswept woods
fearlessly, as they all
cackle their vicious words.
And my own pain stands tall.   200

SCENE 3

Enter Tecmessa° from the building.

TECMESSA
Crewmen of the ship of Aias,
from the earthborn stock of Athens,°
we who care about the distant
house of Telemon have reason

now for grief and lamentation.
Mighty, awesome, savage Aias
lies afflicted, shipwrecked
by a darkly swirling tempest.

CHORUS-LEADER
But what change to even worse
has night now <added
to the anxious> daytime?°
Tell us please, Tecmessa,
child of Phrygian Teleutas.°   210
Since the warrior Aias,
who took you in warfare,
loves you and embraces you,
you might enlighten us with
closer knowledge.

TECMESSA
How to tell of what should not be spoken?
What has happened you will find
as bad as death itself.
Our great Aias, overwhelmed by madness
in the night, has been degraded.
In this building you may witness
such a scene of butchered victims,
blood-bespattered, sacrifices,   220
all the work of that man's hand.

CHORUS
All that you reveal
of our fiery man is hard
news to bear, and yet
too apparent to avoid.
Noisy rumour spread
round by the leading Greeks,
as the taunting grows
louder and still louder speaks.
What's to come brings fear:
the man's bound to die exposed,
since he with frenzied hand   230
brandishing his dusky sword,
has killed the horseback
stockmen and their herd.

TECMESSA

> Ah, so that is where he gathered
> them, from there; then he came back,
> driving on the flock of animals as prisoners.
> Some he slaughtered on the ground here,
> others he dismembered, slashing at their flanks.
> Taking two white rams,° he sheared
> the head and tongue from one, and flung them off;
> then bound the other upright to a pillar,   240
> took a mighty harness-strap for horses,
> and then thrashed the ram with
> whistling doubled leather,
> hurling insults which a god,
> no man, had taught him.

CHORUS

> °Now it is high time
> to cover my head and slip
> stealthily away;
> or getting aboard a ship
> launch her on the sea,   250
> each man at his rowing-bench.
> With such threats unleashed
> by Atreus' Sons against
> Aias and his friends,
> I'm very afraid that I,
> by his side, shall be
> pelted with stones and die—
> all while his mad state
> repels my company.

TECMESSA

> That is over.
> As a scudding south-wind storm goes
> sweeping on with no more flares of
> lightning, he's recovered.
> Now that he's regained his senses,
> he has got new anguish:
> contemplating troubles self-made,   260
> with no one collaborating,
> lays a bed of mighty anguish.

CHORUS-LEADER

    Well, if his fit has passed, I think we should be glad,
    because with troubles gone, there's less cause for concern.

TECMESSA

    Which would you pick, if you could choose:
    to cause pain to your friends and revel in delight yourself,
    or share your grief in common with your company?

CHORUS-LEADER

    Well, lady, double suffering's bound to be the worse.

TECMESSA

    Then we are now afflicted, even though he is not sick,

CHORUS-LEADER

    What do you mean? I cannot understand. 270

TECMESSA

    As long as he was sick, he took delight
    in those dark things that overwhelmed him,
    even though inflicting pain on us, the sane around him.
    But now his sickness has died down, and he's released,
    he's wholly swept along by black despair;
    and we meanwhile are just as burdened as before.
    So is this not a double grief in place of one?

CHORUS-LEADER

    I understand, and fear this is a stroke dealt by some god.
    Because how else could he not be in better spirits,
    now restored, than when he was deranged? 280

TECMESSA

    Yet you must know that that is how he is.

CHORUS-LEADER

    How did this trouble first descend on him?
    Tell us, your fellow-sufferers, what occurred.

TECMESSA

    I'll tell you everything since you're involved as well.
    It was the dead of night, the watch-fires
    were no longer flaring for the evening,
    when he took his sharpened sword,
    all eager to set out upon a mission
    for no apparent reason. I complained:
    'Aias, whatever are you doing now,

embarking on an enterprise without a message
fetching you, and with no trumpet-call?   290
The army is all fast asleep.'
But his reply was pithy, and familiar:
'Woman, for women silence is an ornament.'
So I gave up, and he rushed off alone.
What happened next out there I cannot tell;
but when he came back in, he was corralling bulls,
sheepdogs, and fleecy flocks, all bound with ropes.
He cut the throats of some; others he hung head down,
and chopped them through the spine;
he tortured others in their bonds,
assaulting beasts as he might men.   300
°Then finally he darted out of doors
and blurted speeches to some sort of shadow.
Some words were aimed against the Sons of Atreus,
some about Odysseus, mixed with laughing loud
at what he had inflicted on them
in repayment for their insults.
And then he hurried back indoors again,
and fitfully returned to his right mind.
But when he looked and saw the building full of havoc,
he struck his brow and cried out loud;
then hurled himself among the carcasses
of slaughtered sheep, and sat,
his fingernails clutched tightly in his hair.   310
For quite a time he crouched there silent,
then he threatened me most horribly,
if I did not reveal the whole train of events;
and also asked what part he had in this.°
I was afraid, my friends, and told him everything
that had been done, so far as I could make it out.
Then he at once broke into bitter cries,
a sound I'd never heard from him before.
He always used to say such whining   320
was fit only for dejected cowards:
he groaned himself more like a bellowing bull,
unmixed with any shrill lament.
And now, exhausted by catastrophe,
the man sits where he fell, among the animals
he slaughtered with his sword,

making no noise, refusing food, refusing drink.
And clearly he intends to do some dreadful deed.
[as that is what his words and cries portend]. °
My friends, this is the reason why I came to you:
please come inside and help in any way you can—
for men like him can be prevailed upon
by words from friends.   330

CHORUS-LEADER

By your account, Tecmessa, he, our man,
has been possessed by dark disasters.

AIAS

(*Cry of distress from inside.*)

TECMESSA

Becoming worse, it seems.
You heard that kind of shouting cry that Aias made?

AIAS

(*Repeated cry of distress from inside.*)

CHORUS-LEADER

He seems to be afflicted still,
or else he's feeling pain
because of that affliction past.

AIAS

My boy, my boy!

TECMESSA

Ah, no! Eurysaces,° it's you he's shouting for.   340
What can he want?
And where on earth are you? What misery!

AIAS

Hey, Teucros°. . . where can Teucros be?
Is he to be away collecting spoils for ever,
while I get destroyed?

CHORUS-LEADER

Now he appears to be in his right mind.
So open up the doors;
perhaps when he sees me he'll be restrained.

TECMESSA

All right then, I am opening them.
Now you can see what he has done;
and see what kind of state he's in.

LYRIC DIALOGUE

°*Aias is revealed, sitting among the corpses of slaughtered animals.*

AIAS

> Good friends, my old crew,
> it's you alone preserve   350
> the loyal straight rule.
> See me caught in the wave
> of this blood-storm whirlpool.

CHORUS-LEADER (*to Tecmessa*)

> Your story now seems all too true:
> what he has done shows he is not in his right mind.

AIAS

> My experts at sea,
> you rowers of our boat,
> Only you I see
> to send away this hurt: 360
> help to slaughter me.

CHORUS-LEADER

> Don't say such words. Don't try to cure a wrong
> with wrong, and make the agony yet worse.

AIAS

> See me, fearless in the field,
> dauntless man at arms,
> victor over harmless lambs—
> a laughing-stock, reviled.

TECMESSA

> Aias, my lord, I beg you not to say these things.

AIAS

> Get out of here! Go somewhere else!
> (*Cries in distress.*)   370

TECMESSA

> For heaven's sake, give way. Think sensibly.

AIAS

> Through my fingers I allowed
> devilish men to slip:
> and attacked horned cows and sheep
> spattering black blood.

TECMESSA
Why grieve about what has been done?
it is impossible to have these things undone.

AIAS
All, Odysseus, forge of wrong,   380
all you hear° and see.
Lowlife trickster, you must be
laughing loud and long.

TECMESSA
It is the god that gives to each to laugh or cry.

AIAS
If only, in my ruin, I could watch him too. . .
(*Cries of distress.*)

TECMESSA
No talking big—you surely see how low you are.

AIAS
°Ancestor Zeus, if only I
could kill that vermin fox,
master-crook of tricks,   390
and myself then die.

TECMESSA
When you pray that, then pray for me to die as well.
What cause have I to live if you are dead?

AIAS
Pitch black, my light,
underworld° most bright—
for me: take, oh take
me inside your dark,
hold me in your hall.
No more may I call
any man or god
to ask for some good.   400
The daughter of Zeus°
kills me with misuse.
Where can I escape?
where find somewhere safe?
So if my whole past
is reduced to dust,°
if I've been intent

on a futile hunt,
every soldier should,
both hands, raise his blade
and strike me down dead.

TECMESSA

I'm in despair that this fine man   410
should say such things, things that he never
would have been reduced to say before.

AIAS

Tracks lapped by waves,
and sea-formed coast caves,
thickets by the brine,°
long, long, too long time
you have kept me here
at Troy. But no more,
no more while I have
still the breath of life.
Those with thought should know.
And you nearby flow
of Scamander's° streams,
kindly to the Greeks,   420
no longer shall you see
one to equal me,
whose like, I dare claim,
Troy has never seen
during all this time
come from Greece.° Yet I
now dishonoured lie.

TECMESSA

I have no way to stop your words,
but cannot let you speak,
reduced so low in such disaster.

SCENE 4

AIAS

Aiai, Aias! Who ever would have dreamt my name   430
would chime so closely with the misery of my life,
as now I cry *aiai* redoubled.°

[and tripled, such are the sorrows that I'm in.]°
My father went back home from here,
this land of Troy, bedecked with honourable fame,
rewarded with the prize for highest bravery:°
but I, his son, have come to this same place,
with strength no less than his,
have managed exploits just as great—
and here dishonoured by the Greeks I fall.   440
And yet I reckon this for sure: that if Achilles
were alive, and going to award his armour
as the prize for highest bravery,
then no one else would bear it off but me.
Instead, the Sons of Atreus have purveyed them
to a man who'll stop at nothing,
and pushed aside my powerful claim.
And if these eyes and mind had not spun off,
deflected from my aim, they never would have lived
to cast a vote like that against another man.
But as it is, the unconquerable, fierce-glaring   450
goddess, child of Zeus, has tripped me up,
just as I was about to close my grip on them.
She made me morbidly deranged, so that I dyed
my hands with blood of creatures of this sort.
Meanwhile they cackle and run off, in spite of me.
But when a god decides to harm a stronger man,
then lesser cowards can escape.
And now what should I do?
I'm clearly hated by the gods;
the Greeks feel loathing for me;
the whole of Troy, these plains detest me.
Should I sail home across the wide Aegean Sea,   460
deserting this ship-camp and Atreus' Sons?
And then what kind of face would I present to Telamon?
He could not bear to look at me,
stripped bare, denuded of those glorious prizes
which had crowned his life with highest fame.°
That act would be intolerable.
Well then, suppose I break inside the walls of Troy,
and, fighting solo hand-to-hand,
go down at last engaged in some heroic feat?
But that way I would gratify the Sons of Atreus—

no, that is no use.   470
I have to find some exploit that will show
my aged father that I am his very son,
and not a gutless coward.
I say it's shameful for a man to want long life
when he has no escape from never-ending misery.
What joy in day succeeding day,
with now a move towards life's end and now away?°
Myself, I wouldn't give a penny for the man
who hugs mere empty hope for warmth.
To live well or to die well:
those are the only options for a noble man.
That's all I have to say.   480

CHORUS-LEADER

What you have said could not be called a sham;
you've spoken your own mind.
Yet pause, give up ideas like these,
and let your friends direct your mind.

TECMESSA

°Aias, my lord, there's nothing worse for humans
than to bear a fate imposed by harsh necessity.
I am born of free parentage; my father was as well supplied
with wealth and strength as any man in Phrygia:
yet now I am a slave.
That may have been decided by the gods,
and certainly by your strong arm.   490
Therefore, now that I sleep with you, I wish you well.
And so I beg of you by Zeus, god of the family hearth,
and by your bed, which has joined you
in partnership with me, don't make me have to hear
insulting language from your enemies;
don't let me fall into the hands of someone, anyone.
For on the very day you die and leave me by myself,
you may be sure I shall be violently
manhandled by the Greeks,
and your son too, to bear a life of slavery.
And then some master will let fly a bitter jibe: 500
'Well, look at her, bedfellow once of Aias,
the army's mightiest: now see
what drudgery she bears, instead of being lady luck'—

someone will say that sort of thing.
My fortune will direct my life: but words like these
will mean disgrace for you and your whole house.
Respect your father, don't desert him
in the grimness of old age.
Respect your mother, now allotted many years,
who prays so often you shall come back home alive.
And pity your own boy, my lord,   510
bereft of you, deprived of childhood care,
oppressed by alien guardians.
Think what misery you leave him when you die—
and me as well, for I've nowhere to look but you.
You turned my native land into a waste of war;
and then my mother and my father
both were taken off to join the dead.
What country could have I but you? What wealth?
My whole security depends on you.
And think of me for my own self: 520
a man should clasp the memory,
if he's experienced some lovely joy.
For kindness breeds new kindness,
ever back and forth.
If recollection of the good received
evaporates, that man should lose
the title of a noble man.

CHORUS–LEADER
  If only you felt pity as I do, Aias,
  you would approve the things this woman says.

AIAS
  The way for her to be approved by me
  is if she brings herself to do what I command.

TECMESSA
  I shall obey, dear Aias, everything you say.

AIAS
  Then fetch my son where I can see him.   530

TECMESSA
  I was afraid and so I sent him off.

AIAS
  Because of this disaster here, you mean?

TECMESSA
In case the poor thing crossed your path and met his death.

AIAS
That would have fitted all too well with my unlucky fate.

TECMESSA
At least I took good care preventing that.

AIAS
Yes, that precaution and your action I approve.

TECMESSA
What can I do to help you then, as things are now?

AIAS
This: let me talk to him, and see him clearly here.

TECMESSA
Yes, he's nearby, with servants looking after him.

AIAS
Why this delay? He should be here.   540

TECMESSA (*calling out*)
My son, your father's calling you.
Yes, bring him here, whoever's looking after him.

AIAS
Well, are they coming? Is your word ignored?

TECMESSA
Here is a servant bringing him.

°*Eurysaces is led on by an attendant.*

AIAS
Lift, lift him here to me.
He'll feel no fear at seeing all this fresh-spilt blood,
not if he really is my true-born son.
He must be broken in while young
and learn the tough ways of his father,
so his character's completely formed like mine.

Eurysaces has been handed over to Aias, and set down beside him.

My son, may you be happier than your father,   550
but in other ways the same—
and then you will be fine and brave.
Yet even now I envy you in this,
that you are wholly unperceiving of these troubles—

seeing life is at its sweetest
when it's free from all awareness,
[for being unaware's a painless ill] °
before you learn the sense of joy and grief.
When you arrive at that, then you must show
our enemies what sort of man you are,
and show what sort of father you're bred from.
Till then sustain your innocence upon the tender breeze,
a joyful solace to your mother here.
No single Greek, I'm confident, will try to harm you   560
with degrading violence, even when apart from me,
because I'll leave you such a fearless champion
in Teucros, who will take brave care of you
although he's absent now pursuing enemies.
And you, my warriors, my islanders, I ask this favour
for your share: report these, my commands, to him.
He is to take this boy, my son, back to my home,
and introduce him there to Telamon,
and to my mother, Eriboea, so he may take care of them
throughout the length of their old age,   570
until they reach the chambers of the god below.°
And no one is to be allowed to organize a contest
for my arms among the Greeks—
and not the man who ruined me.°
My son, take this, the armour that explains your name,
Eurysaces;° hold and deploy it by its plaited strap,
my seven-hide impenetrable shield.
The rest of my equipment shall be buried
in the grave along with me.
(*to Tecmessa*) Now quickly, take this child, and close the building up.
And no laments or shedding tears outside—
women are much too liable to pity.   580
Come on, close up the doors.
A well-skilled doctor doesn't warble incantations
for an abscess calling for the knife.

CHORUS-LEADER
  I am alarmed to hear this vehemence,
  and I don't like the sharp edge of your words.

TECMESSA
  Aias my lord, what do you intend to do?

AIAS

Don't ask, don't probe. It's best to be restrained.

TECMESSA

I'm in despair. I beg you by your son and by the gods,
do not, do not be our betrayer.

AIAS

Too much complaint. Do you not see
that I'm no more indebted to the gods in any way?   590

TECMESSA

Don't say such things.

AIAS

Don't speak to me; I am not listening.

TECMESSA

There's no persuading you?

AIAS

You've talked for far too long.

TECMESSA

Because I am afraid.

AIAS

Close up the doors—and quick.

TECMESSA

For gods' sake, soften.

AIAS

I reckon you a fool if you believe that even now
you can re-educate the person that I am.

Aias is shut inside; Tecmessa stays on stage; Eurysaces is taken away.°

CHORAL SONG

CHORUS

    Salamis, my famous island,
    blessed, wave-lapped by the sea,
    you shall stand out bright for ever,
    clear for everyone to see.
    Contrast me, though, in the meadows   600

under Ida° all this time,
sleeping outside in discomfort,
counting endless months in line,
ever in the expectation,
crushed on time's relentless rack,
of descending one day down to
Hades' all-erasing dark.

And I have to stay by Aias,
struck by sickness past relief,
dwelling with his god-sent madness   610
in the sheepfold of his grief.
Salamis, you used to send him,
champion in the blaze of war:
now he pastures lonely thought-flocks,
bringing friends more pain to bear:
all those deeds of highest courage
fallen, fallen down in ruins
with no friendly recognition
paid by Atreus' loathsome sons.   620

Grey with age bred by years,
his mother shall, when she hears
how madness gnaws at her son,
cry *ailinon, ailinon*,
pitiful nightingale;
she shall pour her piteous trill,°
piercing high funeral odes,   630
in time with fists beating thuds
on her breasts in despair,
tearing at her silver hair.

Hidden in Hades dead
is better than live and mad.
Bred from the noblest blood,
he is not true to his breed,
straying outside of it.   640
You, father unfortunate,
yet to learn what a doom
has come upon on your son,
such as has never struck,
apart from him, your high stock.°

SCENE 5

Aias re-emerges from inside, carrying his sword.

AIAS
　　°Long and incalculable Time
　　grows everything from dark into the light,
　　and covers all that has appeared once more.
　　So nothing is unthinkable:
　　even the fiercest oath,
　　even the most inflexible of minds,
　　can be undone.
　　And so with me: I was so fiercely hard before,   650
　　like tempered steel, but now my edge
　　has been new softened by this woman here.°
　　And I feel pity at the thought of leaving her
　　a widow at the mercy of our enemies,
　　my boy an orphan.
　　But I shall go along the shore
　　to where the meadow washing-places are,
　　so I can purge myself of stains,
　　and keep at bay the goddess's oppressive wrath.
　　I'll go and find some place no human foot has trod,
　　and there I'll hide this sword of mine,°
　　detested blade, by digging out a hole
　　where no one can set eyes on it.
　　Let Night and Hades keep it safe below.   660
　　For, ever since I first received this as a gift
　　from Hector, my most deadly enemy,
　　I've had no comfort from the Greeks.
　　There's truth in that old proverb: gifts from enemies
　　are not real gifts, and bring no gain.
　　And so from now on we shall know to yield before the gods;
　　and we shall learn to bow before the Sons of Atreus°—
　　they are rulers, so one's bound to yield. . . no choice!
　　For even things that are most strong and awesome
　　still give way to proper place.°   670
　　The winter thick with snow makes way
　　for summer with its fruitful crops;
　　the dismal round of night retreats

before the day's white horses, blazing light;
the fearsome winds can still to calm
the straining sea; and even sleep all-powerful
lets go of his grip and does not chain
his prisoners for evermore.
So we are surely bound to learn to know our place.
I shall. For I have newly come to realize
an enemy should only earn our enmity
so far as fits one who may yet become a friend;   680
and I shall only give a friend support
so much as suits one who may not remain a friend for good.
The truth is, comradeship turns out for most
to be a faithless anchorage.
As for these matters, they shall be all well;
and you, my woman, go inside
and pray the gods they bring to pass in full
those things my heart desires.

Tecmessa goes silently inside.

And you, my comrades, pay to me the same respect as her:
convey to Teucros, when he comes,
that he should take good care of my affairs,
and show goodwill towards you.
I'm going on the path I have to tread.   690
Do as I say, and soon perhaps you'll find
that, even if I am for now unfortunate,
I shall have been kept safe.

Exit Aias away from the camp, i.e. eastwards along the shore.

CHORAL SONG

CHORUS
        I shiver with desire,
        I fly in ecstasy.
        Yes, Pan, yes, Pan, appear,
        come across the sea
        from snowy mountain-tops
        of wild Arcadia°—
        dancing-master of the gods,
        their choreographer.

So here upon this ground
you may join in and prance
the steps that you have found.°   700
For I have now to dance.
And, lord Apollo, come,
and join us, shining clear,
come from your Delos home,
and always treat us fair.

Ares has removed the pain
that overcast my sight.
Yes, yes, now once again,
now, Zeus, let shine the light,
and let the bright days start
to gleam on our swift boats: 710
now Aias has changed heart,
forgetting his old hurts,
and in good order brings
the gods their sacrifices.
Time's might decays all things,
nothing could surprise us;
of all beyond-hope turns,
Aias has changed his mood,
respecting Atreus' Sons,
rejecting his old feud.

SCENE 6

Enter Teucros' man from the camp direction.

TEUCROS' MAN
    First I shoud tell you, comrades: Teucros is fresh back
    from exploits in the hills of Mysia.°   720
    But as he neared the centre of the camp
    he met abuse from all the Greeks en masse,
    as they had recognized him from afar.
    Encircling him, there was not one who didn't join
    in casting insults from this side and that,
    denouncing him as brother of that maniac

who plotted to attack them all.
There was, they said, no way he could avoid
stark death, reduced to shreds by stoning.
Things reached the stage when swords
were drawn out from their scabbards. . .   730
Once the quarrel reached that far, it was contained
through calming words from senior men.
But where is Aias? I must tell him all of this,
for everything should be conveyed to those concerned.

CHORUS–LEADER

He's not inside. He went away just now,
with new intentions harnessed to new ways.

TEUCROS' MAN

Oh no! Then I've been sent too late
upon this errand, or I've been too slow.

CHORUS–LEADER

Why? What is missing from what must be done?   740

TEUCROS' MAN

Teucros commanded that the man should not be let
outside the house before he had got here himself.

CHORUS–LEADER

Well, he has gone. He turned to thinking positively
how to end his anger with the gods.

TEUCROS' MAN

These words are full of foolishness—
at least if Calchas° is right-minded in his prophesy.

CHORUS–LEADER

What's this? What does he know that bears on this?

TEUCROS' MAN

This much I know as I was there to witness it.
Calchas moved from the council gathered   750
round the chiefs, away from Atreus' Sons;
and taking Teucros by the hand in friendly fashion
urged him to keep Aias shut inside his tent
by every means he could, and not allow him to go out—
just for this daylight shining now,
not if he ever hoped to see him still alive,
because Athena's fury would pursue him
for this single day alone:° that's what he said.

Those men whose presence builds up to excess,
the seer explained, are then brought crashing down   760
through harsh misfortunes planted by the gods—
whoever is begotten as a human, and yet fails
to keep his thoughts within the human scale.
And Aias was revealed to be unsound
right back when he was leaving home.
His father gave him good advice:
'My son,' he said, 'you should aspire to triumph in the field,
but always with a god's support.'
But his reply was arrogant and ill-considered:
'Even some nonentity might triumph, father,
with the gods to help. I can, I trust,
acquire the glory-crown without their aid.'
His bragging took that tone.   770
And then, another time, Athena was supporting him
and told him to charge in and kill the enemy;
but Aias gave a terrible, unspeakable, response:
'My lady, go and take your stand
beside the other Greeks:
the line will never give way where I stand.'
With words like these he's earned unyielding anger
from the goddess, through his thoughts
beyond the human cast of mind.
Yet if he stays alive for this one day,
we may with god's help prove to be the saving of him.
That is what the prophet said.   780
Then Teucros rose at once, and sent me off to you
with these instructions. But if we're thwarted,
then that man no longer lives,
if Calchas has true skill.

CHORUS-LEADER (*calls out*)
    Tecmessa, O poor woman, child of misery,
    come and hear what this man has to say.
    We're just a razor's edge from sorrow.

Tecmessa enters.

TECMESSA
    What? Why disturb me yet again,
    when I have only now found rest from unremitting pain?

CHORUS-LEADER
  Just hear the painful news
  that this man brings about the fate of Aias.   790

TECMESSA
  What is it, man? Are we destroyed?

TEUCROS' MAN
  I cannot know the case with you, but Aias,
  if he's gone away from home. . . I fear for him.

TECMESSA
  He has gone out of doors: your words are torture to me.

TEUCROS' MAN
  Teucros commands that he be kept inside the camp,
  and not allowed to go off by himself.

TECMESSA
  Teucros is where? And why does he say this?

TEUCROS' MAN
  He's just returned. But he anticipates
  this going out will lead to death for Aias.

TECMESSA
  Ah no, whoever did he learn this from?   800

TEUCROS' MAN
  From Calchas, who declares this very day
  is crucial for him—death or life.

TECMESSA
  O friends, protect us from this fate
  which threatens inescapably.
  Some go to Teucros urging him to hurry here,
  while others head along the shore to scour the bays
  towards the west, and others to the east,°
  to follow up the man's ill-omened going off.
  I realize that he's played me false,
  and I have been rejected from
  that long-time favour that I used to know.
  Ah, ah, what should I do, my child?
  It's no use staying here;
  I'll keep on going for as long as I have strength.   810
  Let us be moving then, be swift,

this is no time for inactivity,
not if we want to save a man
who's hastening to death.°

CHORUS-LEADER
  We're ready to set off, as we shall show in deeds,
  not only words, but swift to act and hurry on our way.

°*Exit Teucros' man towards the camp. Tecmessa also goes. The Chorus splits
into two halves, and departs, half in each direction. The empty stage marks
a change of scene to a remote spot along the shore.*

SCENE 7

°*Aias enters alone from the direction of the camp. He is carrying his sword;
going towards the back of the stage-space, he plants it in the ground with blade
pointing up.*

AIAS
  The slaughter-knife: it stands here
  so its blade may cut most clean
  [if there is time for one to calculate].°
  It was a gift from Hector, my worst enemy,
  the man most hated in my sight;
  and here it stands firm fixed
  in hostile Trojan soil, fresh-sharpened
  on the iron-devouring whetstone.   820
  I've planted it myself and fixed it firm around,
  to be most kindly in ensuring me quick death.
  So then, I'm well equipped.
  And now, O Zeus, you rightly should be first to help;
  and it is not a mighty favour that I ask.
  Send someone, please, to take the fatal news
  to Teucros, so that he may be first to raise me up,
  when I lie fallen on this freshly bloodied sword:
  don't let me be discovered by my enemies
  for flinging out as carrion for the dogs and birds.   830

That's what I ask of you, O Zeus.
I also call on Hermes,° who escorts the dead below,
to send me well to sleep,
a leap that's struggle-free and quick,
when I impale my breast upon this blade.
And next I call the ever-virgin helpers,
who forever overview all human suffering,
the striders, dire Erinyes,° to come
and find how I'm destroyed in misery by Atreus' Sons.
°[And may they grasp those wicked men
and evilly destroy them, as they see me   840
here falling in self-slaughter: so may they also die
self-slaughtered by their dearest offspring.]
Come, you vengeful, swift Erinyes,
gulp blood, spare no one from the whole damned army.°
And you, the Sun, steep heaven's charioteer,
when you next see my fatherland,
pull on your golden reins, and give my aged father
news of my catastrophe and death
and my unhappy nurse, poor mother—
once she hears this news, she'll spread   850
a great lament through all the town.
But there's no point in all this futile grief:
the act must be embarked upon—and quickly too.
Now, death, come, death,
it's time for you to tend to me.
°[and yet I'll meet and talk with you down there as well.
And you, this present Light of shining day,
and you the chariot-driving Sun, I call on you
for this last time of all, and never more again.]
O daylight, and you, sacred soil
of my own Salamis, bedrock of my ancestral hearth;   860
and glorious Athens,° with your race akin to mine,
and all you springs and rivers here, and Trojan plain,
I say farewell, my nourishers.
These are the last words Aias has to say to you:
all else I shall address to those below.

He throws himself on his sword.

SCENE 8

Re-enter Chorus in two halves from opposite directions.

HALF-CHORUS A

    Care upon care brings
    yet more care.
    Where, where? For I've been
    everywhere.
    No place gives me clues
    to be sure.
    Look! Do I detect   870
    some footsteps near?

HALF-CHORUS B

    It's us, your friends from on-board ship.

HALF-CHORUS A

    Any sign?

HALF-CHORUS B

    We've searched the whole shore westward of the ships.

HALF-CHORUS A

    Any find?

HALF-CHORUS B

    Just heavy going; nothing else to see.

HALF-CHORUS A

    Nor has the man left any trace
    along the path from eastward shores.

°LYRIC DIALOGUE

CHORUS

    Help me! if only some fisherman
    toiling away at his sleepless net,   880
    or else some goddess of the mountainside
    or nymph of the Bosphorus° riverbed,
    were able to spy him, and tell me where
    the fierce one is wandering—anywhere?
    For I have been seeking him, far and wide,
    yet unsuccessfully; it's a hard
    task tracking a man whose mind is mad.°   890

Tecmessa's voice is heard as she emerges from the background 'thicket' near which the body of Aias lies.

TECMESSA
>Ah no! No!

CHORUS-LEADER
>Who is it I hear calling from this copse nearby?

TECMESSA
>Ah me, my misery!

CHORUS-LEADER
>I see Tecmessa, captured wife of Aias,
>caught up in this cry of grief.

TECMESSA
>I'm lost, I'm dead, I'm desolated, friends.

CHORUS-LEADER
>What do you mean?

TECMESSA (*pointing to the body, which the Chorus have not seen*)
>Here Aias lies, new slaughtered,
>wrapped around his sword deep buried in him.

CHORUS
>It's gone, it's gone,
>my journey home.° 900
>You've killed me, lord,
>your friend on board.
>Unhappy death,
>unhappy wife.

TECMESSA
>All we can do is cry 'Aias, alas!'

CHORUS-LEADER
>Who did he get to help him do this thing?

TECMESSA
>It's clear he turned his hand against himself:
>this sword firm-planted in the earth
>is proof he fell on it.

CHORUS
>I see my blind folly;
>you blood-soaked, lonely,
>no friend, unshielded. 910
>I was so stupid,

                    wholly unwary,
                    I was uncaring.
                    Where is he lying?
                    Unyielding, alas,
                    ill–omened Aias.

TECMESSA
    No, not for looking at. I shall completely
    cover him with this enfolding cloak.°

She covers the body.

    No one who holds him dear could bear to see
    the blackened blood stream from his nostrils,
    and his lethal self–inflicted blow.
    What shall I do? What friend is there
    to raise you up? Where's Teucros now?   920
    If only he would come, he would arrive in time
    to help lay out his brother's body here.
    O poor Aias, how great you were,
    how great your fall; how you deserve,
    even from enemies, lament.

CHORUS
                    So you were bound, then, with time were bound,
                    given your obstinate will, to find
                    death, this uncrossable gulf of pain.
                    All through the night and daylight your mind,
                    fierce from your suffering, growled abuse,   930
                    constantly cursing the Sons of Atreus.
                    It was that time that began our harm,
                    when Achilles' armour was made the claim,
                    set as the prize for the bravest arm.

TECMESSA
                    (*Cry of grief*)

CHORUS–LEADER
                    I know true pain afflicts your heart.

TECMESSA
                    (*Cry of grief*)

CHORUS–LEADER
                    I understand your doubly grieving, lady,   940
                    new–bereaved of one so dear.

TECMESSA
> You may imagine: all too well I know.

CHORUS-LEADER
> I say the same.

TECMESSA
> My child, it's such a heavy yoke of slavery we face;
> just think what warders are set over us.

CHORUS
> You hint at deeds
> too cruel for words,
> ruthless actions
> by Atreus' Sons,
> who have no heart.
> Please gods avert.

TECMESSA
> Things would not be like this, but for the gods.　　　　950

CHORUS-LEADER
> They've made our weight of grief too hard to bear.

TECMESSA
> This is the pain that Zeus' fearsome daughter, Pallas,
> plants to show Odysseus favour.

CHORUS
> That man, much-enduring,°
> he must be sneering,
> happy to mock us
> in his heart's darkness.
> Laughing with gladness
> at all this madness.
> Those Sons of Atreus,
> hearing it later,　　　　960
> will join his laughter.

TECMESSA
> Then let them laugh and take delight
> in this man's sufferings.
> It may be that, although they did not feel
> the want of him alive, they will lament his loss,
> once they're in need without his battle-spear.
> For those who have bad judgement never know
> the good they hold until it's thrown away.

°For me his death's as bitter as for them it's sweet;
but for the man himself it's brought some joy,
because he got his heart's desire,
the death he wished for.
Why should they then stand laughing over him?
It is the gods that killed him, and not them, not them at all.   970
So let Odysseus have his fill of gloating over nothing.
Aias is no more for them: not so for me—
his parting leaves me full of anguish and of tears.

SCENE 9

Teucros approaches from the side of the camp.

TEUCROS
  (*Cry of grief*)

CHORUS-LEADER
  Hold quiet, I think I hear the voice of Teucros,
  crying in a strain that harmonizes with this horror.

TEUCROS
  My dearest brother, Aias, light and comfort to me,
  is it true you've suffered as the rumour says?

CHORUS-LEADER
  The man is dead—you'd better know that, Teucros.

TEUCROS
  Then what a heavy fate that means for me.   980

CHORUS-LEADER
  And in that case. . .

TEUCROS
  I'm lost in grief.

CHORUS-LEADER
  . . . well may we mourn.

TEUCROS
  How fierce a blow.

CHORUS-LEADER
  Yes, yes, too much.

TEUCROS
> Such pain! And what about his son?
> Well? Where on earth is he?

CHORUS-LEADER
> Left by the tents alone.

TEUCROS (*to Tecmessa*)
> Then go and fetch him here at once.
> Make sure no enemy can snatch him,
> like the lost cub of a lioness without her mate.
> Go, hurry, join our effort here.

Exit Tecmessa towards the camp.

> All are inclined to spurn the dead once they are down.

CHORUS-LEADER
> Yes, Aias left instructions when he was alive   990
> for you to take care of the boy, as you do now.

TEUCROS
> Most bitter sight of all the sights
> that I have ever set my eyes upon;
> most painful path of all my paths,
> deep piercing to my core.
> That is the one I have just taken, dearest Aias,
> when I heard about your fate, as I was tracing
> and deciphering your final steps.
> A cutting rumour, as though from a god,
> swept through the Greeks,
> that you were dead and gone.
> When I heard this, while distant still, I sorrowed inwardly: 1000
> but now I look on you, my life is crushed.
> Come now, uncover him,
> so I may see the worst in full.

Aias' body is uncovered.

> Oh how this face is hard to look upon,
> its grimace full of bitter resolution;
> how many agonies your death has sown for me.
> For where can I go now, what people can I turn to,
> when I was no help to you in your dark hour?
> To Telamon perhaps, your father, mine as well?
> Think what a kindly, cheerful face he would receive me with

when I return without you!—Yes,   1010
the man who does not smile too gladly at the best of times!
There's nothing that he'll hold in check,
there's no abuse he'll not let fly against the bastard son,°
got from his conquered enemy, the cowardly,
puny me who proved a traitor to you, dearest Aias—
and even did so through deceit, so, with you dead,
I might usurp your power and property.
That is the kind of thing he'll say, that tetchy man,
grim in old age, quick for a quarrel on no grounds.
And in the end I shall be cast out from my land,°
discarded, made to seem through his abuse
a slave, not a free man.   1020
So much for things at home.
And here at Troy I have a lot of enemies,
and small support, as I have found out through your death.
Ah, now what shall I do? How can I wrench
you from this bitter, gleaming blade?
This is the killer which snuffed out your life;
and so you see how in due time it was still Hector,
even after death, who slaughtered you.
°Consider, by the gods, the fates of these two men.
First Hector with the belt that Aias gave
was tied behind the chariot-rail   1030
and raked along until he breathed his last.
And he received this present here from him,
and with it took his life by his death-dealing fall.
It must have been an Erinys that forged this sword;
and Hades, the cruel craftsman, made that belt.
[I would maintain it is the gods contrive
such things for humans, all of them and always.
And as for anyone who does not like these sentiments,
he can enjoy his own ideas, while I'll keep these.]

SCENE 10

CHORUS-LEADER
Don't talk for long, but think instead   1040
how you will bury him within his grave.

And think what you'll say now, because I see an enemy;
and he's most likely coming here
to mock at our distress, as bad men do.

TEUCROS
Who from the army is it that you see?

CHORUS-LEADER
It's Menelaus, for whose sake
we first embarked on this campaign.

TEUCROS
Yes, now he's near, he is not hard to recognize.

Enter Menelaus from the camp direction.

MENELAUS
You there, I warn you not to try to lift
or move this body—leave it as it is. . .

TEUCROS
Why waste your breath on words like these?

MENELAUS
That's my decision, and the will of him
who is the chief commander.   1050

TEUCROS
Well, tell us what you offer as your explanation.

MENELAUS
Because, when we recruited him from home,
we had supposed that we were bringing here
a friend and ally for the Greeks.
Instead we have discovered him to be
more dangerous than the Trojans are:
the one who hatched a deadly plot
against the army as a whole,
by setting out by night to put us to the sword.
And had some god not smothered this attempt,
it would be us who would have reaped this fate of his—
us lying there in low, humiliating death,
whilst he would be alive.   1060
But, as it is, a god has switched things round,
and turned his violence against the flocks and herds instead.
And that is why there is no man with strength enough
to get this body buried in the tomb:

instead he shall be flung out on the yellow sands
to serve as fodder for the seashore gulls.
So don't you stir up violent fury.
Granted we never could control him while alive,
at least we'll dominate him dead—despite you.
I'll take control by force, because he never used
to pay attention to my words while he still lived.   1070
Indeed, it is the sign of a bad person
when a commoner disdains to pay respect to his superiors.
Good order never could advance in a society
where there is no establishment of fear;
likewise an army can't be ordered properly
unless there's a protective shield of fear and due respect.
A man should know, however brawny
he may grow in bulk, a small affliction
may still bring him down.
It is the person with a proper sense of fear
and modesty who wins security, you know.   1080
And that society where it is possible
for wanton violence and wilfulness to have their way,
though it may run a while before the breeze,
is bound in time to plummet to the depths.
So let there be due fear, say I, and let not those of us
who go indulging pleasure think they'll not
one day be made to pay it back in pain.
They run in alternation, do these things.
This fellow was aflame with insolence before,
but now it is my turn to think ambitiously.
And so I give you notice not to try and bury him,
in case you find it's you who's tumbling in the grave.   1090

CHORUS-LEADER
  Don't, Menelaus, lay out worthy sentiments,
  and then yourself maltreat the dead with arrogance.

TEUCROS
  I'll never be surprised again, my friends,
  if one of humble birth goes wrong,
  when those who are supposed to be of noble blood
  can still go wrong so grossly in their speech.
  Now tell us from the start again:
  you claim you fetched and brought this man

to be an ally for the Greeks?
Yet surely he set sail himself as his own master,
so how can you be his commander?   1100
And what authority have you to rule
the people he recruited here from home?
You came as king of Sparta,° not as master over us.
There's no decree of rank that gives you charge of him,
no more than he of you.
° [You sailed here as subordinate to others, not commander
of the whole with power to order Aias what to do.]
So rule the men you rule, and lambast them with lofty words:
but this man here I'll lay in earth with proper burial;
no matter if you and the other chief say yes or no,
I'll do what's right, and with no fear of your big mouth.   1110
°It wasn't for your wife he came to fight,
unlike your overloaded drudges,
but to keep the oath that he had sworn;
it had nothing to do with you,
because he had no time for nothing-men.
So go and bring some extra heralds here,
and fetch the major-general as well,
I'll never turn my head towards your noise,
not while you are the kind of man you are.

CHORUS-LEADER
  I still don't like this sort of talk in troubled times:
  harsh words, however justified, bite deep.

MENELAUS
  It seems the bow-and-arrow man° aspires to mighty thoughts.   1120

TEUCROS
  I do: it is no vulgar craft I claim as mine.

MENELAUS
  Had you a shield, you might make boastful challenges.

TEUCROS
  Even without, I'd be a match for you in all your gear.

MENELAUS
  Your big talk feeds up your proud fury!

TEUCROS
  There's nothing wrong in being proud with justice on your side.

MENELAUS
  So is it just for him, who murdered me, to get good treatment?

TEUCROS
  Who murdered you? Strange if you're dead and still alive!

MENELAUS
  A god has rescued me: if he had had his way, I would be dead.

TEUCROS
  Then if the gods have saved you, don't dishonour them.

MENELAUS
  And is it me disparaging the sacred laws?   1130

TEUCROS
  Yes, if you won't permit the dead due burial.

MENELAUS
  Because he was my enemy. Is that not right?

TEUCROS
  Did Aias ever stand against you in the field?

MENELAUS
  He hated one who hated him, as you know well.

TEUCROS
  Because you were exposed as having rigged the crooked vote.°

MENELAUS
  He came off worse thanks to the judges, not to me.

TEUCROS
  You could make packs of dirty tricks look good.

MENELAUS
  This talk is going to mean hard blows for somebody.

TEUCROS
  No harsher pain, I think, than I'll inflict myself.

MENELAUS
  One word to you: this man must not be buried.   1140

TEUCROS
  And you shall hear this one word answer: burial.

MENELAUS
  °One day I saw a man, emboldened with big talk,
  who urged his sailors to press on
  their voyage through a tempest.
  But once enveloped in that storm,

you could not hear a word from him,
as he was huddled underneath his cloak,
and let the seamen trample over him at will.
In just that way a mighty storm
grown from a little cloud
may buffet you and your loud mouth,
and smother all your blustering.

TEUCROS
  And I once spied a man stuffed full of foolishness,   1150
  who showed contempt towards
  his neighbours in their darkest hour.
  And then someone like me in form and character
  saw him and said: 'Do not, man,
  treat the dead insultingly, since if you do,
  you can be sure you'll suffer pain yourself.'
  That's what he told the wretch
  straight to his face. I see that man:
  I think he is none other than yourself.
  Now is the moral of my fable clear?

MENELAUS
  I'm off. I would be put to shame if people heard me
  lashing you with words, when I could use straight force.   1160

Menelaus heads off towards camp.

TEUCROS
  Then off you go: it is a deep disgrace for me
  to stand here listening to vacuous speeches from a fool.

SCENE 11

CHORUS-LEADER
  °There is bound to be a mighty conflict.
  Therefore, Teucros, hurry quickly as you can
  to find a hollow grave-trench for this body,
  where he'll take possession
  of his musty sepulchre, memorial
  for mortals evermore.

Tecmessa and her son approach from the camp.

TEUCROS
>And look, here come the man's young child and wife,
>just in good time to lay his wretched body out.   1170
>°My boy, come here, keep close
>beside the father who begot you,
>and as a suppliant take hold of him.
>Stay there in supplication,
>clasping in your hand three locks of hair—
>one mine, one hers, and one your own—
>as treasured tokens of asylum.

The boy and Tecmessa sit by the body.

>If any person from the army should attempt
>to drag you from this corpse by force,
>then may that man be severed from the earth,
>unburied in disgrace, his whole kin
>scythed down at the root as irremediably
>as I cut off this lock of hair.

He cuts a lock of hair; Tecmessa cuts her own and the boy's.

>Take hold of him and stay there, boy;   1180
>and don't let anyone dislodge you.
>If they should try, then throw yourself
>upon the body and hold tight.
>(*To Chorus*) And you, don't stand by helplessly,
>but act as men, not women, and give help
>until I can return from making ready this man's grave—
>no matter who forbids the deed

°*Exit Teucros in the direction away from the camp.*

CHORAL SONG

CHORUS
>What will be the number,
>what the sum of tears,
>which complete the total
>of the fleeting years?
>Years that bring me ceaseless
>battle-toils to face
>through wide Troy, this torment,   1190
>for us Greeks disgrace.

If only he'd been banished
down to Hades first,
or to the high heavens,
that first man accurst,
first pioneer of weapons,
who taught Greeks war-strife,
trouble upon trouble,
blight of human life.

That is the man deprived me
of the wine-cup and its joy,   1200
garlands and music's sweetness,
of the night-time and its joy;
stopped me from love, from loving.
Instead I sleep here at Troy,
hair unkempt, drenched with dewdrops,
tokens of wretched Troy.   1210

Aias was my protection
against stabs, fears in the dark:
now though he's doomed in downfall.
Is there still joy we can take?
I only wish I was by that
wooded cape, sailing on past
sea-beaten Sounion's headland,°   1220
to greet sacred Athens at last.

SCENE 12

Re-enter Teucros, just in time to meet Agamemnon coming from the camp.

TEUCROS
　　I've hurried back because I saw the general,
　　Agamemnon, heading here in our direction:
　　it's clear to me that he'll unleash some stupid talk.

AGAMEMNON
　　It's you, they have been telling me, you
　　who have been impudently sounding off
　　against us, and getting off scot-free.
　　It's you I'm speaking to, the captured slave-girl's son.

Imagine, if you'd had a noble mother, how conceitedly
you'd spout and prance around with strutting steps.   1230
Although you are a nothing, and are championing
the nothing-man, you swear we have no right to act
as the commanders of the Greeks by land or sea:
Aias set sail here on his own authority, you claim.
To have to hear this stuff from slaves is monstrous.
What kind of man was this you fanfare so presumptuously?
Where did he march or make a stand that I did not as well?
And have the Greeks no proper men except for him?
That contest we established for Achilles' arms   1240
will turn out sour, it seems, if we are going to be
disparaged all about the place by Teucros;
and if you who lost will not concede defeat
despite the clear majority of judges.
Yet you, the failures, will persist in blackening us,
or stabbing us by use of trickery.
No rule of law could ever be established
from procedures such as these,
not if we push aside the rightful winners,
and position those who trail behind in front of them.
This has to be prevented.   1250
It's not the burly and broad-shouldered men
who prove to be the most dependable:
it's men of sense who everywhere best exercise control.
A hulking ox can still be kept on straight along the road
by means of a small whip—and I can see
that treatment reaching you quite soon,
if you don't summon up some sense.
Although your man no longer lives, but is a shade,
you nonetheless hurl brazen insults,
and allow your tongue free rein.
It's time you learnt some modesty;
appreciate just who you are, and bring along another,   1260
a free man, to put your case to me on your behalf.
If you start speaking, I'm afraid I would not understand—
I have no knowledge of the lingo of barbarians.

CHORUS
I wish you both would have a mind to be more sensible.
That is the best advice I have to give.

TEUCROS
   How quickly gratitude towards the dead
   can slip away, and can be caught betraying them,
   if this man here has no recall of you at all,
   no word, dear Aias, from him for whom you toiled   1270
   so often, risking your own life in war—
   all gone, discarded, thrown away.
   You have just spoken so much mindless nonsense!
   °Can you really have no recollection
   how you were cooped up inside the wall,
   reduced to nothing by the battle's turn,
   when he, all by himself, arrived and rescued you—
   that time the flames were licking round
   the ships and their top decks,
   and Hector leapt across the ditch to reach the hulls?
   Remember who averted that?   1280
   Not, I suppose, this man, who you assert
   had never ventured anywhere that you had not?
   You will agree he did the right thing by you then?
   °Another time he marched to fight with Hector
   in a single combat, picked by lot, not under orders:
   his lot, no shirking lump of mud, was ready
   to be first to jump out from the helmet's bowl.
   He was the one to do these deeds,
   and I was by his side, the slave,
   the man whose mother was barbarian.
   You fool, can you assert these things with open eyes?   1290
   °You must be well aware that your own father's father,
   Pelops, was by origin a Phrygian, a barbarian;
   and Atreus, who begot you, served his brother up
   a hellish feast concocted of his children's flesh;
   and your own mother came from Crete,
   and when her father found her sleeping with an unknown man,
   he sent her to be silenced by the hungry fish.
   With such a pedigree, you dare discredit me for mine?
   I am the true-born son of Telamon,
   the man who, as the army's highest crown,   1300
   received my mother in his bed;
   and she was royal by birth, the daughter of Laomedon,°
   selected as his special gift by Heracles.
   So I am nobly born from noble parents, both of them;

and I'll not shame my own blood-kin
as he lies here in such great trouble,
while you're for shoving him away unburied,
and you're not ashamed to boast as much.
You may be sure of this, though: if you throw him out,
you'll have to throw the three of us along with him.
For I am proud to die there in full view defending him,   1310
in preference to fighting for your woman—
or, I should have said, your brother's.°
So think about your own position, and not only mine:
if you do me some harm, you'll wish one day
you had been cowardly and not so brash with me.

SCENE 13

Enter Odysseus suddenly from the side of the camp.

CHORUS-LEADER
   My lord Odysseus, you have come at the right time,
   if you are here not to make snags, but to untangle things.

ODYSSEUS
   What is it, men? From far away I heard the Sons of Atreus
   shouting over this brave man, now dead.

AGAMEMNON
   Shouting because, Odysseus, I have had to listen   1320
   to insulting language from this person here.

ODYSSEUS
   What kind of thing? I can forgive a man who bandies insults
   when he has received abuse himself.

AGAMEMNON
   It's true he heard hard words from me,
   but that's because of how he had been treating me.

ODYSSEUS
   What did he do, then, that inflicted harm on you?

AGAMEMNON
   He says he'll not permit this corpse to lie without a tomb,
   and that he'll bury it, though in despite of me.

ODYSSEUS
Then may a close friend speak the truth to you,
and still remain your faithful man, no less than in the past?

AGAMEMNON
Go on. I'd have to be a fool to turn you down, 1330
since I rate you my closest friend among the Greeks.

ODYSSEUS
Then listen: do not go so far
as casting him away unfeelingly, unburied.
Don't let brute force prevail and make your hate
so rabid that you trample justice down.
For me as well he was my greatest enemy,
once I'd become the master of Achilles' arms;
and yet, despite that enmity, I'd not dishonour him
so far as to deny he was the single greatest Greek 1340
of us who came to Troy, but for Achilles.
So there's no way you can with justice
wipe his honour out: for it would not be him
you would be crushing but the values of the gods.
It can't be right to do a fine man hurt,
not once he's dead, regardless of your hate.

AGAMEMNON
Odysseus, are you fighting me and taking this man's side?

ODYSSEUS
I am. I hated him so long as it was right to hate.

AGAMEMNON
And now he's dead should you not tread upon his neck?

ODYSSEUS
Don't revel in advantage, son of Atreus, when it's wrong.

AGAMEMNON
It's not so easy for a monarch to be righteous. 1350

ODYSSEUS
But show respect to friends who give you good advice.

AGAMEMNON
A good man should defer to those who wield authority.

ODYSSEUS
Stop there! You're still in charge if you allow your friends to win.

AGAMEMNON
　This man you're favouring, recall what he was like.

ODYSSEUS
　He was my enemy, but he was noble too.

AGAMEMNON
　What do you mean to do? Revere an enemy corpse?

ODYSSEUS
　Because for me his excellence by far outbids his enmity.

AGAMEMNON
　It's men like this who are the undependable.

ODYSSEUS
　It's true that many present friends may later turn to sour.

AGAMEMNON
　Do you approve of making friends like these?　　　　　　　　　1360

ODYSSEUS
　I don't approve of minds that stay inflexible.

AGAMEMNON
　You'll show us to the world this day as cowards.

ODYSSEUS
　Not so: we shall be seen as just by all the Greeks.

AGAMEMNON
　So you are telling me I should allow this body to be buried?

ODYSSEUS
　I am. Because I too shall come to this.

AGAMEMNON
　It always is the same: each man works for himself.°

ODYSSEUS
　And who is it more apt to work for than myself?

AGAMEMNON
　Well then, the deed will be proclaimed as yours, not mine.

ODYSSEUS
　If you do this, you will be admirable in every way.

AGAMEMNON
　Know this for sure: to you I'd grant　　　　　　　　　　　1370

an even greater favour than this one.
But he shall stay my hated enemy, both here and there below.
You have permission for whatever action you may wish.

Exit Agamemnon towards the camp.

CHORUS-LEADER
Whoever says, Odysseus, you're not wise in judgement,
now you have behaved like this, would be a fool.

ODYSSEUS
And I proclaim to Teucros that from this time on,
I am as great a friend as I was once an enemy.
And I would like to join in burying this man,
to share the rites, and leave undone no task
that people should accomplish for the best of men.   1380

TEUCROS
Noblest Odysseus, I am full of praise for what you say—
you've far exceeded all my hopes.
You were his greatest enemy among the Greeks,
yet you alone have actively stood firm for him.
You did not let yourself, who live,
humiliate this man as he lies dead:
not like that thundering general and his sibling,
who both came and did their best to cast him out
degraded and unburied.
And so I pray to Zeus, lord of Olympus,
and the Erinys who recollects,
and Justice who completes: 1390
consign that vicious pair to a bad end, just as they wished
to thrust him out in undeserved disgrace.
But as for you, good son of old Laertes, I'm reluctant
to allow you to take part directly in this burial,
in case I should offend the dead by doing that.
But in all else please help, and if you'd like to bring
some others from the troops, we shall take no offence.
I shall myself attend to all the other things.
Yet rest assured that in our eyes
you've proved yourself a noble man.

ODYSSEUS

I should have liked to;   1400
but if you're uneasy with my doing that,
then I respect your wish, and go.

Exit Odysseus towards the camp.

TEUCROS

°That's enough. A lot of time has passed already.
Some of you should quickly
clear the hollow grave-trench;
others set a lofty tripod
where the fire will heat it,
ready for the ritual cleansing.

Some men go off in the direction away from the camp.

And a troop should bring
his body-armour from his quarters.

Some men go off in the direction of the camp.

(*To Eurysaces*) You, my boy, as best as you are able,
lovingly approach and help me
in the task of raising up your father's body,   1410
as his still-warm vessels flow with livid fluid.°

Teucros, Eurysaces, and others lift the body and form a procession.

Come now, everybody who is
here with claims to friendship,
hurry, let us all be moving;
add your efforts to do honour
to this man, in every way outstanding.
°[No one ever was superior to Aias
when he was among us, I assert that.]

CHORUS

°After they've seen,
then humans can learn
many things from the past.
Before they have seen
how their future will turn,
there's no one can forecast.   1420

*All, including Teucros, Eurysaces, Tecmessa, and the Chorus, take the body
of Aias off in the direction of his grave.*

PHILOCTETES

INTRODUCTION TO
PHILOCTETES

The Personal and Ethical Triangle

ALL the best Greek tragedies are in some respects untypical, but *Philoctetes* is even more untypical than most. It is set in a barren terrain with no local inhabitants; it is the only surviving tragedy with no female roles whatsoever; it has a cast-list of only five parts (eight would be more standard); and almost all the play is occupied with the relations between just three of those five, Philoctetes, Odysseus,[1] and Neoptolemus. It is their twisting-and-turning interactions and clashes that make the stuff of the play. In keeping with this spotlight on the individual human feelings and dilemmas, the chorus has a relatively interactive role, which diminishes its distinctive voice; indeed, it has only one fully fledged choral lyric (676–729).

The tensions between the three characters produce a kind of triangle of human forces. Philoctetes, at the apex so to speak, has been consumed with his loathing of Odysseus throughout the last nine, lonesome years, ever since he was abandoned by him and the leaders of the Greek expedition against Troy. When Neoptolemus turns up, Philoctetes is, by contrast, captivated by his youthful freshness, his resemblance to his father Achilles, and his (alleged) hatred of the same *bêtes noires*. His instinctive trust of Neoptolemus makes his eventual betrayal all the more disillusioning ("the doing of a man / who seemed incapable of wrong", 960). After that, it is then hugely heartening that Neoptolemus comes good after all. Even so, Philoctetes' settled hate is yet stronger than his new friend's good-will, as he explains in his speech at 1348 ff. His resolution is so implacable that it takes his dearest old friend Heracles, now transformed into an Olympian god, to dissolve it.

Odysseus is comparably single-minded, but in an utterly different style. He never wavers from his determination to be victorious by bringing about the defeat of Troy ("It's my instinct always to reach out for victory . . .", 1052). He is prepared to do and say whatever it takes to deceive Philoctetes, regardless of all his old-fashioned high-mindedness. He confidently manipulates young Neoptolemus, and intervenes whenever

---

[1] And the false "merchant" is, in effect, a surrogate for Odysseus.

he wavers. His duplicity is so self-aware that it verges on disarming (1049–51):

> . . . whatever sort of man is called for, that is me.
> So when the challenge is for righteous folk,
> you will not find one single person more high-minded.

There may even be some temptation to admire him; there is, after all, a level of truth to his claim that what he is doing is what Zeus wills (989–90). That does not mean, however, that Zeus endorses his methods. And in the end, he is dismissed humiliatingly, and has to run for his life (1302). The play ultimately dismisses his ethics along with the man.[2]

The third point of this triangle, caught between the pull of the two very different yet single-minded old hands, is the malleable, vacillating Neoptolemus. As is brought out clearly in the prologue-scene with Odysseus, he has a natural bent towards honesty and direct action (88–91):

> It is my nature not to manage anything
> by means of sordid guile;
> . . .
> I'm quite prepared to catch the man by force,
> but not by tricks. . .

But he is not able to hold out against Odysseus' manipulation, and eventually agrees to collaborate in the deceit. There may be some traces of compunction when he is first confronted with the outer squalor and inner integrity of Philoctetes (239–41), and he does avoid telling too many outright lies; nonetheless, he proves very effective in taking in the older man with his show of youthful artlessness. His moral unease recurs, however, and throughout the scene in which Philoctetes is suffering agonies of pain (730 ff.) it is subtly suggested that Neoptolemus is uncomfortable with his duplicity. This is confirmed by his refusal at 839–40 to desert Philoctetes while he lies oblivious in a coma.

The scene between lines 895 and 974, in which Neoptolemus first reveals his dilemma and is then faced with Philoctetes' plea for the return of the bow, is in many ways the core of the play. It takes the direct intervention of Odysseus to break Neoptolemus' dilemma, at least temporarily. For the rest of the scene after that his state of mind is left

---

[2] There have been those who maintain that Heracles at the end is actually Odysseus in disguise. At first glance this twist, with its cynical manipulation of power, might seem appealing. The trouble is that it would in effect bleed the entire play of its power: all those agonizing dilemmas for nothing! And it is, in any case, utterly implausible to have Odysseus fabricate all the things that only Heracles could have the perspective to be able to express.

tantalizingly unrevealed.[3] It is this very reticence that makes possible an unpredictable and highly unusual turn of events: Neoptolemus undergoes a crucial change of heart while off-stage. He then returns (at 1222) with his mind already made up to do the right thing by Philoctetes. So it comes about that his Achillean nature is finally triumphant over the double-crossing of Odysseus. He is even prepared to return to Greece along with the old warrior, and ready for the two of them to defy the allied forces from a kind of two-man citadel of integrity.

Heroic Models

The basic story of how Philoctetes was marooned on the island of Lemnos and fetched to Troy only towards the end of the ten-year siege, was ancient and well known. The participation of Neoptolemus was, however, an innovation by Sophocles. We know this because in earlier versions, including tragedies by both Aeschylus and Euripides, it was Odysseus and Diomedes who were sent to fetch him.[4] This innovation sets up one of the central features of the play: the young man's dilemma between the two "role-models" of behaviour. This is explicitly set out as the choice between two kinds of hero. Philoctetes is firmly associated with Achilles, whom he always praises. And there is also a sort of "roll-call" at 410 ff. of others who share that kind of old-fashioned integrity and open courage: Aias, Patroclus, and Antilochus, all of them now dead at Troy. Odysseus is, of course, the exemplar of the other, new sort of hero, the pragmatic strategist, and he is associated in the same scene with the Sons of Atreus, Diomedes, and Thersites. Philoctetes bitterly detects a pattern in all this (448–50):

> The gods spend special care on this,
> and take a strange delight in turning back
> the crooks and tricksters from the doors of Hades,
> whilst for ever packing off the just and virtuous.

Behind the "old-style" heroes looms another great model: Heracles. Philoctetes was his close friend, and, as a kind of token of their shared values, Heracles passed on to him his supernatural bow and arrows that never miss their target. The handover had occurred high on Mount Oeta,

---

[3] It is still much disputed whether the desertion of Philoctetes is genuine or a bluff, and whether Neoptolemus is colluding with Odysseus. See note on 1080.

[4] This is thanks to an essay (*Oration* 52) by Dio Chrysostom (first century AD), which compared the three dramatizations. It is interesting that in the other two there were local inhabitants of Lemnos who formed the chorus.

Philoctetes' home territory, when he alone was prepared to light the
pyre while Heracles was still alive on it, suffering unrelenting agonies.[5]
Philoctetes is willing to contemplate allowing Neoptolemus to handle the
bow only because he sees in him a virtue worthy of Hercules (667–70):

> . . . it shall be yours to take the bow
> into your hands, to give it back again,
> and to proclaim the boast that you alone of men
> have handled it, by virtue of your goodness.
> It was by doing a good deed
> that I myself first came by it.

This assurance is then turned into actuality when Philoctetes, knowing
that he is about to fall into unconsciousness, hands the bow over for
safe-keeping. Even as it changes hands, he draws attention to its power
and to its possible danger (776–8):

> Here, take it, son.
> And pray to keep resentment off,
> so that it does not prove for you a thing
> weighed down with pains, such as it has been to me,
> and to the one who was its owner previous to me.

Awareness of this potential is an important factor in bringing Neoptolemus
to feel pain and regret at what he is doing. At the same time, he is reluctant
to let the bow go, now that he actually has it in his hands: in fact he keeps
possession of it all the way from line 776 until line 1292 (this includes
1081–1217, when he is off-stage). So, although he does eventually return
it, there is, arguably, an ominous suggestion that by obtaining the bow by
unworthy means, Neoptolemus has incurred some sort of indelible black
mark. In the longer-term myth he will participate in the sack of Troy, but
will commit a sacrilege by killing Priam, and will die young after his return
to Greece. The ending of the play may hint at this future: see note on
1440–1. If this interpretation is right, it suggests that Heraclean heroism
needs to be so uncompromisingly honest that even a temporary contam-
ination by Odyssean neo-heroism will damage it irrevocably.

Destiny and Human Will

Philoctetes presents an unkempt, scarcely human, figure; he has been,
as he says, "turned to something wild" (226). All that he still retains to

---

[5] The story leading up to this (but with no mention of Philoctetes) is dramatized in
Sophocles' *Women of Trachis*.

show that he was once an aristocratic warrior is his eloquent use of the Greek language—and the magnificent bow of Heracles. He draws attention to this awe-inspiring token before he even gives his name (261–3). But he has another distinguishing sign, no less conspicuous: one of his legs is bound round the calf and foot with old, improvised bandages, all discoloured with the stains of infection. The wound and the bow,[6] the degradation and the sign of exceptionality, are indivisible. It is this above all that makes Philoctetes such an unusual and striking tragic figure.

While the dilemmas of Neoptolemus form one interwoven strand holding the concentration of this play together, the intransigent figure of Philoctetes is no less, perhaps even more, fascinating. How, it is asked repeatedly, how could he have survived in these conditions with such hardship and pain for so long? Two things have, it seems, filled his mind during this time: his hatred for the leaders who abandoned him, and his command of language. This man, who seems at first to have been reduced to a less-than-human figure, delivers no fewer than five magnificent speeches during the course of the play.[7]

But why does Philoctetes have the wound? There is no suggestion that he has done something wrong to deserve it. He simply had the bad luck, it seems, to have trodden too close to the sacred snake in the sanctuary of Chryse. It is small wonder that he finds the ways of the gods incomprehensible (451–2). All that is offered in the way of explanation within the play is a belief that the gods must have determined it this way. Neoptolemus twice voices the sentiment. Early on he explains to the chorus that it must be the will of the gods that Philoctetes should not take Troy with the invincible bow before the fated time (192–200). And towards the end, when he finally tells Philoctetes about the prophet Helenus at 1325 ff., he says that all the agony has been "from a higher fate", and that he will never be rid of it until he goes willingly to Troy. There is no underlying moral shape offered for this, it is simply the inscrutable way that the gods work. The same dispensation is confirmed by the divinized Heracles at the end. He does, it is true, draw an analogy between the way that his labours have led in the end to immortal stature and the way that Philoctetes' sufferings will emerge into "a life of glory". But this is not laid down as some sort of pattern of higher justice, it is

---

[6] The title of a famous, if somewhat dated, essay (1941) on the effect of childhood traumas on famous writers, by Edmund Wilson.

[7] These are: (i) the story of his abandonment (254–316); (ii) his plea to be taken home (468–503); (iii) the great plea for the return of his bow (927–60); (iv) his damning indictment of Odysseus (1004–49); (v) the unacceptability of going to Troy (1348–72).

simply a comforting analogy in this particular case. The play *Philoctetes* tells how it is, but does not explain why.

As often in Greek tragedy, the narrative as determined by the will of the gods and the sequence of actions as achieved or attempted by the humans are kept as two separate levels of explanation. In *Philoctetes* they are more than usually divergent and hard to reconcile. The evidence for divine will is provided by the prophesies of Helenus: it is through these that the Greeks know in the first place that they have to get Philoctetes and the bow to Troy before the city can be finally conquered. The significance of Helenus is first reported by the false "merchant", but he is far from a wholly reliable source. Helenus' pronouncements are not conveyed in a trustworthy form until Neoptolemus brings them to bear in his final appeal. Elements that become newly clear at this late stage are that Philoctetes must come of his free will; that he will definitely be cured; and that it needs the two of them together to defeat Troy. It would be a mistake, however, to read awareness of these "facts" back into what has transpired earlier in the play. It is true that there are oblique hints, most notably in Neoptolemus' reference to the instruction of the 'god' in his hexameter lines at 839–42 (see note); and Helenus' prophesies may also be implicit in Odysseus' claim to the authority of Zeus at 989–90. But there is never a definitive citation of what Helenus said, and thus no definitive answer to questions such as: are both the bow and man essential? Does Philoctetes need to come willingly? As often in Sophocles, the oracles are divulged piecemeal and not fully consistently; his plays tend to reveal oracular elements in snatches that are not completely consistent, and in a sequence that serves the drama, not "the truth". For the audience they present an enigma almost as much as they reveal divine will.

Philoctetes has no doubt that it is the gods who have brought about this new interest in him (1037–9):

> . . . you never would
> have set out on this quest for such a wretch,
> unless some prodding from the gods
> had sent you after me.

But that does not mean that he accepts Helenus' prophesies as the last word. On the contrary, his belief that the gods must ultimately be just leads him to quite a different conclusion: they must want to pun- ish Odysseus and the Sons of Atreus—the gods cannot possibly want him to support those villains! He is so confident of the justice of his case that it leads him to insist on a course of action that is actually con- trary to the prophesy of Helenus: he will go back to Greece. He even persuades Neoptolemus to come along with him. In this way Sophocles shows human judgement and will making a strong case for a course of action which is in direct conflict with what must be, with "destiny". If Philoctetes goes to Greece then Troy will not fall: the myth will not happen.

Sophocles deliberately pushes this "anti-destiny" to the verge of being enacted before he allows "what must be" to be asserted in the end. Heracles only appears at the moment when Philoctetes, and Neoptolemus with him, are beginning to set off for Greece. He has come, as he says (1415–16):

> . . .to tell you Zeus' purpose,
> and to stop you from the journey
> that you have just started out on.

It takes the external, superhuman intervention to reassert destiny; it was not reached through human choice.

Possible Endings

The "human" ending is brought so close to happening at line 1408, before the "divine" ending is superimposed on it, that some have felt that Sophocles offers it as somehow a more real conclusion. We might well be disinclined to regard the departure to Troy as *more* satisfactory, at least at first sight. Philoctetes and the conscience-stricken Neoptolemus were about to go off to set up a kind of bastion of truth and loyalty, free of corruption: instead they have to join the world of intrigue, compromise, and unfairness that will eventually manage to achieve victory at Troy. It would be hard to accept that that is a morally better world, although it may be maintained that it is more realistic and less isolated.

Taking a longer perspective on the lead-up to this ending, it makes sense to see *Philoctetes* as tracing a whole series of possible endings, all but the last of them rejected or averted. The first comes at line 1217. Whether we view the departure of Odysseus and Neoptolemus with the bow as genuine or as a bluff, there is no doubting that Philoctetes' departure into his cave is in earnest. He believes he is going to his death; he foresees that he will starve in there, and that his body will, with a sort of reciprocal justice, be consumed by the wild creatures that he himself has been feeding on (see 954–8, 1155–7). This might, indeed, have made an ending: the stubborn old hero is left to die on his island, while the others triumph (maybe) at Troy with the help of his bow. It is not Philoctetes, but the conscience of Neoptolemus that reopens the play.

Next, two possibilities are briefly glimpsed in the flurry of action at 1293–1303. For a moment it seems possible that Odysseus might seize the bow by force. What might have happened in that case? Almost immediately after that, at 1299, it seems a real possibility that Philoctetes will shoot and kill Odysseus. The consequences of that denouement are not explored either—it all happens too fast.

After this Neoptolemus makes his deeply serious plea to persuade Philoctetes to come to Troy of his own free will. When he finishes his speech at 1347 there is, I suggest, a real possibility that Philoctetes will be persuaded: he himself regards this moment as a tough dilemma (1348–51). Had Philoctetes agreed, had the harsh old hero softened before the entreaties of his young friend, then the prophesy of Helenus would have been gladly fulfilled. This would, in a sense, have been the "happy ending". But it would also have been too easy, too bland to satisfy the complexity of the play.

Instead, Philoctetes is not able to yield, and puts the pressure on Neoptolemus to yield instead. And so it comes about that before long the pair are about to embark together on the "anti-destiny" discussed above. It would have been a fully human ending, but also one which would have to confront unresolved strife and violent recriminations. And the bow of Heracles would have been put to deadly use in a kind of civil war. So the attractions of this ending become much more ambivalent on further thought.

Last of all comes the ending imposed by Heracles "from the machine". Before disparaging this as contrived or authoritarian, there are some considerations worth taking on board. Heracles not only confirms the cure at Troy,[8] and the glory of the victory, he also assures Philoctetes that he will return home in triumph. And there he will find his old father Poias still alive. And the bow will be put to proper use, to kill Paris, to defeat Troy, and to be honoured at the site of the pyre of its ultimate owner. In response to this, Philoctetes puts up no protest or resistance: he recognizes that this is what has to be, regardless of the flaws of the other leaders at Troy (who are carefully not mentioned).

His final farewell to Lemnos (1452–68) is deeply moving. He calls with a kind of wistful affection on his rocky cave, the breaking sea and wind-swept spray, the lonely echoes, and his sustaining sources of life. And so:

> Farewell, sea-encircled land of
> Lemnos, send me

---

[8] *The Cure at Troy* is the title of Seamus Heaney's version of the play, first performed in Derry in 1990.

on a fair and faultless voyage,
where strong fate conveys me,
and the good advice of comrades,
and the all-subduing godhead
who has brought these things to pass.

PHILOCTETES

LIST OF CHARACTERS

ODYSSEUS, experienced strategist for the Greek siege of Troy

NEOPTOLEMUS, son of Achilles, still young and inexperienced

PHILOCTETES, old warrior from Thessaly who has been marooned on
Lemnos for nearly ten years

'MERCHANT', a member of the crew, disguised as a merchant sea-captain

HERACLES, great hero who has now become one of the celestial gods

CHORUS of loyal members of Neoptolemus' crew from Scyros

Place: a deserted part of the island of Lemnos, near the entrance to the
cave where Philoctetes has been living.

Odysseus enters cautiously from the direction of the ship, followed by Neoptolemus with an attendant.

ODYSSEUS
  This is the place:
  this is the shore of Lemnos isle,° encircled by the sea,
  not trodden or inhabited by men.
  And it was here, son of Achilles,° greatest of the Greeks,
  young Neoptolemus, here that I once deposited
  the man from Malis, son of Poias.°
  I was acting under orders set by my superiors:
  his foot was suppurating with a flesh-devouring ulcer,
  and this meant that we could undertake
  no offering or sacrifice in peace and quiet
  without his constantly distracting the whole fleet   10
  with his wild, ill-omened swearing, howlings, screams.
  No need for detail—this is not the time for chattering,
  that way I'd spoil the whole device
  by which I plan to catch him quick.
  But now it is your task to serve by spying
  whereabouts round here there is a double-entrance cave,°
  one with two seats so as to catch the sun in winter,
  while in summer months a breeze that's good for sleep
  blows through the hollow gallery.
  A little lower down towards the left   20
  you may make out a spring of drinking-water,
  if it is still good.
  Now make your way there—silently—
  and signal whether he still lives in this same spot,
  or if he's moved elsewhere.
  Then I can tell you all the rest of what we plan,
  and you can hear it, so that we proceed in step.

Neoptolemus starts exploring.

NEOPTOLEMUS
  Your task, my lord Odysseus, need not take me long:

I think I see a cave that fits with your description.

ODYSSEUS

Above you, or below? I see no sign of it.

NEOPTOLEMUS

Here, higher up. . . and there are footprints at the entrance.°

ODYSSEUS

Look out in case he's sleeping there inside.　　　　　　　　　30

NEOPTOLEMUS

An empty chamber's all I see: no human here.

ODYSSEUS

And are there not some traces of domestic life?

NEOPTOLEMUS

Yes, here's a pressed–down mass of leaves,
like there would be for someone bedding down.

ODYSSEUS

But otherwise all bare? There's nothing else inside?

NEOPTOLEMUS

Ah, here's a cup–shaped lump of wood—
a piece of clumsy craftsmanship.
And some material for kindling fire.

ODYSSEUS

These must be his, these treasures you describe.

NEOPTOLEMUS

Ugh! And here as well there are some rags hung up to dry,
all stained with some revolting discharge.

ODYSSEUS

It's clear that this must be the place he lives,　　　　　　　40
He can't be far away:
how could a man whose leg is maimed
by that long-time infection ever venture far?
He might have gone to search for food,
or he may know of some medicinal plant.
Dispatch your man to keep a look-out,
and make sure he doesn't pounce
upon me by surprise: he'd rather get his hands
on me than all the other Greeks.

Neoptolemus sends his attendant off, and comes back close to Odysseus.

NEOPTOLEMUS
   He's gone now and will guard the path.
   If there is more you want to tell me,
   go on with the second part.

ODYSSEUS
   Son of Achilles, you must show your breeding   50
   in this mission, and not only through your strength.
   So if you now hear something of a novel kind,
   something you've never heard before,
   you must still do your bit—you're here to serve, you know.

NEOPTOLEMUS
   What then do you require?

ODYSSEUS
   The soul of Philoctetes:
   you must inveigle him by telling tales.
   So when he asks you who you are and where you're from,
   reply 'Achilles' son'—no need to juggle that—
   but say you're sailing home,
   and that you've left behind the naval expedition
   of the Greeks because you loathe them utterly.
   Say that they sent and begged you to leave home   60
   and join with them, because you were
   their only way of taking Troy.
   But then when you arrived and asked, as was your right,
   that they should pass to you the armour of Achilles,
   they did not agree, but made them over to Odysseus.
   And add whatever nasty things you like of me,
   the foulest of the foul—that won't hurt me a bit.
   But if you don't succeed in this,
   then that will do real harm to all the Greeks,
   because, if that man's bow is not acquired,°
   then you shall never conquer Troy.
   Now I'll explain the reason you can hold a conversation   70
   with him that is credible and safe, while I cannot.
   When you set sail for Troy, you were not bound
   by oath° to anyone, nor were you forced to go,
   nor were you part of the campaign that went at first:
   whereas for me all these are undeniable.
   So if he catches me while he controls his bow,
   I am a dead man—

and I am bound to drag you down along with me.
So this is what we have to work out cleverly:
a way that you can rob him of that unconquerable bow.
Now I know well, my son, it does not come to you
by nature to design or weave this sort of sordid trick;   80
but victory's a pleasant prize to grasp, so steel yourself—
we can emerge as righteous at another time.
For now, though, give yourself to me
for one brief hour or two, devoid of shame.
And then for ever more you can be famed
as the most virtuous of mortal men.

NEOPTOLEMUS

For me the things I find a pain to hear, son of Laertes,
I also find abhorrent to convert to deeds.
It is my nature not to manage anything
by means of sordid guile; it's not my way,
and not my father's either, so they say.
I'm quite prepared to catch the man by force,   90
but not by tricks: no need—
he couldn't get the better of our numbers,
not by force, with only one good leg.
I was sent here to be your helper, and I've no wish
to be known as the one who let you down;
but I had rather fail while acting honourably
than win success dishonestly.

ODYSSEUS

You are your noble father's son.
I was young once as well, and I was slow with speech,
but had a ready hand for deeds.
But now that I have gained experience,
I see that in the human world it is your speech
and not your deeds that manage everything.

NEOPTOLEMUS

So your command is simply that I should tell lies?   100

ODYSSEUS

I'm saying you should capture Philoctetes by deceit.

NEOPTOLEMUS

But why by trickery rather than persuasion?°

ODYSSEUS
Because he will not be persuaded.
And you'll never capture him by force.

NEOPTOLEMUS
Has he the strength to fill him with such confidence?

ODYSSEUS
He has: his arrows always hit the mark, and kill.

NEOPTOLEMUS
So much that no one even dares get near to him?

ODYSSEUS
None, not unless they catch him by a trick, as I am telling you.

NEOPTOLEMUS
So you don't think it wrong to peddle lies?

ODYSSEUS
Not if those lies lead safely to success.

NEOPTOLEMUS
How can one have the face to blurt out things like that?   110

ODYSSEUS
To gain advantage you should never flinch.

NEOPTOLEMUS
What is the gain for me if that man comes to Troy?

ODYSSEUS
Troy falls before this bow of his, no other way.

NEOPTOLEMUS
So I am not to be the conqueror, as you have claimed?°

ODYSSEUS
Not you without the bow; and not the bow apart from you.

NEOPTOLEMUS
If that's the case, we have to track it down.

ODYSSEUS
If you can manage that, you bear off two awards.

NEOPTOLEMUS
What two? If I was sure, I'd not refuse this deed.

ODYSSEUS
You would be famous as both brave and clever too.

NEOPTOLEMUS
All right. I'll do it, and I'll lay aside all sense of shame.   120

ODYSSEUS

You do remember, then, the briefing that I gave to you?

NEOPTOLEMUS

Don't worry, yes—now that I've properly agreed.

ODYSSEUS

All right: stay here now ready to encounter him,
while I head off to make quite sure that I'm not seen.
I'll send your look-out to the ship again;
°and if I think you're taking too much time,
I'll send the same man here, disguised to play
a merchant seaman's role, so that he'll not be recognized.
Then as he spins his crafty yarn, you can, my son,   130
pick up some helpful leads from anything he says.
I'm going to the ship and leaving things to you.
May Hermes, the great escort-trickster, be our guide.
[also Athena Victory Polias, who always keeps me safe.]°

Exit Odysseus, as the chorus of Neptolemus' crewmen enter.

°CHORAL ENTRY WITH LYRIC DIALOGUE

CHORUS

Tell me, master, what to hide;
I'm alien on alien ground.
Tell me what to say out loud
to face a man who's on his guard.
Those like you have greater skill,
and judgement too, than others have—
one who's given power to rule
with sceptre, gift of Zeus, in hand.   140
And it's come, my son, to you,
this sovereign ancestral power:
tell me therefore what to do
in useful service for you now.

NEOPTOLEMUS

If you want to inspect his
habitat out in the wilds,
now is the time to look.
Whenever that frightening, strange
wanderer comes back here,°

follow my signs and provide
whatever the moment needs.

CHORUS

That's the leading task, my lord,   150
that has long been my concern,
keeping out a watchful eye
to serve your call at every turn.
Tell me now what sort of home
he's managed to inhabit here,
and the ground he occupies.
It is timely I should know,
to make sure he doesn't spring
in ambush on me from some place.
Where's his place, and where's his path?
Is he inside or somewhere else?

NEOPTOLEMUS

Here you can see his tunnel abode,
his mattress of rock.   160

CHORUS

But where has the sorry wretch gone?

NEOPTOLEMUS

This seems obvious to me:
he has gone out and drags
his trailing furrow nearby,
as he searches for food.
This is how he endures
his primitive life, it is said,
shooting at prey
with his feather-swift shafts.
But no healer of wounds
comes anywhere near.

CHORUS

For my part I'm sorry for him,
with nobody caring for him,   170
no eye companionable,
but loneliness perpetual.
He suffers a savage disease,
constantly dazed by surprise.
How could the poor man survive?

O gods,° what devices you serve;
O race of unfortunate men,
whose lives never keep to the mean.

This man is inferior to none   180
from families that are high-born;
yet lacking the good things of life,
he lies isolated, alone,
his company beasts of the wild,
dappled, or bristling hostile.
I pity his hunger and grief
incurable, with no relief—
and Echo's loose, faraway noise
the only response to his cries   190

NEOPTOLEMUS

None of this rouses wonder in me,
because, if I understand aright,
it all was willed by the gods,
this suffering that he has had
from Chryse's raw cruelty.°
And now all this agony,
with nobody here to help:
it must be the work of a god
to make double-sure he couldn't unleash
his invincible arrows at Troy,
before the right time had arrived,
the day it is prophesied
the city should fall to them.   200

Distant cries can be heard.

CHORUS

°Hush, keep quiet, my son. . .

NEOPTOLEMUS

What's this?

CHORUS

A clear, piercing sound
as though from the mouth
of one who is ground
down by pain. . . somewhere
here. . . or over there.

That voice has shaken me,
in truth shaken me:
one whose footsteps limp
beneath crushing cramp.
From far to my ear
that call cries despair,
anguish loud and clear.

The cries are coming closer.

CHORUS
Time to consider, my child. . .   210

NEOPTOLEMUS
Tell me.

CHORUS
. . . a new strategy.
Not so far away,
he sounds closer by.
Not the music that floats
from the piping flutes
playing shepherds' notes:
no, his stumblings force
out from crushing stress
blood-curdling cries.
Or maybe he hates
the beach with no boats°—
such horrific shouts!

SCENE 2

°*Philoctetes has been slowly limping on from the 'wild' island side; he has the bow and arrows with him.*

PHILOCTETES
Ah. . . strangers!
Who may you be and from what land,°   220
that you have put in at this shore
which has no harbour, no inhabitants?
As from what land or race should I address you?

Your style of dress is Greek,
a highly welcome sight to me,
but let me hear your speech.

They shrink from him in silence.

Don't be afraid and flinch away in horror
at the way that I've been turned
to something wild:
instead, take pity on a fellow-man
who's wretched and alone,
degraded, desolate, bereft of friends. (*silence*)
So speak – if you are well disposed, that is. (*silence*)°   230
Please answer me. It can't be right
that we should disappoint each other so.

NEOPTOLEMUS
First, stranger, rest assured that we are Greeks—
since you're so keen to know.

PHILOCTETES
The language I most love!
Dear god, to think that after all these years
I'd hear the voice of someone such as this!
What purpose brought you here, my child,
what impulse, what supremely welcome wind?
Come, tell me everything, so I may find out who you are.

NEOPTOLEMUS
I am from Skyros, isle encircled by the sea.
I'm sailing home.   240
My name is Neoptolemus, son of Achilles.
There. . . now you know everything.°

PHILOCTETES
Son of a father much beloved, and of a much-loved land,
and raised by old King Lycomedes!
What voyage has brought you to this place?
Where are you sailing from?

NEOPTOLEMUS
Just now I'm sailing back from Troy.

PHILOCTETES
What's that you say? You were not one of us
when we were first embarked for Troy.

NEOPTOLEMUS
> You mean that you were part of that great task?

PHILOCTETES
> Can you, my son, not recognize the man before your eyes?

NEOPTOLEMUS
> How could I know a man I've never met before?   250

PHILOCTETES
> You mean you've heard no story of my name?
> no inkling of these troubles I've been tortured with?

NEOPTOLEMUS
> I tell you I know nothing of these things you ask about.

PHILOCTETES
> Oh what a wretched man I am, and hateful to the gods!
> To think no story of my sufferings
> has filtered through to home,
> nor anywhere in Greece.
> But those who viciously abandoned me
> just chuckle, and keep quiet;
> meanwhile my sickness flourishes
> and keeps on getting worse.
> My boy, Achilles' son, I am the one. . .   260
> the man you may have heard of
> as the master of this bow of Heracles:°

He holds the bow up.

> Philoctetes, son of Poias.
> That pair of generals and the lord of Ithaca°
> despicably cast me ashore, marooned here,
> devastated by this savage ulcer-wound
> which was inflicted by the lethal serpent's savage fangs.
> When they had sailed on from the isle of Chryse,
> and the fleet had put in here, those creatures   270
> cast me off, left all alone except for that affliction.
> How glad they must have been when, after all the waves,
> they saw me sleeping soundly on the shore
> beneath the cover of the rock.
> And off they went and left,
> supplying me with just some meagre rags,
> and token modicum of food—
> I wish to god that they could get the same!

Imagine, son, what it was like to waken from my sleep,
when I sat up to find they'd gone.
Oh how I wept, how I bemoaned my lot,
when I could see how all the ships
I had embarked with had sailed off—
and not one person in the place,   280
not one to help me or support me in my suffering.
When I searched all around I could find nothing here—
except for agony, and that was all too plentiful!
And so, as season followed season by,
I had to serve myself as I survived
alone in this small shelter.
For my belly's needs this bow provided,
shooting at the birds as they flew by.
Whatever my drawn bowstring might bring down,   290
I had to fetch it for myself, and drag my wretched leg.
And if I needed to fetch water,
or, with frost upon the ground in wintertime,
I had to break some firewood, I simply had
to crawl along and manage for myself.
Then there's no fire, and I must strike with stone on stone
until the hidden spark appeared and caught—
and that has kept me going all along.
A roof above my head along with fire
supply the sum of what I want. . .
except the end of my disease.
Now let me tell you all about this coast, my son.   300
No sailor comes near here deliberately;
there is no port, nowhere to ply
some gainful trade, nor hospitality.
No people of good sense make voyages here.°
Occasionally someone lands by accident
(for such things happen in the longer run of human life);
and when they come, these visitors feel sorry for me,
so they say, and may well give me scraps of food
or clothing. But there is one thing
that no one wants to offer, when I mention it:
to take me safe back home.   310
So this is the tenth year that I've been wasting here,
downcast and hungry, feeding up this ever-greedy ulcer.
This is the way those Sons of Atreus and Odysseus°

dealt with me, my boy.
I only wish the Olympian gods would make them
suffer likewise as a recompense for me.

CHORUS-LEADER
And I feel pity for you, son of Poias,
in the same way as those others who came here.

NEOPTOLEMUS
And I myself can testify that what you tell to us is true:
I have received bad treatment at their hands as well.   320
[from the Sons of Atreus and Odysseus].°

PHILOCTETES
You mean you too have reason to accuse
those cursed Sons of Atreus, and to rage against them?

NEOPTOLEMUS
I hope one day to satisfy my fury with strong action,
so that Mycene may concede, and Sparta too,°
that Skyros is the motherland to men of courage.

PHILOCTETES
Bravo, my son! What provocation, then,
has brought you to denounce them with such passion?

NEOPTOLEMUS
Although it's hard, I'll tell you of the gross humiliation
that I was subjected to when I arrived.   330
When fate had brought to pass Achilles' death. . .°

PHILOCTETES
Ah no! Tell me your tale no further till I have this clear:
Achilles, he is dead?

NEOPTOLEMUS
He's dead, brought down, they say, not by the hand of man,
but by the arrow of a god, Apollo.°

PHILOCTETES
Well, both the killer and the killed were noble then.
But now I'm torn, my son, between first asking
what you've suffered, or else mourning for the man.

NEOPTOLEMUS
I think your anguish is enough for you, poor soul,
without lamenting other men as well.   340

PHILOCTETES

You're right. So start again about the way
they treated you contemptuously.

NEOPTOLEMUS

Their ship with ceremonial decorations came for me,
the great Odysseus and my father's teacher, Phoenix.°
They told me—whether true or false, I am not sure—
that, with my father dead, it would be wrong
for anyone but me to overcome the famous towers.
Their story, stranger, far from dampened down my haste
to get embarked—especially because of my desire   350
to see his corpse before the burial,
for I had never looked on him alive.
And then there was the tempting promise that, by going,
I would take the towers of Troy.
The second day of voyaging with sail and oars
we reached Sigeion,° bitter shore.
There the whole army crowded round and greeted me,
and swore that they were looking at
Achilles back alive again.
Himself he lay there dead.
When I had wept for him, it was not long   360
before I went to call on Atreus' Sons,
in friendly spirit, as you would expect,
and claimed my father's arms, and any other thing he'd left.
°But their response was harsh and shameless:
'You, as offspring of Achilles, are at liberty to take
all of your father's other things—except the armour.
Another has possession over that, Laertes' son.'
Then I burst into furious tears,
and rising up in pain and anger said:
'You brutes, how could you dare to give my arms
to someone else without consulting me?'   370
Odysseus happened to be standing near, and said:
'Believe me, boy, they've rightly passed them on to me,
since I was there, and could retrieve both them and him.'
In fury I berated them with every filthy insult at the prospect
that that man was going to take my arms away from me.
Then he, though slow to anger, was so far provoked
by my abuse, that he made this riposte:

'You were not here with us;
you were away when you should not have been.
And now you've blurted out such brazen talk,   380
you'll never take these back with you to Scyros.'
So now I've heard myself insulted so abusively,
I'm sailing home, denuded of my rightful heritage
by him, the lowest bastard of the low,° Odysseus.
°[And yet I don't blame him as much as those in charge,
because a city and an army are entirely in the hands
of those who rule. And people who disrupt good order
come to be rotten on instructions from their leaders.]
Well, that is my whole story told.
And may that man who hates the Sons of Atreus
be favoured by the gods as warmly as by me.   390

CHORUS
            °All-feeding Mother Earth,
            mother of Zeus himself,
            goddess of mountainside,
            and mighty Pactolus,°
            the river flecked with gold,
            at Troy I called to you.
            When utter insolence
            advanced from Atreus' sons
            against my master here,
            as they were passing on
            his father's famous arms,
            that highest glory-sign,
            to please Laertes' son,
            you, blessed charioteer   400
            of bull-devouring lions,
            I called out to you there.

PHILOCTETES
    It would seem, strangers, that your voyage is laden
    with a source of grief that closely matches mine;
    indeed your song is so in tune
    that I can recognize the kind of work that stems
    from those two Sons of Atreus and Odysseus
    (for I know that man would put his voice
    behind all sorts of dirty tricks and criminality,
    as long as it advances some nefarious end).

But it's not this surprises me, but that the greater Aias°   410
could stand by and watch this happening.

NEOPTOLEMUS
He was not still alive. I never would have been
defrauded in this way, had he been living.

PHILOCTETES
You mean he too is dead and gone?

NEOPTOLEMUS
Don't think of him as any longer in the light of day.

PHILOCTETES
That's bad. While Diomedes and the son that Sisyphus
had palmed off on Laertes,° they will not be dead—oh no!—
because they are the ones who should not be alive.

NEOPTOLEMUS
You are too right: they are still there among
the Greek battalions, and greatly flourishing.   420

PHILOCTETES
And what about my dear old friend, good Nestor?
Is he still alive? He used to stop those people
from their mischief with his good advice.

NEOPTOLEMUS
He's in a poor state nowadays: his son Antilochus,°
who was with him, was taken off by death.

PHILOCTETES
These names are two I should least want to hear as killed.
Ah me! What can we hope for, when these men are dead,
and yet Odysseus is still here: whereas he is the one
who should be numbered as a corpse instead of them.   430

NEOPTOLEMUS
He is a clever wrestler, that one, Philoctetes—
yet even clever plans can get tripped up.

PHILOCTETES
But where on earth then was Patroclus,
your own father's closest friend?

NEOPTOLEMUS
He too was dead.
I tell you in a word: war does not care to snatch
the criminals, but every time the good.

PHILOCTETES

    I too can vouch for that—which prompts me to enquire
    about the fortunes of a certain man, worthless,
    yet dangerous and clever with his powers of speech.   440

NEOPTOLEMUS

    You can't mean any other than Odysseus?

PHILOCTETES

    Not him: but there was someone called Thersites,°
    who never would stop speaking, even when none wanted it.
    Maybe you know if he is still alive?

NEOPTOLEMUS

    I never saw him, but I heard that he still is.

PHILOCTETES

    He would be—nothing sordid ever seems to die.
    The gods spend special care on this,
    and take a strange delight in turning back
    the crooks and tricksters from the doors of Hades,
    whilst for ever packing off the just and virtuous.   450
    What can one make of this? How give approval, if,
    when I investigate divinity,° I find the gods are bad?

NEOPTOLEMUS

    Well, offspring from the fatherland of Oeta,°
    from henceforth I shall be keeping well away from Troy
    and Atreus' Sons, and be on guard.
    A world where lesser men have power
    above the good, where honesty deteriorates,
    and where the coward rules: these are the sort of people
    that I never shall embrace.
    No, rocky Scyros will be good enough for me,
    and keep me happily at home.   460
    And now it's time I should be going to my ship.

Neoptolemus makes moves towards departing.

    Farewell, then, son of Poias, and I wish you all the best;
    and may the gods deliver you from sickness as you hope.
    (*to Chorus*) But now let's go, so that we're set to leave,
    whenever god may make it fair for setting sail.

PHILOCTETES

    You are already heading off, my son?

NEOPTOLEMUS
   We are: we need to watch out for the opportunity
   to sail from on board ship not from afar.

PHILOCTETES
   Now by your father and your mother, child,
   by anything at home that you hold dear,
   I beg you as your suppliant:
   don't leave me here alone like this,   470
   in isolation with these troubles you have seen,
   and even more that you have heard I have to live with.
   Take me on board as extra cargo:
   this will, I'm well aware, be burdensome,
   but make the effort to put up with it.
   For men of noble character the wrong is hateful,
   and the good is glorious.
   And so for you: if you refuse me this,
   it will bring you disgrace: while if you do it, son,
   and I come safely to the land of Oeta,
   you will win a noble reputation in reward.
   Take courage! The ordeal will last not even   480
   one whole day.° So steel yourself:
   and stow me where you think it best—
   down in the hold, up on the prow, the stern,
   wherever I would cause the least offence to those on board.
   By Zeus, the god of suppliants, consent,
   give way to my persuasion—
   I go down upon my knees to you,
   weak and disabled as I am.

Philoctetes kneels.°

   Don't leave me here deserted, off the track of human life:
   no, rescue me, and take me to your home,
   or to Chalcedon's kingdom in Euboea.°
   From there the leg to Oeta is not far,   490
   and to the range of Trachis, and the wide Spercheius,
   where you may present me to my dear old father.
   For long I've been afraid he's dead and gone,
   since I have often sent him messages
   with those who put in here, imploring him
   to sail here for himself and take me safe back home.

But either he has died, or—as is likely, I suppose—
the messengers have made a low priority of my concerns,
and pressed on with their journey home.
But now I have in you an escort and a messenger in one,   500
so, please, you rescue me, take pity on me, you.
And bear in mind how everything in human life
is threatening and dangerous;
and after time experiencing the good,
the opposite may come along in turn.
°[A person needs to see the threat, while clear of troubles;
when he's doing well, he should then look most closely
at his life in case he comes to grief, while off his guard.]

CHORUS

    °Take pity on him, lord:
    he's told us of his pains,
    so great and hard to bear
    (may such not strike my friends!)
    But if you hate that pair   510
    of Atreus' spiteful sons,
    then I would turn their wrongs
    to this man's greater gains;
    and would convey him safe
    on board our nimble ship
    well fitted for the wave,
    and take him to the hearth
    where he so longs to live.
    That way we should escape
    resentment from above.

NEOPTOLEMUS

Take care! You're easy-going now,
while merely standing by, but when you've had your fill   520
of closer contact with the malady,
you may well find you change your tune.

CHORUS

No, not at all. There is no way that you'll prove
justified in aiming that reproach at me.

NEOPTOLEMUS

Well, I would be disgraced if I appeared
less diligent than you in striving hard
to help the stranger in his hour of need.

So, if you think this course is right, let's set our sails.
And he should move at once as well—
at least the ship will take him on without refusal.
I only hope the gods will waft us safely from this land
wherever we may wish to voyage next.

PHILOCTETES

Oh what a welcome day!   530
Delightful man! Dear sailors!
I wish that I could clearly show you now
how much you have endeared yourselves to me.
Come on then, let's be going, son.
But first we'll pay respects to this unhomely home of mine,
and you may see what means I had for my survival,
and how stout-hearted I have been.
I don't believe that anyone except for me,
once they had taken a good look in there,
could have endured this life.
But I have had to find a way to put up with these miseries.

SCENE 3

CHORUS

Stop there. I see two men approaching here:
one is a crewman from your ship, the other foreign.   540
Listen first to them, and then go in.

°*Enter attendant disguised as a merchant seaman, with a crewman. He addresses himself to Neoptolemus, not paying attention to Philoctetes.*

'MERCHANT'

Achilles' son, I found this fellow-sailor
and two others keeping watch on board your ship.
So I requested them to tell me where you were,
seeing that I'd come upon you unexpectedly
by chancing to drop anchor at this selfsame place.
I'm skipper of a modest merchant ship,
and on my way from Troy back home
towards Peparethos° with its rich vines.
And when I heard the sailors were your crew,   550

I thought I should not sail off on my way
without informing you—and getting due reward.
You may know nothing of your situation,
plans the Greeks have hatched concerning you.
And not just plans, but actions launched without delay.

NEOPTOLEMUS

I shall stay truly grateful for
the friendly forethought you have taken
for me, stranger. But tell me, what are these actions
that you speak of? I want to know
what is this latest plan concocted by the Greeks.   560

'MERCHANT'

They've set out with a fleet to follow you,
old Phoenix and the sons of Theseus.°

NEOPTOLEMUS

To fetch me back by force or power of words?

'MERCHANT'

Don't know: I'm only here to tell you what I've heard.

NEOPTOLEMUS

Are Phoenix and his shipmates doing this so readily
to gratify the sons of Atreus?

'MERCHANT'

The point is that it's being done, and now.

NEOPTOLEMUS

How come Odysseus was not keen to sail
with his own message? Was he constrained by fear?

'MERCHANT'

That man and Diomedes were, as I was on my way,
just setting out to fetch some other man.   570

NEOPTOLEMUS

Who was this that Odysseus set his sights upon?

'MERCHANT'

There was a man. . .
but wait, first tell me who this is.
And keep your voice down as you tell me.

NEOPTOLEMUS

This, stranger, is the celebrated Philoctetes.

'Merchant' speaks in fake asides.

'MERCHANT'
> Then question me no more.
> Set sail and get yourself away
> from here as quickly as you can.

PHILOCTETES
> What is he saying, son?
> What is this undercover deal
> the sailor's bargaining with you?

NEOPTOLEMUS (*with false openness*)
> I can't be sure yet
> But whatever he may have to say, he'll have to say it
> openly to me and you and these men here.

'MERCHANT'
> Child of Achilles, don't denounce me to the army-chiefs
> for speaking out of turn. I offer them a lot of benefits
> and they reward me back. I'm poor, you understand.

NEOPTOLEMUS
> I'm ill-disposed to them. And this man's my good friend
> because he hates the Sons of Atreus too.
> Since you have come to me in friendly fashion,
> you should not hide from us whatever you have heard.

'MERCHANT'
> Be careful what you do, my boy.

NEOPTOLEMUS
> I have been taking care.

'MERCHANT'
> I shall hold you responsible.

NEOPTOLEMUS
> All right—but speak.

'MERCHANT'
> Then speak I shall. This is the man,
> the man those two—Odysseus, Diomedes—sailed to fetch.
> And they have sworn an oath
> that they'll persuade him with their words,
> or else will master him by force.
> The Greeks all heard Odysseus
> clearly make the claim; he was the one
> more confident that they would bring this off.

580

590

NEOPTOLEMUS

But what's the reason why, when such a long time
has elapsed, the sons of Atreus should have turned
attention to this man, the man they cast away so long ago?   600
Why such a rush of fervent longing?
Is it some compulsion or resentment
from the gods who see to it
that past wrongs get their punishment?

'MERCHANT

°Well, since you may not yet have heard the tale,
I'll tell you everything. There is a noble prophet,
son of Priam, Helenus by name.
That man who has the shameless, shady reputation,°
Odysseus, set out all alone one night to capture him
by stealth, and then paraded him in chains
before the Greeks, a splendid catch.
Among his other prophesies he said   610
that they would never take the walls of Troy,
unless by their persuasive words
they were to bring this man
from off this island where for now he lives.
Odysseus, when he heard the prophesy
at once proclaimed a promise he would fetch the man,
and show him off before the Greeks.
He reckoned he could fetch him of his own free will—
but, if not, then against his will.
And he'd let anyone cut off his head if he did not succeed.°
That's the whole story, lad.   620
I would urge you and anyone you care about
to set off on your way, and quick.

PHILOCTETES

Good god! How could that man, that utter filth,
declare on oath that he would fetch me
to the Greeks by means of his persuasion?
I am as likely to end up persuaded
to return to earth from Hades—like his father Sisyphus.°

'MERCHANT'

I know nothing of that. But I am off now to my ship,
and may the god be with you for the best.

He goes.

PHILOCTETES

This is outrageous, isn't it, my son, that he,
Odysseus, should have harboured hopes
of luring me with sugared talk,
and then displaying me before the gathered Greeks? 630
No, no. I'd rather listen to the hated snake,
the one that crippled me like this.
That man would utter anything, try any scheme;
and now for sure he's coming here.
Come on my boy, let's go,
so we can put a wide expanse of sea
between ourselves and that man's ship.
Come on then; haste when haste is needed
can bring sleep and relaxation once the work is done.°

NEOPTOLEMUS

Then once this head-wind has let up, we'll sail;
for now it's set against us. 640

PHILOCTETES

But sailing's always fair when you're escaping trouble.

NEOPTOLEMUS

That's true: but it's unfavourable for them as well.

PHILOCTETES

No wind is contrary for pirates when they see
the chance to raid and seize by violence.

NEOPTOLEMUS

All right then, let's be going,
once you've fetched from inside
whatever you most need and might still miss.

PHILOCTETES

I don't have much, but there are things I want.

NEOPTOLEMUS

What could there be that I won't have on board?

PHILOCTETES

I have a certain herb, which I find best
to soothe this ulcer and relieve the pain. 650

NEOPTOLEMUS

Then fetch it out. And is there something else you want to take?

PHILOCTETES
   Yes, any of these arrows here
   that have been dropped and lie unnoticed,
   so they're not left for anyone to take.

NEOPTOLEMUS
   Is this in fact the celebrated bow that you have there?

PHILOCTETES
   Yes, this is it:
   there is no other, just this one I'm carrying.

NEOPTOLEMUS
   And is it possible for me to look at it close up?
   and handle and revere it as a god?

PHILOCTETES
   For you it is, my son; and any other thing
   I can provide that's for your benefit.

NEOPTOLEMUS
   °I long for that, yes.
   This is how I feel. . .   660
   if it's permitted, that is what I want:
   if not, then let it be.

PHILOCTETES
   Your words are pious; and it is permitted.
   For you alone have given me the chance
   to look upon the light of day, to see the land of Oeta;
   you, to see my aged father and my friends;
   and you who set me on my feet, released
   from underneath oppression by my enemies.
   So rest assured, it shall be yours to take the bow
   into your hands, to give it back again,°
   and to proclaim the boast
   that you alone of men have handled it,
   by virtue of your goodness.
   It was by doing a good deed
   that I myself first came by it.°   670

NEOPTOLEMUS
   °I am so pleased to have set eyes on you
   and gained you as my friend.
   The person who knows how to do good deeds
   in due return for being done some good,

becomes a friend more precious
than an object of however high a price.
Now, if you will, go in.

PHILOCTETES

And I shall take you in as well.
My malady has need of you to stand firm by my side.

They both go inside the cave.

CHORAL SONG

CHORUS

°I've heard, but never seen, how Ixion,
who tried to violate the marriage-bed
of high all-mighty Zeus, was clamped upon
a whirling wheel instead.
No other have I heard about nor seen,   680
no human come to such a hateful doom
as this just man, who did no wrong, no harm,
dragged so unfairly down.
I am amazed to think of how, of how
he lives alone, how he forever hears
the waves that crash all round, yet still endures
this life so full of tears.   690

All by himself, no other footfall near,
no local people, no one by to share
his agony, or join with him to weep
his blood-drunk, hungry sore.
No one to soothe to sleep the burning flux,
which oozes from his foot, with healing bath
in time of need, or pain-relieving herbs
picked from the fertile earth.   700
But he has had to crawl this way and that,
child-like, but with no nurse affectionate,
and search out needs of life for when the stab
of anguish might abate.

Never feeding from the earth's rich harvest,
or what humans raise by farming,
but for when his arrows flying deadly   710
might fetch food to fill his belly.
Poor soul, ten years with no wine to warm him,

never sipping from the cup-brim,
ever thirsty seeking after
stores of stagnant puddle-water.

°Now by meeting with a noble offspring
he shall end up strong and prosperous.   720
He'll take him on board his ship for sailing,
after many months of waiting,
home at last to his ancestral palace
by Spercheius, nymphs of Malis,
where that man, with god's fire brighter,
was deified above Mount Oeta.

SCENE 4

Neoptolemus and Philoctetes re-enter from the cave; Philoctetes is in pain.°

NEOPTOLEMUS
  Please come along.
  Why have you fallen silent over nothing?   730
  Why stop as though you're paralysed?

PHILOCTETES (*cries out in pain*)

NEOPTOLEMUS
  What is the matter?

PHILOCTETES
  Nothing. . . nothing serious. Keep on, my son.

NEOPTOLEMUS
  Is this some pain brought on by your old malady?

PHILOCTETES
  No, no. . . I think it's getting better even now. . .
  (*cries of pain. . .*)
  Oh gods!

NEOPTOLEMUS
  What makes you groan like this and call upon the gods?

PHILOCTETES
  I'm begging them to come down gently and to rescue me. . .
  (*cries of pain*)

NEOPTOLEMUS

    What is the trouble with you?

    Speak up and don't hold back like this.   740

    It's obvious that something's wrong with you.

PHILOCTETES

    This is the end, my son—

    I cannot hide my pain from you. . .

    (*cries of pain. . .*)

    It's piercing through. . . it's piercing through—

    what a wretched thing I am.

    This is the end, my son. . . I'm being eaten through, my son. . .

    (*long cries of pain. . .*)

    For god's sake, son, if you have got a sword to hand,

    hack at my foot, cut quickly, amputate,

    use all your strength, do not hold back.°

    Come on, my boy.   750

NEOPTOLEMUS

    What is this sudden new attack

    that's makes you howl and groan like this?

PHILOCTETES

    You know, my son.

NEOPTOLEMUS

    Know what?

PHILOCTETES

    You know, my boy.

NEOPTOLEMUS

    What do you mean? I do not know.

PHILOCTETES

    You've got to know. . .

    (*cries of pain. . .*)

NEOPTOLEMUS

    This sickness bears down on you horribly.

PHILOCTETES

    Yes, horrible, unspeakable! Oh pity me!

NEOPTOLEMUS

    Then what am I to do?

PHILOCTETES

    Do not get frightened and abandon me.

    It comes and goes from time to time,

perhaps when it has had enough
of fluctuating, this disease.

NEOPTOLEMUS
Poor man, unfortunate in every way.   760
Shall I take hold of you and give you some support?

PHILOCTETES
No don't do that. But take this bow of mine,
as you requested me not long ago.
Keep it secure until this present onset of my agony is over.
For when the fit is tailing off a coma comes upon me:
it will not cease till after that.
And then you have to let me have the peace to sleep.
But if those people come ashore while this is happening,
then, by the gods, I give you this command: 770
do not give up this bow to them,
not willingly, unwillingly, no, not by any means.
For if you do, you'll prove the cause of your own death,
as well as mine, your suppliant.

NEOPTOLEMUS
You can be sure I'll take good care.
No one is going to get it given them
except for you and me. So hand it me—
and may good fortune go with it.

He hands over the bow.

PHILOCTETES
Here, take it, son.
And pray to keep resentment off,°
so that it does not prove for you a thing
weighed down with pains, as it has been to me,
and to the one who was its owner previous to me.

NEOPTOLEMUS
May these our prayers be granted.
And may our voyage prove prosperous and swift,   780
whatever place the god and our intentions carry us.

PHILOCTETES (*cries of pain. . .*)
I fear, my son, your prayer will come to nothing:
as here come the ulcer-oozings
mixed with blood from deep inside.
I know it will get worse. . .

(*cries of pain. . .*)
It's you, my foot, what would you do to me?
It's creeping up. . . it's getting near. . .
Hold on, don't run away, no no!
(*cries of pain. . .*)   790
O you, my friend from Ithaca,
oh how I wish this agony of mine
would pierce you through the breast
(*even worse cries of pain. . .*)
And you, you pair of generals,
[you Agamemnon, Menelaus, instead of me]°
I wish that you might feed this plague, and for as long as me. . .
(*cries of pain. . .*)
O death, death, how is it that,
although I call on you like this day after day,
you're never able to appear?
My child, take hold of me, and immolate me
in this famous fire of Lemnos.°   800
Yes, my noble child. I once saw fit
to do this very thing for Heracles, the son of Zeus,
and got this bow that you are holding now in recompense,
What do you say to that, my child? (*Silence*)
What do you say? Why are you silent? (*Still silent*)
Where are you, son? Say where. . .?

NEOPTOLEMUS
   I have been feeling anguish for your sufferings.

PHILOCTETES
   Hold on, be brave, my son.
   This thing here overwhelms me fiercely,
   then as quickly goes away again.
   But listen: do not leave me here alone.

NEOPTOLEMUS
   No—rest assured, we're staying.

PHILOCTETES
   You will stay?   810

NEOPTOLEMUS
   You can be sure of that.

PHILOCTETES
   I do not want to put you under oath, my son,

NEOPTOLEMUS
No need: it would be wrong for me to leave you.

PHILOCTETES
Give me your hand in confirmation.

NEOPTOLEMUS
I promise I shall stay.

They join hands.

PHILOCTETES
°Now take me there. . . there. . .

NEOPTOLEMUS
Where do you mean?

PHILOCTETES
Up, up. . .

NEOPTOLEMUS
Are you delirious? Why look up at the heavens?

PHILOCTETES
Let go now. . . let me go. . .

NEOPTOLEMUS
Let you go where?

PHILOCTETES
Just let me go. . .

NEOPTOLEMUS
No, I refuse.

PHILOCTETES
Your touch will murder me. . .

NEOPTOLEMUS
All right. I'm letting go, now that you're more coherent.

PHILOCTETES (*sinking to the ground*)
Earth, earth, accept me as I am, as dead.
This trouble will not let me stand,
not upright any more. . .   820

NEOPTOLEMUS
It looks as though deep sleep
is shortly going to grip the man—

yes, look at how his head is tipping back.
And now a sweat is breaking out all over him;
a swollen vein down in his lower leg has broken open
with a rush of dark-brown blood.
Come, friends, we'll let him lie down undisturbed,
so he may sink into deep sleep.

°CHORUS

°Come, Sleep forgetful of torment,
come, Sleep forgetful of pain;
breathe, breathe with lenient breezes,   830
great Lord of radiant peace.
Spread shadow over his eyelids;
here, Healer, over him now.

They turn to Neoptolemus, and change tone.

Think, son, of where you are standing,
consider where you will step.
What are your plans from here onward?
Look, he is deeply asleep.°
Right timing is all-decisive,
and wins by seizing the moment.

NEOPTOLEMUS

°His ears hear nothing, no, but now I understand this capture:
this bow we hold is void, a futile trophy, if we sail without him.   840
The crown is his to claim; god told us: get this man.
Disgrace to brag of deeds incomplete and patched with lies.

CHORUS

Well, god can oversee that, then.
Tell me now cautiously, son—
hush, hush now!—keeping your voice down.
The sleep of all who are sick
can be so easily wakeful,
sleep that hardly is sleep.
°That thing, so far as you're able,   850
think how to do it by stealth—
you're well aware of what that means.
Take care, since if you maintain
this kind of thinking, then surely
there'll be insoluble strains.

Friendly wind, friendly wind, blow now—
come, my boy, time to be going.
He lies there helpless, unsighted,
stretched at full length and benighted,
sleeping, forgetful,° not moving,
not a hand, not a foot, nothing,   860
deathly as one down in Hades.
Think if your words show good timing.
This makes best sense to my seeming:
labours that are the least fearful
turn out to be the most powerful.

Philoctetes begins to stir.

NEOPTOLEMUS

Be quiet, I tell you, don't be foolish.
The man is opening his eyes, and lifting up his head.

PHILOCTETES

The light that follows sleep!
And here, beyond my wildest hopes,
these strangers have kept watch.
I never really thought, my son,
you would be able to put up with my distress,   870
to pity, and to stay and give me aid.
The Sons of Atreus did not bear these things
so staunchly, those valiant commanders—no!
But you, my child, you have inherited your noble nature,
and so you could make light of this,
despite my cries and stink.
And now I seem to have some respite and relief,
my child, would you please help me to my feet—
yes, you, support me as I stand, my child.
Then once the dizziness has gone away,   880
we may get going for the ship and sail without delay.

NEOPTOLEMUS

I am so glad to see you back awake
and breathing free from pain.
I had not hoped as much:
the symptoms of your sickness at their height
appeared to show you at the point of death.
Now, raise yourself and get up to your feet;

or, if you like, these men can carry you.
Now you and I are firmly set upon this course,
they will not shy back from the task.

PHILOCTETES

Thank you, my son; and help me up as you suggest.
But let them be, so they are not tormented   890
by the dreadful stench before they have to be.
It will be bad enough for them to have to share
the space with me once I'm on board the ship.

NEOPTOLEMUS

All right, stand up and lean your weight on me.

PHILOCTETES

Getting up and putting his arm round Neoptolemus.

Don't worry. Force of habit will enable me to stand.

NEOPTOLEMUS *(stops)*

Ah, ah! What am I going to do? What next?°

PHILOCTETES

What is it, son? Where have your words gone wandering?

NEOPTOLEMUS

I don't know what to say. . . I'm at a loss which way to turn.

PHILOCTETES

You're at a loss? No, don't say that, my child.

NEOPTOLEMUS

But that's the place my pain has brought me to.

PHILOCTETES

I hope disgust at my disease has not so struck you   900
that you're not going to take me on board ship?

NEOPTOLEMUS

Everything stirs up disgust
when someone fails his better nature,
and behaves untrue to self.

PHILOCTETES

By helping a good man, you have not done
or spoken anything unfitting for your father.

NEOPTOLEMUS

I shall be found unworthy:
that is what has been tormenting me.

PHILOCTETES
> Not in these deeds at least.
> But I have qualms about the things you say.

NEOPTOLEMUS
> O Zeus, what should I do?

Pulling away from Philoctetes.

> Shall I be stigmatized as doubly guilty,
> both hiding things I should not hide
> and speaking words of utmost shame?

PHILOCTETES
> Unless I'm very wrong, this man is going to play me false   910
> by sailing off and leaving me behind.

NEOPTOLEMUS
> It's not by leaving you, but more by taking you
> along a way that you'll detest:
> that's what has been tormenting me.

PHILOCTETES
> Whatever are you saying, child? I do not understand.

NEOPTOLEMUS
> I shall hide nothing:
> you have got to sail to Troy and join the Greeks,
> the Sons of Atreus and their troops.

PHILOCTETES
> No, no! What's this you say?

NEOPTOLEMUS
> Do not complain before you know.

PHILOCTETES
> Know what? What d'you intend to do with me?

NEOPTOLEMUS
> First to release you from this misery,
> and then, along with you, to take the land of Troy.   920

PHILOCTETES
> This is the truth? This is your aim?

NEOPTOLEMUS
> A strong compulsion drives these things.
> So don't be angry over them.

PHILOCTETES

This is disaster, I'm betrayed!
What, stranger, have you done to me?
Return my bow immediately.

NEOPTOLEMUS

Impossible. Both what is just and what is prudent
mean I must obey those in authority.

PHILOCTETES

You hell-fire you,
monstrosity, abhorrent demon of atrocity,
how you have used me, how deluded me!
Do you not feel ashamed to look at me,
your suppliant, with your hard heart?   930
By capturing my bow you have unstrung my life.
Give it me back, I beg you, give it back, I say.
By your ancestral gods, do not, my son,
deprive me of my bow, my life.°

Neoptolemus is turned away, and makes no response.

Ay me, he has no more to say to me,
he turns away, like one who's never going to give.
You inlets and you headlands,
and companion creatures of the hillsides,
and you jagged cliffs:
I call on you, familiar company,
since I have no one else to turn to.
Witness how Achilles' son has dealt with me.   940
He swore that he would take me home:
instead he's hauling me to Troy.
He reached his right hand out to me in promise,
but then snatched my bow with it,
the sacred bow of Heracles the son of Zeus;
and he intends to show it off before the Greeks.
He's caught me out as if he'd had to use his strength
against a mighty man, and doesn't realize that
he's snuffing out a corpse,
the shade of smoke, a phantom merely.
He never would have captured me, had I my strength,
nor even in my present state, except by trickery.
But now in misery I've been miserably deceived.

What should I do?

Turns back to Neoptolemus.

                Give, give it back.
Even now be your true self. (*Silence*)   950
Say something. . . (*Silence*) Silent.
I'm as good as dead.
Well then, my rock-formed double cave,
I shall return once more to you,
disarmed, deprived of any source of food.
Instead I shall just shrivel up
inside this chamber, all alone,
since I can't use this bow he holds
to kill a flying bird or mountain-running animal.
In fact, in death I shall lay on a feast
for those I used to feed upon;
and those I used to hunt shall now hunt me.
And so I'll pay the price for blood with blood—
and all the doing of a man
who seemed incapable of wrong.   960
°To hell then, damn you. . .
no, not yet, not till I find out if you'll change your mind.
If not, then may you die in agony.

CHORUS
  What should we do? It lies with you, my lord, to choose:
  are we to sail away, or go along with what he asks?

NEOPTOLEMUS
  I have been shaken by a potent sense of pity
  for this man—and not just now, before as well.

PHILOCTETES
  For gods' sake pity me, my son.
  Don't let yourself become a byword for your tricking me.

NEOPTOLEMUS
  Ay me, what shall I do?
  I wish I'd never sailed from Scyros: 970
  this dilemma pierces me so painfully.

PHILOCTETES
  You're not corrupt yourself:
  it seems, though, that you've come here

after learning vicious ways from men who *are*.
So give those others what belongs to them,
and sail away, but first return my bow to me.

NEOPTOLEMUS
What should we do, my friends?

SCENE 5

°*Neoptolemus begins to reach out; but Odysseus, followed by a couple of men, jumps out of ambush; he comes up behind Philoctetes.*

ODYSSEUS
You lowest scum, what *are* you doing?
Back: return that bow to me!

PHILOCTETES
Ah, who is this? Is that his voice. . . Odysseus' voice?

ODYSSEUS
Odysseus, yes, that's me: as now you see.

PHILOCTETES
Oh no! I have been bought, sold—I am finished!
Here is the man who caught me out,
and stripped me of my bow.

ODYSSEUS
Yes me, and no one else—I'll go along with that.   980

PHILOCTETES
Give back, give me, my boy, my bow.

ODYSSEUS
That he shall not do, not even if he wants to.
But you must come along with it as well;
or else these men will make you.

PHILOCTETES
Me, you lowest, stop-at-nothing filth?
These men will drag me off by force?

ODYSSEUS
Yes, if you won't come willingly.

PHILOCTETES
O land of Lemnos,

with your all-consuming fire created by Hephaestus,°
are you going to let this be?
Will you allow this creature to abduct me
from your care by force?

ODYSSEUS
    It's Zeus, I tell you, Zeus, lord of this island,
    Zeus, who has decreed this. I serve him.   990

PHILOCTETES
    How I hate you! The pretexts that you manage to invent!
    By holding up the gods as your authority
    you turn them into lies.

ODYSSEUS
    Oh no, they are the truth.
    And now this is the road you have to take.

PHILOCTETES
    No, no, I say!

ODYSSEUS
    And I say yes. And I am in command.

PHILOCTETES
    So much for me! It's all too clear
    that I was born to be a slave, not free.

ODYSSEUS
    Not so, but to be side by side with the elite:
    as one of us you must take Troy and lay it waste.

PHILOCTETES
    No, never. Even if I have to undergo the worst,
    not while I have the precipices of this land.   1000

ODYSSEUS
    What do you mean to do?

PHILOCTETES
    °I'll throw myself from off a cliff,
    and smash my skull upon the rocks below.

ODYSSEUS (*to his men*)
    Get hold of him. Don't let him try that way.

PHILOCTETES
    Hands, hands, the things you have to suffer,
    ensnared now by this person,
    through the lack of your dear bowstring.

(*to Odysseus*) You have no touch of wholesomeness or generosity:
look at the way you have crept up on me,
the way you've netted me.
And as your cover you have used
this lad I did not know before
—not right for you, but more my kind—
and he knew nothing better than to do as he was told.   1010
But now he's clearly feeling pain
at his own errors and my sufferings.°
But your low spirit, peering from the murky depths,
instructed him, although he was not willing or adept;
you trained him fully in the arts of wickedness.
And now you mean to chain me up
and take me from this shore, the place
where you abandoned me without a friend,
no neighbour, no society, a living corpse.
To hell with you! And yet no use:
although I have so often prayed for that,
the gods grant nothing that I want.   1020
And so you flourish and enjoy yourself,
while I endure a life of pain with many miseries,
still ridiculed by you and those two generals,
the Sons of Atreus, your operators for this job.
And yet this is the irony: you only sailed with them,
when subjugated by a trick and force:°
while I, poor fool, set sail of my free will
with seven ships, and only *then* was cast away,
demeaned by them—or so you say, while they say you.
And now why are you taking me? Why drag me off?
I am a nothing; I've been dead to you for ages.   1030
How is it, hell-hound, that I'm now not lame?
how can you make your sacrifices to the gods,
how pour your offerings?
Since that was your excuse for putting me ashore.°
Damn you, I hope you rot! And rot you shall,
to make up for the way you've treated me.
That's if the gods have any care for justice;
and I'm sure they have, because you never would
have set out on this quest for such a wretch,
unless some prodding from the gods
had sent you after me.

I call upon my fatherland, and on you gods who watch: 1040
oh make them pay, yes, make them pay,
although so late, the whole damn pack of them,
if you feel any pity on my side.
My life is pitiable, yes, but could I see them crushed,
I'd feel as though I'd won remission from my plague.

CHORUS
  The man's still grim, and grim this speech of his,
  Odysseus; he remains impervious to his troubles.

ODYSSEUS
  There are a lot of things that I could say
  in answer to his talk, had I the leisure.
  But for now I'll give just one supreme account:
  whatever sort of man is called for, that is me.
  So when the challenge is for righteous folk, 1050
  you will not find one single person more high-minded.
  It's my instinct always to reach out for victory—
  excepting in your case.
  I'm happy to give way to you right now.
  (*to his men*) Yes, let him go; do not restrain him.
  Let him stay here.
  (*to Philoctetes*) We don't have any use for you,
  not now we have this bow, since we have Teucros°
  on our side, and he's well practised in this skill.
  And there is me: I reckon that I'm just as good as you
  in handling this and aiming true. No need of you.
  Farewell, and go on limping round your Lemnos! 1060
  We must be on our way.
  Perhaps your trophy will bring *me*
  the glory that by rights was yours.

PHILOCTETES
  Oh no, what can I do now in my misery?
  Are you to strut among the Greeks,
  embellished with my weapons?

ODYSSEUS
  No answering back. I'm on my way.

PHILOCTETES (*to Neoptolemus*)
  Son of Achilles, say, am I to stay unspoken to
  by even you? Will you be going just like this?

ODYSSEUS (*to Neoptolemus*)
    Get moving, you. Don't look at him.
    We must not let your noble-mindedness
    go spoiling our good luck.

PHILOCTETES (*to Chorus*)
    And you, my friends?   1070
    Am I to be deserted here by you as well?
    Will you not pity me?

CHORUS
    This youth is our commander.
    Whatever he may say to you, we say to you as well.

NEOPTOLEMUS
    I shall be told I am too liable to pity.
    All the same, if this man wishes,
    you may stay here for as long as it will take
    the sailors to rig out our ship all trim,
    and to complete our prayers to the gods.
    Perhaps he'll come to thinking
    better things of us within this time.
    So let's be going then;
    and you, come quickly when we summon you.   1080

°*Odysseus and Neoptolemus, still holding the bow, depart together.*

SCENE 6—°LYRIC DIALOGUE

PHILOCTETES
        O my rock-vault cavern—
        ice winter, summer hot—
        so it seems that I was not
        meant to leave you ever.
        You'll be at my death-day,
        old shelter from the rain,
        overflowing with my pain:
        how am I to live each day?   1090
        with what hope of nurture?
        No longer cower, you birds,
        fly on through the whistling winds;
        I've no means to hurt you.

CHORUS
        It was you who fixed this fate,

not imposed by outside force.
With the chance to show good sense,
you still chose to take the worse
rather than the better lot.   1100

PHILOCTETES

What a wretched figure,
mortified by pain,
uncompanioned by man,
henceforth and for ever.
Staying here to perish,
no longer getting game
brought down by my steady aim   1110
and my flighted arrows.
Falsehood from a fraudster
crept up behind my back:
would that I could see that crook
suffer equal torture.

CHORUS

Fate from gods, no sleight of hand
from me, brought you to this pass.
So at others aim your curse   1120
full of hate: for it's my wish
you should keep me as your friend.

PHILOCTETES

He is sitting somewhere
beside the deep gray sea,
brandishing my arrows
and making mock of me,
plucking with his fingers
my means of livelihood,
bowstring that no one else
except for me has pulled.
Roughly wrenched away
from my hands, bow so dear,
you would view with pity,
could you become aware,   1130
Heracles' companion,
who'll hold you nevermore.
With this change of owner,
from now on you'll be strung

by that man of many
devices,° lord of wrong;
you will witness trickery,
worked by that hated man,
who has planned so much deceit
twisted to bring me pain.

CHORUS

A man should speak out what is just,   1140
and after that should not then thrust
resentful spikes of sharp invective.
That person was the one selected
to keep the common good defended. °

PHILOCTETES

Birds that wing above me
and beasts with gleaming eyes,
creatures of these hillsides,
no longer in surprise
start up from your cover.
I've lost my strength, my bow,   1150
lost my matchless arrows:
I am the victim now.
This terrain no longer
holds any fear for you,
and you may roam in freedom.
This is your chance to feast,
fix your teeth in vengeance
upon my mottled meat.
Soon I shall be fading,
for how can I retrieve
what I need for feeding?
Can anyone survive   1160
nourished by the breezes?
How can a creature live
with no power to gather
what the earth may give?

CHORUS

Have some respect towards a friend
who comes here with your good in mind.
Know this, know sure, you *can* escape
this deadly plague that eats you up

so cruelly; there's no way to learn
to live here with this endless pain.

PHILOCTETES

There it is—again, again—
you remind me of that pain. 1170
Best of those who've come to me,
why do you have to torture me?
What is it you've done to me?

CHORUS

But what makes you speak this way?

PHILOCTETES

You hope to carry me away
to the hateful land of Troy?

CHORUS

Yes, since I believe that's best.

PHILOCTETES

Go then, leave me here at last

CHORUS

Good, I welcome what you say;
I am eager to agree.
Come on then, let's take the road 1180
to our duties on ship-board.

The Chorus make moves towards departure.

PHILOCTETES

Do not go. I call on Zeus,
god of curses. . .

CHORUS

. . . don't abuse. . .°

PHILOCTETES

Friends, don't go.

CHORUS

Why recall us?

PHILOCTETES

I'm destroyed! Oh god, oh god!
How to live, oh foot, oh foot,
live with you in future days?
Strangers, here, return back, please. 1190

CHORUS

> For what? Have you some idea
> different from your wish before?

PHILOCTETES

> There's no cause to take offence
> if a man lashed round with pains
> says some things that are unwise.

CHORUS

> Come on then, as we advise.

PHILOCTETES

> Never, never, that's assured,
> even if the lightning-lord
> were to blast me with his fire.
> To hell with the Trojan war   1200
> and the leaders of the siege,
> who abandoned my disease.
> Strangers, grant me this, I plead.

CHORUS

> What is it you want to say?

PHILOCTETES

> Somehow find for me a sword
> or an axe or any blade.

CHORUS

> What attempt are you about?

PHILOCTETES

> Slash my limbs or cut my throat.
> Death, death is my only thought.

CHORUS

> Why?

PHILOCTETES

> To seek my father out.   1210

CHORUS

> Where on earth?

PHILOCTETES

> In Hades' night,
> since he's not still in the light.
> Fatherland and native town,
> oh to see you once again!

Fool to leave your sacred flow,
and join the Greeks that I abhor.
I am gone. I am no more.

Philoctetes goes into the cave.°

[CHORUS-LEADER
°I would have long ago departed,
and would be getting near my ship,
had we not seen Odysseus and Achilles' son   1220
here coming on their way towards us.]

SCENE 7

Re-enter Odysseus and Neoptolemus, who is still holding the bow.

ODYSSEUS
°I'd be obliged if you would tell me
why you've come back along this path;
and why in such a hurry too!

NEOPTOLEMUS
I must undo the error that I made a while ago.

ODYSSEUS
That is strange talk. What error do you mean?

NEOPTOLEMUS
I mean obeying you and all the others.

ODYSSEUS
Is anything amiss in what you've done?

NEOPTOLEMUS
I took a man by low deceit and trickery.

ODYSSEUS
What man? Oh! Are you up to some new scheme?

NEOPTOLEMUS
No nothing new. And yet for Philoctetes...   1230

ODYSSEUS
What are you doing? I've a growing fear.

NEOPTOLEMUS
I took this bow from him: and back to him again. . .

ODYSSEUS
Good god, what's this? You can't intend to give it him?

NEOPTOLEMUS
I can, because I got it wrongly, by foul play.

ODYSSEUS
Can you be saying this to make a fool of me?

NEOPTOLEMUS
If it is making fools to speak the truth.

ODYSSEUS
What's this, Achilles' son? What can you mean?

NEOPTOLEMUS
D'you want me to repeat it twice? Three times?

ODYSSEUS
I'd rather not have heard it even once.

NEOPTOLEMUS
Well, get this clear: all that I have to say, you've heard.   1240

ODYSSEUS
There is somebody who will stop you doing this.

NEOPTOLEMUS
Oh yes? And who is this who can prevent me?

ODYSSEUS
The whole Greek army, and, among them, me.

NEOPTOLEMUS
You may be clever, but what you say is not.

ODYSSEUS
Your talk's not clever either. Nor what you mean to do.

NEOPTOLEMUS
Well, if it's just, that's better than mere cleverness.

ODYSSEUS
And how's it just to give up what you have obtained
thanks to my planning?

NEOPTOLEMUS
I did a wrong, a shameful wrong,
and now I shall attempt to set it right.

ODYSSEUS

    Have you no fear of our Greek army as you act?   1250

NEOPTOLEMUS

    I do not dread your army, not so long as I am in the right.

ODYSSEUS

    <It would be sensible to fear the threat of force.>°

NEOPTOLEMUS

    I'll not agree to do your work, not even under threat.

ODYSSEUS

    So it's not Troy we shall be fighting with, but you.

NEOPTOLEMUS

    So be it then.

ODYSSEUS

    You see my hand is on my sword-hilt?

Odysseus threatens to draw his sword; Neoptolemus does the same.

NEOPTOLEMUS

    You see me making that same move,
    and I'll not hesitate. . .

ODYSSEUS

    All right, I'll let you be.
    But I shall go and tell our forces about this,
    and they shall make you pay for it.

Odysseus goes.

NEOPTOLEMUS (*calling after him*)

    That shows good sense.
    And if you stay as sensible in future,
    then possibly you may steer clear of getting hurt.   1260

Turns to cave and calls out.

    You, son of Poias, Philoctetes, come out;
    come, leave this rocky home of yours.

PHILOCTETES (*emerging*)

    What's this new shouting from outside my cave?
    Why summon me? What is it, strangers, that you want?

Sees Neoptolemus.

    Ah no, this is not good. Why are you here?

to add new troubles to the old?

NEOPTOLEMUS
   Don't be alarmed—just hear the words I've come to say.

PHILOCTETES
   I *am* afraid, though, since I came to grief
   through listening to your fine words before.

NEOPTOLEMUS
   Is it not possible for me to change my mind?   1270

PHILOCTETES
   This was your way with words before,
   when you were kidnapping my bow:
   all plausible yet vicious underneath.

NEOPTOLEMUS
   Yet not so now. But tell me this:
   are you determined to endure by staying here?
   or will you sail with us?

PHILOCTETES
   Stop your words there.
   Whatever you may say, it will be pointless.

NEOPTOLEMUS
   You are decided then?

PHILOCTETES
   More firmly than I can express.

NEOPTOLEMUS
   I wish you'd been persuaded by my words.
   But if there's nothing I can say
   that's to the point, then I stop there.   1280

PHILOCTETES
   Nothing you say will be of any use.
   You'll never win me round to wish you well,
   not you who stole my life away through trickery.
   Yet, even after that, you come and lecture me,
   detested son born of the finest father.
   To hell with all of you—the Sons of Atreus first,
   then that Odysseus, and then you.

NEOPTOLEMUS
   Enough of cursing.

He holds out the bow.

Here: your bow and arrows,
take them from my hand.

PHILOCTETES
What's this? Are you deceiving me a second time?

NEOPTOLEMUS
No, by the sanctity of Zeus most high, I swear I'm not.

PHILOCTETES
What welcome words!—provided you speak true.   1290

NEOPTOLEMUS
I'll put them into action.
Here, reach out your hand,
and take your weapon for your own. . .

°*Odysseus comes out of hiding just as the bow changes hands.*

ODYSSEUS
Stop! I forbid this, on the authority of Atreus' Sons,
and of the whole Greek force—the gods be my support.

PHILOCTETES
My son, whose voice is this I hear? Odysseus?

ODYSSEUS
Too right! And now you see me too!
And I am taking you away to Troy by force,
whether Achilles' son agrees with this or not.

Philoctetes draws his bow.

PHILOCTETES
You'll not succeed, not if this arrow-tip flies true.

Neoptolemus restrains Philoctetes.

NEOPTOLEMUS
Ah, no, no, stop! For gods' sake, do not shoot!   1300

PHILOCTETES
For gods' sake, let go of my arm, dear son. . .

NEOPTOLEMUS
I shall not.

Odysseus runs off.

SCENE 8

PHILOCTETES

Damn! Why prevent me firing off an arrow
through the man who is my deadly enemy?

NEOPTOLEMUS

That would not have been right, for me or you.

PHILOCTETES

At least we have proved this: the officers,
the phony envoys of the Greeks, are cowards
in the face of weapons, manly only in their talk.

NEOPTOLEMUS

You're right! And now you have your bow,   1310
you have no cause to aim your anger or reproach at me.

PHILOCTETES

I grant you that. You have displayed
your inborn nature, son, your pedigree:
no bastard son of Sisyphus, but offspring of Achilles,
the man who had the highest reputation when alive,
and has so still among the dead.

NEOPTOLEMUS

I am so glad to hear your words of praise
about my father and myself.
Now listen while I tell you what I hope to win from you.
Humans inevitably have to bear
the circumstances given to them by the gods:
but towards those who still cling to the traumas
they have chosen for themselves, as you do,
it is not justified to feel with sympathy or pity.   1320
You have become dehumanized,
and will let no one offer you advice;
if someone does, in friendly spirit, you still hate him,
and regard him as your deadly enemy.
Yet I shall speak out, all the same,
and I invoke Zeus, god of oaths,
so listen carefully, and then inscribe this in your heart.
This malady of yours comes from a higher fate,
incurred when you walked near the guard of Chryse,°
the hidden serpent which protects that roofless precinct.

You need to know that you shall never
have a cure from this appalling plague—   1330
not while the sun's orb rises here, and then sets over there—
until you come to Troy of your free will.
There you shall meet Asclepius' sons,° who are with us,
and thanks to them be nursed free of this malady.
Then with the arrows of this bow, and with me too,
you shall emerge as victor over Troy.
And I shall tell you how I know that this is how it is:
we hold a man, a prisoner from Troy, called Helenus.°
He is a master-seer, and foretells clearly
that these things must come to pass;   1340
and furthermore that Troy is bound to be
completely conquered by this summertime.
And he will yield himself for death
if what he says prove false.
So now you know all this, please follow willingly.
It adds up to a fine success:
to be adjudged the greatest of the Greeks;
to come into the care of healing hands;
and then to sack the city that has brought
so many sorrows, Troy; and win the highest glory too.

PHILOCTETES
I hate you, life—why keep me up here in the light,
and not deliver me to Hades' dark?
What shall I do?   1350
How can I possibly dismiss this man's account,
when he has given me advice and means me well?
So should I yield?
How, after doing that, could I then show my face?
Who could I possibly converse with?
How could my eyes, that have seen everything,
be able to put up with this, and tolerate the company
of Atreus' Sons, the men who brought me down?
How could they bear to see that damned Odysseus?
And yet it's not so much resentments
for things past that sting me, but the kind of things
that I imagine I shall to have to undergo
at those men's hands in future   1360
(for if a person's mind has given birth to bad,

it trains him to be bad in everything).
And you, I am surprised at you,
since you should not yourself be going back to Troy;
you should be keeping me away from there.
Those men insulted you by pilfering your father's trophies;
[rating wretched Aias as inferior to Odysseus
in the competition for your father's arms]°
and are you, after that, to go and fight for them,
and make me do the same?
Do not do this, my son:
instead escort me home as you have promised me,°
and leave those filthy crooks to rot in filth.
That way you'll mark up double gratitude   1370
from me and from my father too.
And you will not appear, through helping them,
to have a nature like those criminals.

NEOPTOLEMUS

The things you say are fair enough. But all the same
I still want you to trust the gods and my account,
and sail from here alongside me, your friend.

PHILOCTETES

What? Go to Troy and to the hateful Sons of Atreus?
And with my wretched foot like this?

NEOPTOLEMUS

No, but to take your ulcer-wound
to those who can relieve it,
and release you from this plague.

PHILOCTETES

This is such dark advice: what can you mean?   1380

NEOPTOLEMUS

The best conclusion that I see for you and me.

PHILOCTETES

Have you no shame before the gods as you say this?

NEOPTOLEMUS

Why feel ashamed at offering to help my friends?

PHILOCTETES

Is what you say a favour for the Sons of Atreus, or for me?

NEOPTOLEMUS

For you, of course. I'm speaking as the friend I am.

PHILOCTETES
How so, when you still want
to hand me over to my enemies?

NEOPTOLEMUS
My friend, you ought to learn
to be less absolute amid your troubles.

PHILOCTETES
You shall destroy me giving this advice, I know you will.

NEOPTOLEMUS
No I shall not. You do not understand, I tell you.

PHILOCTETES
So I don't know that it was Atreus' Sons marooned me?   1390

NEOPTOLEMUS
They did: but see how they'll become your rescuers.

PHILOCTETES
Never, not if that means I must set eyes
on Troy of my free will.

NEOPTOLEMUS
What can I do if I'm not able to convince you
over anything by using words?
The time has come° for me to give up talking,
and for you to go on living as you are, without a cure.

PHILOCTETES
Then let me suffer as I have to.
And you do the thing you promised me,
your hand held clasped with mine:
to take me home.
Do that and don't delay; and mention Troy no more;   1400
I've had enough of talking on and on.

°NEOPTOLEMUS
If you're certain, let's be going.

PHILOCTETES
That's a fine thing to have spoken.

Neoptolemus supports Philoctetes as he makes some first steps.

NEOPTOLEMUS
Lean, then, on me as you're stepping.

PHILOCTETES
Yes, as well as I am able.

NEOPTOLEMUS
How shall I avoid the Greeks' reproaches?

PHILOCTETES
Do not let that be a worry.

NEOPTOLEMUS
But suppose they devastate my country.

PHILOCTETES
I'll support you. . .

NEOPTOLEMUS
But what kind of help can you provide me?

PHILOCTETES
. . . using Heracles' own arrows.

NEOPTOLEMUS
What is this you're saying?

PHILOCTETES
I'll deter them from approaching near your country.

NEOPTOLEMUS
°Very well then, if you can fulfil your words in action,
come along and make your farewells to this island.

As they begin to depart, the vision of Heracles appears above them.°

°SCENE 9

HERACLES
Not so hasty, son of Poias,   1410
not before you've heard my message.
Yes, it's Heracles whose voice you're
hearing, and whose face you see here.
It's for your sake I've descended,
coming from my place in heaven
here to tell you Zeus' purpose;
and to stop you from the journey
that you have just started out on.
Therefore listen to my message.

And first I'll tell you what has happened in my story:
once I had completed all those labours
I attained immortal status,° as you now can see.   1420
This progression is confirmed for you as well:
emerging from these painful labours
you shall win a life that's crowned with glory.
You must go to Troy, and keep this man beside you.
There, first, you'll be delivered from this gruesome plague;
and then you shall be chosen for the valour-prize,
reward for taking life away from Paris,°
cause of all these troubles, with an arrow from my bow,
and then for going on to conquer Troy.
And after you have been awarded special honours
by the Greeks, you shall convey the trophies
home to Poias, your old father,
high on Oeta, your ancestral mountain home.   1430
And you shall offer any plunder you have taken
from this war before my pyre-mound°
in commemoration of my bow.
(*to Neoptolemus*) To you, Achilles' son, I offer this advice:
because you do not have the strength to conquer Troy
without this man, nor he apart from you,
you should protect each other
like a pair of prowling lions.
(*to Philoctetes again*) I'll send Asclepius° to Troy
to be the healer of your malady,
since it is destined to be taken
with my bow a second time.°
And do remember this
when you are laying low that land: 1440
respect the province of the gods.°
The Father rates all other matters
of less weight than this.
[that's Zeus. For piety does not perish when people die;
among the living and the dead it's indestructible.]°

PHILOCTETES
Oh how keenly I have longed to
hear you speaking; now at last you
have appeared before me. All that
you have ordered I shall follow.

NEOPTOLEMUS
  I too give you my agreement.

HERACLES
  No delay then, turn to action.
  For this wind is in your favour,   1450
  right for urging on your voyage.

PHILOCTETES (*prepares himself to leave*)
        Then I call out to this island
        as I start on my departure.
        Fare you well, my home, my look-out,
        and you nymphs of water-meadows,
        and you bass-voiced booming
        of the ocean breakers.
        Farewell, place where often,
        though inside, my hair was wetted
        by the south-wind's sea-spray;
        and where often Mount Hermaion°
        would resound with echoes
        to my own tempestuous howling.   1460
        Now, you springs and Lycian well-head,°
        I am leaving you, yes,
        leaving you for ever—
        which I thought would never happen.
        Farewell, sea-encircled land of
        Lemnos, send me
        on a fair and faultless voyage,
        where strong fate conveys me,
        and the good advice of comrades,
        and the all-subduing godhead
        who has brought these things to pass.

CHORUS
        Come along then on our way
        all together; and we pray,   1470
        Nymphs of Ocean, please convey
        us safely back to home° one day.

They all set off for the ship.

OEDIPUS
AT COLONUS

INTRODUCTION TO
OEDIPUS AT COLONUS

The New Hero at Colonus

THE chief appeal of *Oedipus at Colonus* (*OC*)[1] lies, arguably, in features which we do not generally think of as characteristic of Greek tragedy. First, there is a very particular and numinous locality, one blessed with bird-thronged thickets and other detailed local features. Into this settled rural landscape there intrudes the figure of a blind old man, unkempt and ragged, who dominates the play with an uncanny mixture of wisdom and irascibility. Oedipus is on-stage the whole way from the opening until line 1555 (but for a few lines, when he hides on the approach of the chorus). During this time he displays a huge range of dispositions and emotions, from weakness to imperiousness, from gratitude to defiance, and from devotion to virulent hate. He starts the play a helpless beggar, and he ends it as a superhuman "hero", one of the powerful dead. The mysterious transition between the two is both sublime and disturbing.

A strong sense of "last things" hangs over *OC*. While it is usually hazardous to infer anything about the artist's actual biography from a work of art, this is something of an exception.[2] The tragedy is so concerned with old age, its sufferings and its occasional compensations, that it would have been tempting to guess from that alone that it was composed in Sophocles' old age. As it is, external evidence confirms that it was composed at the very end of his life, at the age of about ninety, and first performed only after his death in 406 BC. Even after years of physical dependence and deterioration Oedipus is still assailed by fresh conflicts and dilemmas, as is epitomized in the famous "Old Age Ode" at 1211 ff. But he is also staunchly defended by Athens and its king, Theseus. And he still has the love and loyalty of his two daughters, a love he returns (1615–18):

> It has been harsh, I know, my girls,
> but there is one small word

---

[1] The first syllable of Colonus is a short o, the second, which should carry the stress, is long (coll-**lone**-us). In Greek *Oidipous epi Kolono*, but the "subtitle" almost certainly does not go back to Sophocles and was added later to distinguish this play from the earlier *Oidipous*, subtitled *Tyrannos*; see p. 3.

[2] The story that he had a legal dispute with his sons in his old age is most probably a fiction derived from this very play.

> redeems these many sufferings:
> you never could have had a *love*
> more full than from this heart of mine. . . .

The insistent attention lavished on the locality of Colonus, a rural settlement not far out from (ancient) Athens to the north-west, is another
biographical connection which is confirmed by external evidence: it
was Sophocles' home village. This affectionate "landscape-painting" is
introduced right at the beginning (14–18), when the scene is set in front
of a burgeoning sacred grove. There is even a whole ode devoted to the
praises of Colonus and its landscape at 668–719, sung by the chorus of
elders who are proud of their home "parish". It is an attractive idea that
the aged Sophocles has even worked himself into this song with the lines
(691–3):

> The Muses favour this Colonus
> with poetry and song and dances—
> and Aphrodite's golden harness.[3]

And he was, indeed, famous for his feats in the sphere of Aphrodite as
well as that of the Muses.

Cultic details about the religious observances of Colonus prolifer-
ate both in the Colonus Ode and in several passages elsewhere. In fact,
practical religious pieties are probably more pervasively incorporated
into *OC* than any other surviving Greek tragedy. While this may reflect
Sophocles' personal religious concerns, it is also fully relevant to the
subject-matter of the play. Within its course a new superhuman power
will be added to the divine favours that already inhabit Colonus. Oedipus
will himself become a kind of local god, or, more precisely, a "hero".

Ancient Greece was polytheistic, and had room for a wide variety of
divinities. Among them, the most important were undoubtedly the familiar Olympian gods, presided over by Zeus, immortal powers inhabiting the
celestial sphere above, and honoured appropriately through the savours
that went upwards from sacrificial offerings. Heroes, on the other hand,
belong below the earth: they were mortals and they are now dead. They
retain power and could exert it, benign or malign, among the humans
living in the upper world; and so they too were honoured and placated
through cult. This characteristically took the form of offerings, blood and
other liquids that were poured down into the earth. And their cult was
usually tied closely to the place of their death and location of their bones.[4]

---

[3] More literally: "The choruses of the Muses do not spurn it, nor does Aphrodite of the
golden rein."

[4] See also pp. 83–4 on *Aias*.

It is uncertain whether or not there was a hero–cult of Oedipus at Colonus before Sophocles' play; in other words, it is possible that the cult which undoubtedly existed in later times was first inaugurated by the tragedy. The prediction of Oedipus' heroic status and powers are very clearly explicit in the play. As soon as he finds out where he is, he says that he will die there; and he speaks again and again of the benefit that he will bring Athens as recompense for protecting him and giving him a resting-place after death. Oedipus spells out his future demonic power when he tells Theseus that one day Athens will be on bad terms with Thebes (621–2):

> Then shall my hidden, sleeping corpse,
> though cold, gulp down their warm life-blood. . .

Above all, though, there is the wonder and mystery of Oedipus' own ending. First, he supervises what is, in effect, his own funeral procession, the blind man leading the way (1538 ff., 1586 ff.). Finally, as the messenger relates (1623 ff.), he is summoned by a supernatural voice, and tells everyone to turn away except for Theseus. When they turn around, they see Theseus reacting to some awesome sight, while Oedipus himself has disappeared. There is no doubt that he is dead, but there has been no physical death; and what has happened to him must remain a sacred secret. While hero–cult is germane to several Greek tragedies, including Sophocles' *Aias* and *Women of Trachis*, it is nowhere else so closely worked into the story and the matter of the play.

The Unburdening of Oedipus' Guilt

The progression through which Oedipus, after many years of humbled suffering, attains a serene and miraculous death and a future cult may sound attractively analogous to Christian sanctification and saint-cult.[5] But this should not be pressed: Oedipus is far from saint-like. While there are suggestions that the pollutions and agonies of his life-history are in some sense cancelled or "redeemed", he remains at the same time a deeply ambivalent and problematic figure. This perspective emerges more clearly once this play is set in relation to earlier portrayals of Oedipus, especially by Sophocles himself. For, although there were other plays by other poets, the figure of Oedipus was evidently above all a Sophoclean creation, and it is highly likely that it was *Oedipus the King*

---

[5] It is telling that the best-known modern adaptation of *OC* is Lee Breuer's *Gospel at Colonus*, which is explicitly and insistently christianized.

(*OT*), dating from (probably) at least twenty-five years earlier than *OC*, that turned him into the archetypally tragic figure, the great king who is reduced to the lowest state of powerlessness and misery.

The most prominent shift between *OT* and *OC* is towards the matter of Oedipus' guilt or innocence. In *OT* the question of whether Oedipus deserves his terrible fate is left conspicuously unresolved: he is no paragon, indeed he has serious faults, but these are not seen as explaining or justifying his sufferings, which may seem disproportionate (see further pp. 8–9). The past deeds that he discovers are straight horrific facts, they are not excused or explained; and while there is no assertion anywhere that they were his own fault, there is also no attempt to mitigate the horror or to exonerate him, the agent. In *OC* it is quite different: the issues about whether his past acts were deliberate or not, and whether he is guilty or not, are prominently raised.[6] They are disputed in two sequences in the first part of the play, at 265–74 and more fully in the lyric exchange at 534–48; and then most fully at 960–1003, where he is inclined to attribute them to the inscrutable ways of the gods (see 964–5, 998). Oedipus maintains that he is not to blame because there was no way he could have known that the old man he killed on the road was his father; and that he did not choose Iocasta as his wife, but was given her by the city of Thebes as a reward for getting rid of the Sphinx. He insists that he is "pure before the law" (548).

The big question of whether Oedipus becomes pure and purged in *OC* is far from settled. I believe that the roles of his children, Antigone and Polynices, and their fates imposed by Oedipus just before his death, are crucial for this issue. First, then, Antigone, who stays loyally by her father's side, shining with constancy through the stormy vicissitudes of the play. Young though she is (around twenty, it is implied), she is far from passive, and when her father is in danger of ejection from Colonus by the chorus, she sings a moving plea (237–53). Throughout she does not hesitate to give Oedipus advice, and in the final scenes she really comes into her own, especially in relation to her beloved brother Polynices. Antigone was almost entirely a Sophoclean invention, and it is very likely (though not ultimately provable) that Sophocles himself, in his earlier *Antigone*, had invented the whole story of the sister who gives her life in order to ensure that her brother Polynices gets buried. So she is established long before *OC* as the brave young woman who sacrifices herself for her family. But there is no hint either in *Antigone* or *OT* of her going into exile with her father.[7]

---

[6] Especially through the deployment of the word *akon* (unwillingly, unknowingly), as opposed to *hekon* (willingly, deliberately).

It seems, however, that the inventor of this strand of the story, telling of Antigone's role as her blind father's companion in exile, was not Sophocles at all, but Euripides in his *Phoenician Women* (of about 409 BC). The story there is that Oedipus is still in Thebes at the time of the fatal battle between his two sons; and then in the closing scenes he goes into exile accompanied by Antigone.[8] It would seem, then, that in *OC* Sophocles is responding to Euripides' new twist to the story, and reconfigures it yet again by having Oedipus and Antigone go into exile *before* the battle between the sons at Thebes. This new sequence means that Antigone is present at the cursing of her brother, Polynices, and is closely tied up in its significance and its practical consequences.

What, then, are we to make of Polynices? How just is Oedipus' treatment of him? Does he fully deserve his father's deadly curse? This ethical and emotional assessment is a central question in the interpretation of the whole play. Polynices is usually seen as a thoroughly nasty piece of work who merits all the condemnation and grim fate that Oedipus calls down on him. But there is a case for seeing him as a more ambivalent figure whose case should at least gain some sympathy and consideration. Oedipus' utter condemnation, which calls on Justice to trump Mercy (see note on 1268), may arguably be viewed as excessive. It is true that no one within the play questions or condemns his vindictive fury, but that does not necessarily mean that it is to be admired or endorsed.

When Theseus tells Oedipus that a young man wants to talk to him, Oedipus immediately identifies this as Polynices and refuses to see him. Antigone intervenes on her brother's behalf (1189–92):

> You are his father, which means that no matter
> how appallingly he has behaved to you,
> it still would not be true and right
> for you to wrong him in return.
> And so allow him here.

And when Oedipus, contrary to this forgiving sentiment, not only refuses to help Polynices' cause, but lays terrible curses upon him, it is to his sisters that the devastated son turns (1399 ff.). He accepts that he is doomed, and begs them to make sure, if they can, that his dead body receives proper burial. There is then a dialogue between him and Antigone (1414–49) in which, despite their mutual affection, she is

---

[7] In fact, at the end of *OT* there is some prevarication over whether Oedipus will go into exile at all, or whether he will stay in Thebes (see pp. 304–5).

[8] There is a further complication that the authenticity of some relevant passages in *Phoenician Women* is in dispute

unable to persuade him to turn away from the prospect of certain death. So, even if there is nothing else to be said for Polynices, Antigone is devoted to him and stands up for him. Her loyalty might, indeed, be offered as a consideration to suggest that Polynices is not entirely rotten, and that Oedipus' damnation of him is not unequivocally admirable.

Another factor is the contrast with Creon. Creon claims to represent the whole city of Thebes, but is in fact partisan (for a reason never given) in favour of the younger brother, Eteocles.[9] He is portrayed as a thoroughly nasty piece of work, close to an outright villain, in a fashion not usual in Greek tragedy. He lies and threatens, while hiding behind a veneer of righteous indignation; and, when he does not succeed, he reverts to crude physical force, abducting the helpless Antigone and even laying hands on Oedipus himself. This all earns unreserved condemnation from the good King Theseus. Contrast this with Polynices, who arrives alone without military support, and who approaches hesitantly. He tells the truth, however much it may be to his discredit,[10] and there is no reason to doubt that his regrets are sincere. Unlike Creon, he does not put up any defiance in the face of Oedipus' crushing condemnation: on the contrary he accepts that he is doomed.

It is surely significant that, as soon as Polynices has gone, the thunder sounds (1456 ff.), marking the beginning of Oedipus' final scenes. In the course of these he miraculously leads all the sighted people off to the designated sacred place. Then a messenger arrives and tells of his mysterious and thrilling last minutes among the living (1663–5):

> sent on without distress,
> not by disease, no cries of pain,
> but in a way, for any human, wonderful.

Because of the close sequence, this redemptive release from life seems to be almost, in some sense, a kind of "reward" for his treatment of Polynices. Or at least it suggests that the business of Polynices had to be cleared out of the way before the gods concerned are ready to let Oedipus go to this extraordinary death.

Had the play ended at line 1666 then Oedipus' treatment of his son might possibly have been viewed as the triumphant crowning act of his rehabilitation. But the closing scene that follows complicates and darkens the picture. In this the two daughters indulge in lamentation, before

---

[9] This is contrary to the usual seniority of Eteocles, see note on 374–6.
[10] Particularly his cataloguing of the leaders he has recruited to march against Thebes. The balance of assessment might be altered if these lines were not authentic—see note on 1313–25.

Theseus returns at 1751 to tell them that such grief is inappropriate when their father's death has been so painless and extraordinary. Then, in the closing lines of the whole play (1768 ff.), Antigone asks Theseus to help her and Ismene to go back to Thebes, where they will try to stop the fatal battle between their brothers. Theseus replies (1773–6):

> I shall do that, and whatever
> other favour I can offer
> to assist you, and respect the
> one below, the new-departed.

Anyone who knows Sophocles' *Antigone* will know what terrible things are going to happen once Antigone does get to Thebes: they will recall how she will die for burying Polynices' body, contrary to the authority of Creon. This very tragedy has been foreshadowed by Polynices' own plea for burial before he departed (1405 ff.). This ending does not (of course) cancel out the splendour of Oedipus' departure—and it most certainly does not diminish his cultic stature as a hero—but it does cast a shadow over the closure, and disturb what might otherwise have been exalted in a kind of celestial light.

Oedipus loved Antigone with all his heart and wished the very best for her, yet the compulsion he feels to damn Polynices drags his daughter down along with her brother. Even though he does not pay for it himself, there is a kind of price that is exacted for such unrelenting fervour. There is perhaps even a suggestion that Oedipus can only win his release by "unloading" some of his burden onto Polynices. But this means also onto his beloved Antigone. In this way Sophocles does not let his play become a straightforward tale of purification and redemption. It remains true to the complexity of human life, which is never completely free from dark shadows.

Athens and Thebes

There is a lot about Athens in *OC*, and it is represented as very much the Good City. Her people are well ordered and pious; their king is wise and considerate while also being brave and decisive. Oedipus, when his daughters have been rescued, is unequivocal in his praise (1124–7):

> So may the gods reward you as I wish,
> both you and this your country,
> since alone of all mankind
> among your people I've discovered piety,
> a sense of fairness, and refusal to speak false.

This does not necessarily mean, though, that the play is "all about" Athens, nor even that it is some kind of patriotic or ideological propaganda.

Oedipus' initial arrival at Colonus is, in effect, an arrival at Athens; and in terms of stage-space the city itself is to be thought of as not far away down one of the two side-entrances (see p. xx). That is the direction of safety. The other direction leads away "elsewhere", and above all to Thebes, which was, in geographical reality, some 60 km away, northwest over the mountains (see Map 2). It is from there, the direction of danger, that Oedipus arrives at the start of the play; and it is from there, of course, that the villainous Creon arrives, and away towards there that he drags Antigone.[11] It is also, therefore, away from Athens and towards the perils of Thebes that she departs at the very end of the play.

But while it is the direction towards Thebes that threatens danger, and which is opposed to the piety and strength of Athens, does this mean that Thebes itself is on the side of evil, so to speak? Creon claims to represent the city as a whole, but this directly contradicted by Theseus (919–21, 929–30):

> And yet it is not Thebes has trained you in bad ways:
> the Thebans don't encourage men to be corrupt,
> and they would not approve if they found out
> . . .
> But you are a disgrace to your own well-deserving city. . . .

It is emphasized that Thebes once was—and might again be—a worthy friend of Athens; and it is an underlying assumption that, back in the mythical era in which the play is set, Thebes was an admirable place and on good terms with Athens. Oedipus has to warn Theseus that, although this is now the case, it will not necessarily always stay like that (616–20):

> So even if for now the sunny days between
> yourself and Thebes are shining fair,
> innumerable time begets innumerable days and nights,
> and as these pass they shall, though for some trivial cause,
> shatter in pieces with the sword
> these now harmonious bonds.

And it is the historical case that, at the time the play was performed, and for nearly a century and more before that, Athens had been on distinctly hostile terms with Thebes. They had even descended into outright conflict, especially in the years of the Peloponnesian War that had consumed

---

[11] It is interesting that Polynices very probably arrives from the Athens direction, but then departs towards Thebes—see note on 1249 ff.

the energy and manpower of Athens for the last generation. In the light of that, the exoneration of Thebes in *OC* is indeed rather striking.

It has been claimed that Thebes is almost invariably portrayed in tragedy as a distorted and corrupted place, a kind of "evil empire", locus of dark, introverted perversion in opposition to the light, openness, and justice of Athens. While there are undeniably some plays where Thebes is portrayed in a generally negative light, this by no means amounts to a predominant pattern. Terrible things do happen at Thebes in quite a few tragedies, but that is because a good number of them are set there, and terrible things do tend to occur in tragedies!

It is not, in fact, the city of Thebes that is at the epicentre of the conflicts that are worked through in *OC*, but the royal family of Thebes. The guilt or non-guilt of Oedipus' past life, the involvement of his mother/wife's brother Creon, the fratricidal rivalry for power between his two sons, the contrast between them and his daughters: all these convoluted struggles are at play here. Sophocles has, however, transported them away from Thebes, and set them in the idyllic locality of Colonus. And here they are largely purged of their venom. There is a strong suggestion that it takes this beautiful and god-haunted place to draw the poison out of this family's terrible history. A sense of purification and even of sublimity is achieved. Even then, though, Sophocles, at the very end of his life, is too honest to embrace a transcendent redemption: there is still Antigone's tragedy to be enacted.

So, while Athens is warmly praised in *OC*, it is not the core of the play. There is a more universal, and less exclusive, appeal. This lies both in its stark realization that past troubles can never be completely purged, and in its suggestion that certain rural, numinous places have a special power for absorbing human suffering into a more harmonious continuum.

OEDIPUS AT COLONUS

LIST OF CHARACTERS

OEDIPUS, the former king of Thebes, now old, blind and a wandering beggar

ANTIGONE, Oedipus' young daughter, accompanying him in exile

MAN OF COLONUS, a local inhabitant

ISMENE, Oedipus' other daughter, who has remained in Thebes

THESEUS, noble king of Athens

CREON, Oedipus' brother-in-law, the power behind the throne of Eteocles, younger son of Oedipus, who is ruling at Thebes

POLYNICES, elder son of Oedipus, who, in exile, has raised an army to conquer Thebes

ATTENDANT OF THESEUS (often known as 'Messenger')

CHORUS of local elders of the community of Colonus

Place: in front of a sacred grove at Colonus, a rural settlement (about 1½ km to the NNW of the walls of Athens).

Oedipus comes on slowly, led by Antigone, from the direction of 'abroad'.
Both are meanly clothed and unkempt.

OEDIPUS
    My daughter, child of this old sightless man,
    Antigone, say whereabouts have we arrived,
    what people's land? Who for this day will cater
    for the wanderer, Oedipus, with meagre offerings?
    I beg for little, and receive still less,
    and rest content with that.
    For sufferings, and the long companionship of time,
    and, third, my dignity have taught me to be satisfied.
    So, daughter, if you see a place to rest,
    upon some common ground, or by some sacred grove,   10
    stop there and sit me down,
    so we can question where we are.
    As strangers we are bound to find things out from local folk,
    and then to act on what we hear from them.

ANTIGONE
    My father, trouble-stricken Oedipus,
    the towers that crown the city look quite far away,°
    but this spot here is clearly sacred,°
    flourishing with laurel, olive tress, and vines;
    within it flocks of feathered songbirds,
    make their harmony.
    So rest your limbs on this unchiselled ledge of rock;°
    since you have covered a long way for one so old.   20

OEDIPUS
    Then sit me here, and take care of the blind.

ANTIGONE
    I hardly need to study that, not after all this time.

She guides him to the rock, where he sits.

OEDIPUS
    Can you say where we have arrived?

ANTIGONE

Although I cannot name this neighbourhood,
I know this land is Athens.

OEDIPUS

Yes, everyone we've met has told us this.

ANTIGONE

Well, shall I go and find the name of this locality?

OEDIPUS

Yes, child, supposing it's inhabited.

ANTIGONE

It is inhabited. And there's no need to go, I think—
I see a man close by us here.

OEDIPUS

And is he on the move in our direction?   30

Enter Man of Colonus from the 'home' direction.

ANTIGONE

He is already with us. So say whatever
you may have in mind right now—here is the man.

OEDIPUS

Good stranger, this young woman,
who has sight for me as well as for herself,
informs me your attention has directed you to here
at just the moment when you can enlighten us. . .

MAN OF COLONUS

Before you ask me any more, get up from off this seat:
you're on a place where it's not pure to tread.

OEDIPUS

What is this place? Which of the gods is it assigned to?

MAN OF COLONUS

The ground must never be disturbed or settled on,
since it belongs to fearsome goddesses,
the daughters of the Earth and Dark.   40

OEDIPUS

What is their solemn title that I should invoke?

MAN OF COLONUS

The people hereabouts entitle them
'Eumenides all-seeing, goddesses benign'.°
But other names stand good for them elsewhere.

OEDIPUS
  Then may they kindly welcome me, their suppliant,
  as I shall never leave this place of rest.

MAN OF COLONUS
  What can you mean?

OEDIPUS
  This is the password of my destiny.°

MAN OF COLONUS
  Then I would not myself be bold enough
  to make you move without due sanction from the city,
  not until I tell them what I mean to do.

OEDIPUS
  I beg you, stranger, don't refuse me, vagrant though I am,
  but answer me the things that I ask.   50

MAN OF COLONUS
  Go on; you shall not meet with disrespect from me.

OEDIPUS
  What is this ground that we have stepped upon?

MAN OF COLONUS
  I'll tell you all, so far as I have knowledge:
  all this area here is sacred ground,
  the sanctuary of dread Poseidon,
  also of Prometheus, fire-supplying Titan-god.°
  The spot you're treading near is called
  the bronze-stepped threshold° of this land,
  the underpin of Athens.
  The neighbouring fields proclaim
  this horse-rider Colonus° here to be their founder,
  and the local people all employ his name as theirs.   60
  That is the way things are here, stranger—
  not celebrated in the famous tales so much
  as by our constant being here.

OEDIPUS
  So there are people who inhabit this locality?

MAN OF COLONUS
  They do; and take their title from this god.

OEDIPUS
  And do they have a ruler,
  or do the common people have authority?

MAN OF COLONUS
The ruling power° rests with the king who's in the city.

OEDIPUS
Who is this holds command in word and strength?

MAN OF COLONUS
His name is Theseus, son of Aegeus, king before him.

OEDIPUS
I wonder if a messenger might go to him from you?   70

MAN OF COLONUS
To tell him what? Or to arrange for him to come?

OEDIPUS
For him to grant a little favour,
and so gain great benefit.

MAN OF COLONUS
What help might come from one who cannot see?

OEDIPUS
All words I utter shall be filled with sight.

MAN OF COLONUS
I tell you, stranger, what's the safest course for you,
because you have the bearing of nobility,
were it not for your fate: stay here,
just where you first appeared, while I go off
and tell the local, not the city, men.
For they're the ones who shall decide if you should stay,   80
or set off on your way again.

Exit man of Colonus towards town.

OEDIPUS
Say, daughter, has the stranger gone?

ANTIGONE
He's gone: so say whatever you may wish
secure in peace, as I'm the only person near.

OEDIPUS (*calls on the Eumenides*)
You goddess-queens so fierce to face, your rock-seat
was the first place in this land I bent my knees.
Do not refuse consideration, then,
for Phoebus and for me. He told me,
when he prophesied those many gruesome things,

that this would be my respite after years and years:
that I would reach my ending at that place
where I would find a seat and sanctuary   90
belonging to the Solemn Goddesses.°
And there I should complete my stricken life's last lap,
and, by my dwelling, I should bring reward
to those who harboured me, and doom to those
who had expelled and driven me away.
He pledged that there would be some signals of fulfilment:
earthquake, or loud thunder, or the lightning-bolt of Zeus.
And so I knew it had to be an omen I could trust
that brought my footsteps to this grove of yours.
That is the only way I could have possibly
encountered you the first as I went on my way
—me abstinent with you who take no wine°—   100
and sat upon this sacred unshaped pedestal.
So, goddesses, please grant me passing
and completion to my life, to fit Apollo's word—
unless, that is, I seem beneath your notice,
ever labouring at the basest human toils.
Hear me, sweet daughters of primeval Dark;
hear me, most honoured city,
titled after mighty Pallas, Athens:
take pity on this sorry phantom of the person Oedipus,
since this is not the body that I used to be.   110

ANTIGONE
Keep quiet. Here come some men, advanced in years,
approaching to investigate your resting-place.

OEDIPUS
Then I'll keep quiet. And you conceal me in the grove,
clear of the road, until I find what they are going to say.
We need to know, if we're to act with proper caution.

°*Antigone helps Oedipus hide in the entrance to the grove; the chorus of local elders arrives from the 'home' direction.*

°CHORAL ENTRANCE-SONG, WITH LYRIC DIALOGUE

CHORUS (*urgently searching*)
              Look! Who was the man?
              Where's he got his lair?

Where's he run away?
—utter recklessness.
Look around for him, 120
search about for him,
here and everywhere.
Vagrant, that old man,
vagrant, not from here,
or he never would
have disturbed this ground,
breached the sacred wood,
forbidden to tread down,
which belongs to these
undefeated powers—
names we dread to sound,
those we hurry past,
turning eyes away, 130
silencing our voice,
framing holy thoughts.
Now I hear that one
with no fear has come;
though I scour the shrine,
still I cannot find
where he's gone to ground.

OEDIPUS (*revealing himself*)
Here he is, that person.
Voices, goes the saying,
offer vision to the sightless.

CHORUS
Oh, oh, horrible to see, and horrible to hear! 140

OEDIPUS
I implore you, don't regard me as an outlaw.

CHORUS
Zeus protect us! Who on earth is this old person?

OEDIPUS
Not a body to call happy for his flawless
fortune, guardians of this country.
This is plain, as otherwise I'd not rely on
eyes of others, and, though greater,
fasten on a little anchor.

CHORUS

> Were you born with eyes 150
> that were ever blind?
> I can tell your life
> has been long with grief,
> grief as much as years.
> At least I'll hold you
> back from further curse:
> you have gone too far,
> too far. Yet make sure
> not to press on more
> in this grassy grove,
> where no voice should sound,
> where the water bowl
> mixes with the drops 160
> poured from honey-cups.
> Stranger, take good care;
> move, step further back,
> keep a wider track.
> Wanderer, tired with toils,
> do you hear my voice?
> If you've any words
> to exchange with us,
> leave forbidden soil;
> speak where it's allowed:
> until then hold back.

OEDIPUS

> Daughter, what direction 170
> should we turn our thoughts to?

ANTIGONE

> We should take due notice
> of the local people, father,
> giving way with full attention.

OEDIPUS

> Well then, reach and touch me.

ANTIGONE

> Here you are, I'm holding onto you.

OEDIPUS

> Strangers, don't let anyone maltreat me,

once I have left this ground and put my trust in you.

°*During the following lyric Oedipus leaves the sacred ground.*

CHORUS

> No one shall remove you
> from this place of refuge,
> not if you refuse it.

OEDIPUS

> More yet?

CHORUS

> Step on forward.

OEDIPUS

> Further?

CHORUS

> You, young woman,   180
> guide him; you can hear us.

ANTIGONE

> Follow this way, follow
> with your darkened footstep,
> where I lead you, father.
> °. . .

CHORUS

> In a strange land, stranger,
> bring yourself to loathing
> what the country holds as
> hateful, and to honour
> what it finds worth loving.

OEDIPUS

> Lead me then, my daughter,
> to a place that's pious,
> somewhere we may speak and listen.   190
> There's no point in fighting
> what has got to happen.

They have by now come to the edge of the rock-ledge.

CHORUS

> Stop there. Step no further,
> stay there on that rocky
> bedrock formed by nature.

OEDIPUS
>   This way?

CHORUS
>   Far enough, yes.

OEDIPUS
>   Sit here?

CHORUS
>   There beside you,
>   low down on the outcrop.

ANTIGONE
>   I can help you, father;
>   calmly plant your footstep
>   here beside my footstep.

OEDIPUS
>   Ah, my. . .

ANTIGONE
>   Lean your poor old body   200
>   on my loving arm here.

OEDIPUS
>   . . . ah, my grim confusion.

Oedipus is now on the outcrop outside the sacred ground.

CHORUS
>   Now that you are settled:
>   who you are—inform us.
>   Led upon your wandering
>   with such pain, we wonder,
>   what place is your homeland?

OEDIPUS
>   Cityless, strangers. Do not. . .

CHORUS
>   What is it you're forbidding?

OEDIPUS
>   Not who I am: don't ask me.   210
>   Do not pursue, no searching.

CHORUS
>   Why is this?

OEDIPUS

> Birth distorted.

CHORUS

> Tell of it.

OEDIPUS

> Oh, my daughter
> whatever should I tell them?

CHORUS

> Whose seed sowed you, stranger?
> Speak to us: name your father.

OEDIPUS

> What is to happen, daughter?

CHORUS

> Speak, as you've reached the margin.

OEDIPUS

> Tell it I must, because I
> have no escape for cover.

CHORUS

> Too long delay; now quickly!

OEDIPUS

> You may have heard about a
> son of Laius°. . .   220

CHORUS

> Oh god!

OEDIPUS

> . . . offspring of Labdacus. . .

CHORUS

> Oh Zeus!

OEDIPUS

> Oedipus, man of sorrow.

CHORUS

> You are that man, you're saying?

OEDIPUS

> Don't let my words alarm you.

CHORUS

> No, no, no!

OEDIPUS
> Misery!

CHORUS
> No, no!

OEDIPUS
> What is to happen, daughter?

CHORUS
> °Go away. Leave my country!

OEDIPUS
> But what about your promise?
> Surely you ought to keep that?

CHORUS
> Fate inflicts no harm
> for committing wrong
> which repays the harm
> that began the wrong.   230
> So if new deceit
> challenges deceit,
> it repays with hurt,
> not with benefit.
> You! Get out of here!
> Get up from this seat,
> quick from off my ground;
> and don't make my land
> liable to face
> some yet greater price.

ANTIGONE
> °Strangers, men of respect,
> since you could not bear
> to be kindly towards
> my old father here—
> not now that you have heard
> rumour of his deeds,
> though not willingly done—   240
> listen to my words.
> Pity me, I beg you,
> in my misery,
> here appealing for my
> father in misery.

Eyes meet yours in appeal,
mine that are not blind;
I look into your eyes,
one of your own kind,
as though of your blood.
Give him your respect;
we rely upon you,
god-like, to protect.
Grant us this benefit,
feel for us, as I,
hoping against all hope,
plead for favour by
what you hold most dear: 250
by that thing I plead,
child, or wife that you love,
treasure, or a god.
Search, no matter how hard,
you will never see
someone dragged by a god
able to break free.

SCENE 2

CHORUS-LEADER
Know clearly, child of Oedipus, we do feel pity,
both for you and him for what's befallen you.
But still we fear the gods, and do not have the power
to speak beyond the things we have just said.

OEDIPUS
So what's the good of fame and glorious repute,
if it becomes dispersed in uselessness?
Why bother with the claim that Athens
is supremely god-fearing, and stands uniquely strong   260
to rescue and protect the persecuted stranger?°
How is this true in my own case,
when you've dislodged me from my rock-seat here,
and now are driving me away, in fear of my mere name?
It can't be for my person or my deeds,
since, rest assured, you'd find my acts lay more

in passive suffering than active doing,
were I to tell you of my mother and my father—
which is what frightens you, I have no doubt.
And yet how was I evil in my essence,   270
when what I did was to retaliate at being harmed,
in such a way that, even if I'd acted knowingly,
I still would not have qualified as bad?
Yet, as it was, I came to where I came to
knowing nothing, while I suffered at the hands
of those who knowingly attempted to kill me.
In view of this, I beg you, strangers, by the gods,
just as you made me stand and move, so keep me safe.
Don't grant the gods due honour,
and then treat them as benighted.°
You should believe that they examine both the pious
and the impious, and that a godless person   280
has never yet escaped scot-free.
Do not employ them just to darken Athens' blessed fame
by reinforcing impious acts.
No: as you first accepted me, a dedicated suppliant,
now rescue me, and keep me safe.
Don't simply look at my disfigured face,
and treat me with contempt.
I come to you, I tell you, as one sacred,
as a special benefactor to the people of this city here.
And when the man who wields authority shall come,
whoever is your leader, he shall hear   290
and gather everything. Till then, do not
at any cost disgrace yourselves.

CHORUS-LEADER
  There is, we see, a heavy obligation
  laid upon us to respect these sentiments
  of yours with awe, now you have put them
  in such weighty terms. So I am satisfied
  the ruler of this land should arbitrate.

OEDIPUS
  Where is he, then, this country's governor?

CHORUS-LEADER
  He lives in the ancestral capital. That warden
  who called us together here has gone to fetch him.

OEDIPUS

Do you suppose he'll show enough attentive care
towards the blind to come here for himself?   300

CHORUS-LEADER

I'm sure he will, once he has learned your name.

OEDIPUS

But who is there will take him word of that?

CHORUS-LEADER

It is some distance; but the busy talk
of travellers is liable to spread.
And when he hears, then rest assured, he'll come.
Your name, old man, is well known far and wide.
So even if he's resting at his ease, when he hears
it is you he'll come here quick enough.

OEDIPUS

Well, may his coming bring good fortune to his country
and to me—for good men can still benefit themselves.

SCENE 3

Antigone, who is looking off, interrupts.

ANTIGONE

O Zeus, what shall I say? What, father, can I think?   310

OEDIPUS

What is it, child Antigone?

ANTIGONE

I see a woman riding here towards us on an Etna pony,
with a wide Thessalian hat° to shade her face.
What can I say? Her?. . . Can it be?
Not her? Or has my mind run wild?
I say it is. . . it's not. . . I don't know what to say.
It surely must be her: she's throwing me bright looks
of greeting now she's getting close;   320
and this could only come from her, Ismene.

OEDIPUS

What's that, my child?

ANTIGONE
It is your daughter, my own sister, that I see.
And now she's close enough to recognize her voice.

Enter Ismene, with one attendant, from the 'foreign' direction.

ISMENE
My father and my sister,
sweetest pair of names for me to sound.
What pain and trouble I have had to track you down;
and now, afresh, to see you blinds my eyes with tears.

OEDIPUS
Can you be here, my child?

ISMENE
Oh father, what a dreadful sight.

OEDIPUS
You really have appeared, my child?

ISMENE
It's been no easy task for me

OEDIPUS
Reach out, my daughter.

Ismene embraces them both.

ISMENE
I hold the two of you together.

OEDIPUS
O children, kindred sisters.°   330

ISMENE
What a dismal way of life!

OEDIPUS
You mean for her and me?

ISMENE
My own has hardship too.

OEDIPUS
Why have you come, my child?

ISMENE
Because I was concerned for you.

OEDIPUS
You mean through missing me?

ISMENE

    Yes that, and so that I could bring you news myself
    (with the one person in the house that I could trust).

OEDIPUS

    And those young men, your brothers,
    where are they helping with this task?

ISMENE

    Well, where they are, they are.
    These times are dark for them.

OEDIPUS

    Those two behave in just the way they do in Egypt, °
    both in their inner and their outer lives.
    For in that land the males sit tight indoors
    and labour at the weaving, while their females   340
    venture out to win their daily bread.
    And so with you, my daughters:
    those who should have laboured at these tasks
    just lounge around at home like girls,
    while you take on the burdens
    of my wretched care instead of them.
    Antigone, since she first ceased to be a child,
    and reached her adult strength, has led
    a constant vagrant life with me, poor thing,
    and catered for an old man's daily needs.
    She's wandered through the wild terrain,
    deprived of food, barefoot,
    and often has put up with pelting rains and scorching sun,   350
    regarding homely comforts as a second best,
    provided that her father gets good care.
    And you, my other daughter, set out once before,
    without the Thebans knowing it, to tell your father
    all the oracles concerning this poor frame of mine;
    and you remained my trusty guard
    when I was being driven from the land.
    So now, Ismene, what's the news you bring?
    what task has taken you away from home?
    For I am sure you have not come with empty hands:
    might you be bringing me some cause for fear?   360

ISMENE

    I shall pass over all the troubles, father,

that I've met in searching to discover
where you have found lodging to survive.
I have no wish to suffer twice, repeating them in words.
But the disasters that right now surround
your two ill-fated sons:
it's those I've come to tell you of.
In former times it was agreed to leave the throne
for Creon,° and so clear the city of pollution,
considering the ancient blighting of the dynasty,
which kept its hold upon your ill-starred house.   370
But now an evil conflict has invaded them,
the wretched fools, deriving from some god,
and from their own distorted minds,°
and this has made them both grasp after total power.
The younger, later-born, has stripped
his elder brother, Polynices,° of the throne,
and forced him from his native land.
And he—or so the rumour spreads among us—
has gone off in exile to the plain of Argos,
where he has contracted a new marriage-bond,
and friends to battle at his side;
this will ensure, he claims, that either he will
occupy the land of Thebes with honour,   380
or else send it smoking to the sky.°
This is not merely piling up of words, dear father:
this is appalling action.
I cannot tell what is the way the gods
shall take some pity on your sufferings.

OEDIPUS

Why then, have you some cause to hope
the gods intend I shall one day be saved?

ISMENE

I have, according, father, to these present oracles.

OEDIPUS

What kind of oracles?
What has been prophesied, my child?

ISMENE

They say that one day you shall be sought out
by them, those people there in Thebes,
alive or dead, as key to their security.   390

OEDIPUS

   But who might gather benefit from such a one as me?

ISMENE

   It's said that power over them will rest with *you*.

OEDIPUS

   So when I cease to be, that's when I am the man!

ISMENE

   Yes, that's because the gods are now uplifting you,
   although they brought you down before.

OEDIPUS

   It's trifling to raise up an old man, who fell young.

ISMENE

   Yet still this is the reason Creon will be coming—
   not far in the future, very soon.

OEDIPUS

   But what to do? Explain to me, my daughter.

ISMENE

   So they can plant you near the Theban land,
   and have control of you,   400
   without your setting foot across the frontier.

OEDIPUS

   What benefit for them from my remaining
   kept outside their gates?

ISMENE

   Your tomb: if it's unfavourable, then it will do them harm.

OEDIPUS

   One could tell that without a god's advice.

ISMENE

   That's why they want to settle you
   close to their land, and yet not where
   you shall have charge of your own power.

OEDIPUS

   But would they shade me under Theban soil?

ISMENE

   Your family blood-guilt would not permit that, father.

OEDIPUS

   In that case they shall never gain control of me.

ISMENE
That shall one day prove grievous for the Thebans.

OEDIPUS
What will conspire to bring about that day?   410

ISMENE
Your anger, when they take their stand beside your tomb.°

OEDIPUS
Who did you hear this from, the things you tell?

ISMENE
From those who had consulted at the Delphic shrine.

OEDIPUS
So did Apollo ratify these things concerning me?

ISMENE
That's what they told us on return to Thebes.

OEDIPUS
And did my sons get wind of this at all?

ISMENE
Yes, both of them, and they are well aware of it.

OEDIPUS
And even when they'd heard, the vermin valued
total power above the wish to have me back?

ISMENE
It gives me pain to bring this message,° yet I must.   420

OEDIPUS
Then may the gods not quench their fated clash,
and may the outcome of this coming fight,
where they are set to join in battle
spear to spear, depend on me.
For then the one who occupies the throne for now
would not stay there; nor would the one
who went away return back home again.
They are the sons, who, when their father,
I, was being scornfully ejected from our fatherland,
did nothing to protect or keep me there,
but stood and watched me driven into homelessness,   430
proclaimed in public as a fugitive.
You might suppose the city fairly granted me
my wishes at that time? No, not at all.

°Back on that day when my emotions seethed,
I fiercely longed to die by stoning,
yet nobody emerged to help me to that fervent wish.
But in the course of time, when all that anguish
had subsided, and I realized my passion
had been too drastic for the wrongs done in the past,
the city then was set upon expelling me by force.   440
And they, their father's sons, who had the power
to help their father, were not willing to do anything;
and for the lack of just a little word from them,
I've been condemned to lead a vagrant beggar's life.
And so it is from these unmarried girls,
so far as nature will allow them,
that I get my nourishment, and my protection
in the world, and family affection:
whilst those two boys have seized the sceptre and the throne,
and opted for unbridled power above their father's claims.
But they'll not win this person as their fellow-fighter,   450
no, nor ever harvest profit from this ruling over Thebes.
I am assured of this, now that I've heard the oracle she brings,
along with thinking through Apollo's prophesies
from long ago, which he has finally confirmed.
And so they're welcome to send Creon on my trail,
and any other who has power in their state,
because, if you are willing, strangers, to protect me,
with these solemn goddesses of your locality,
you will recruit a strong preserver for this city here,
and troubles for this country's enemies.°   460

CHORUS-LEADER
　　You do deserve our pity, Oedipus,
　　you and your daughters here. And since, by this account,
　　you pledge yourself to be a saviour for this land,
　　I wish to offer you instructions for your benefit.

OEDIPUS
　　Good friend, speak as my host, and I'll do all you say.

CHORUS-LEADER
　　You should perform a purifying ritual
　　for these goddesses you came to first,
　　whose ground you've trespassed on.

OEDIPUS
Instruct me, strangers: say what sort of rite.

CHORUS-LEADER
First draw libations from the ever-flowing spring,
touched only by pure hands.   470

OEDIPUS
And when I have this unpolluted draught?

CHORUS-LEADER
There are the mixing-bowls, an expert craftsmen's work:
drape these around the handles and the rim.

OEDIPUS
With olive boughs, or woven wool, or in what way?

CHORUS-LEADER
Using the new-shorn fleece of a ewe-lamb.

OEDIPUS
That's good. How should I then complete the ritual?

CHORUS-LEADER
Pour out libations, facing where the dawn first lights.

OEDIPUS
And do I pour them from these vessels that you speak of?

CHORUS-LEADER
Yes, with three tippings, and the last one every drop.

OEDIPUS
What should I fill that with? Instruct me.   480

CHORUS-LEADER
With water, honey too, but don't add wine.

OEDIPUS
And when the Earth, dark-shadowed, has accepted these?

CHORUS-LEADER
Lay down three-times-nine olive branches
with both hands, and make this prayer:

OEDIPUS
I wish to hear these words, for this is cardinal.

CHORUS-LEADER
'As we name them "Benign",° may they accept
this suppliant and keep him safe with hearts that are benign.'
Pronounce this prayer yourself, or one on your behalf,

but speak it quietly, don't declaim out loud.
Then leave and do not turn around.   490
Do this and I would stand firm by your side:
but, stranger, otherwise I would be full of fear for you.

OEDIPUS

My daughters, you have heard the things
these local people have explained?

ISMENE

We have. So tell us what we should do now.

OEDIPUS

I cannot go myself. I lack the strength to manage it,
and lack my sight, a double ill.
So one of you should go and do these things.
I'm confident one soul is adequate
to pay this debt for thousands,
so long as one approaches with good will.
So set about this quickly.   500
But do not leave me here alone;
my body does not have the strength
to move without a guiding hand.

ISMENE

Then I will go and carry out the ritual.
But first I need to know where I'm to find the place.

CHORUS-LEADER

It's on the further side of this grove here, young woman.
If you are in need of anything, there is a warden
lives right by, and he will give advice.

ISMENE

Then I'll be going. But, Antigone,
stay here and guard our father well.
Troubles undertaken for our parents
should not be seen as burdensome.

Exit Ismene in the 'foreign' direction.

°LYRIC DIALOGUE

CHORUS

    I know that it is hard
    to waken from their bed   510

evils of long ago.
And yet I long to know. . .

OEDIPUS

Waken? What. . . ?

CHORUS

That racking, helpless grief
which you were tangled with. . .

OEDIPUS

Be good hosts; don't expose
the pains I've had to face.

CHORUS

The stories spread about—
I long to hear them straight

OEDIPUS

A, a!

CHORUS

Indulge me, I implore. . .

OEDIPUS

No, no!

CHORUS

I gave what *you* begged for.   520

OEDIPUS

°Bad things I have endured,
excessively° endured;
and yet not one of those
was action that I chose.

CHORUS

Not chose? How?

OEDIPUS

I could not know the wife
the city gave brought grief.

CHORUS

Your mother, I have heard:
you lay in her cursed bed?

OEDIPUS

That's death for me to hear.
And, friends, these two girls are. . .

CHORUS

What? Say.

OEDIPUS

. . . doomed children, birth-pains from. . .

CHORUS

Oh Zeus!

OEDIPUS

. . . my mother, the same womb.

CHORUS

So for you they're daughters. . .

OEDIPUS

. . . and their father's sisters.

CHORUS

A, a!

OEDIPUS

Wrongs in thousands wheel.

CHORUS

You have suffered.

OEDIPUS

Wounds that never heal.

CHORUS

The acts you did!

OEDIPUS

I did not act.

CHORUS

How can that be?

OEDIPUS

°I received a gift
offered by the town,   540
rewarded by that gift
I wish I'd never won.

CHORUS

You went on to slaughter. . .

OEDIPUS

What trail are you after?

CHORUS

. . . your own father?

OEDIPUS
>Second wound on wound.

CHORUS
>You did it. . . .

OEDIPUS
>I did, and yet that deed. . .

CHORUS
>What can you plead?

OEDIPUS
>. . . was justified.

CHORUS
>How could that be?

OEDIPUS
>°He tried to murder me:
>I, in self-defence,
>pure before the law,
>moved in innocence.

SCENE 4

Enter Theseus from the side of the city.

CHORUS-LEADER
>Here comes our ruler, Theseus son of Aegeus,
>answering the message that you sent. 550

THESEUS
>I've often heard before today about the gory gouging
>of your eyes, and so could recognize you, son of Laius.
>And now I've made this journey here
>and look at you,° I am more certain,
>since your clothing and your ravaged face
>make it quite obvious to me just who you are.
>And out of pity for you, wretched Oedipus,
>I want to know what is the plea
>that you have come to put to Athens
>and to me, you and your poor companion.
>Enlighten me: for you would have to tell

a truly fearsome history for me to turn my back. 560
°I have in mind that I, like you, was brought up
as an alien, and that I had to struggle in a foreign land
with dangers threatening my life, as great as any man.
And so I never would recoil from rescuing
a foreign alien such as you are now,
because I know full well that I am human,
and I have no greater share
than you in what tomorrow brings.

OEDIPUS

You've shown such noble understanding, Theseus,
in few words, that I need not say much. 570
You have correctly stated who I am,
whose son, and where I'm from;
and so there's nothing left for me to say
except for what I want—and then that's all.

THESEUS

Then tell me what that is: I'm keen to know.

OEDIPUS

I've come to give my wretched self to you,
my body, nothing nice to look upon, and yet
it offers benefits far finer than external beauty.

THESUES

What is this benefit you claim to bring?

OEDIPUS

You shall learn that in time, but not just yet. 580

THESEUS

When is it, then, your offer shall be clearly shown?

OEDIPUS

When I have died and you have buried me.

THESEUS

What you are asking for concerns the final acts of life;
but you're forgetting all the things that intervene—
or do you hold them of no weight?

OEDIPUS

That's right, because they are all gathered at that point.

THESEUS

And yet this favour that you ask is light.

OEDIPUS
  Be careful though. This issue is not slight, no, not at all.

THESEUS
  Are you referring to your sons, or what?

OEDIPUS
  They will attempt to force me to go back.

THESEUS
  If you are ready, then it would be wrong   590
  for you to stay in exile.

OEDIPUS
  But when I wanted to stay there, they would not let me.

THESEUS
  Unwise! This anger's not appropriate
  for someone in misfortune.

OEDIPUS
  When you know all, then criticize—till then let be.

THESEUS
  Then tell me: I should not rebuke if I'm not well informed.

OEDIPUS
  I've suffered, Theseus, fearsome wrong on wrong.

THESEUS
  You mean the ancient troubles of your line?

OEDIPUS
  Not that: the whole of Greece can tell of those.

THESEUS
  This worse-than-human pestilence, what can it be?

OEDIPUS
  Well, this is how I stand: I was ejected
  from my land by my own progeny, and now   600
  I never can go back, because I am the parricide.

THESEUS
  How can they fetch you, then,
  when you are bound to live apart?

OEDIPUS
  The sacred oracle is making them do this.

THESEUS
  What frightening prospect does the oracle reveal?

OEDIPUS

That they are fated to be blasted in *this* land.

THESEUS

But how could my relationship with them get soured?

OEDIPUS

°My dearest son of Aegeus, gods alone are free
from aging and from death.
All other things are put in flux by all-controlling Time.
The vigour of the earth decays,   610
so does the body's strength;
trust wilts and dies, and distrust germinates.
The spirit that binds men as friends
does not remain the same for ever,
nor does that between one city and another.
For some men now, and some in later time,
delightful friendships turn to bitterness, and back again.
So even if for now the sunny days between
yourself and Thebes are shining fair,
innumerable time begets innumerable days and nights,
and as these pass they shall, though for some trivial cause,
shatter in pieces with the sword
these now harmonious bonds.   620
Then shall my hidden, sleeping corpse,
though cold, gulp down their warm life-blood,
if Zeus remains still Zeus,
and if his son Apollo still holds true.
But it's unpleasant voicing words that should not be unleashed,
so let me settle at my starting-point:
that you should simply keep good faith.
Then shall you never need to say
that, by receiving Oedipus in this locality,
you welcomed in a useless resident—
so long as I'm not cheated by the gods.

CHORUS

My lord, this man has all along made clear
he will fulfil such promises as these to help this land.   630

THESEUS

Then who would throw away
benevolence from such a man?

For one thing, there has always been alliance
forged between our houses;
and he has arrived, a suppliant of the gods,
with no small compensation for this land and me.
Out of respect for these concerns I shall not cast away
his favour, but shall settle him at home in this domain.
(*to the Chorus*) Now, if it is the stranger's wish to stay
in this place here, I shall entrust you
with protecting him; or he can come with me.
I leave it, Oedipus, to you, which course you choose;   640
I shall respect your preference either way.

OEDIPUS
O Zeus, may you reward men such as this.

THESEUS
What would you like? To travel with me to my house?

OEDIPUS
I would if that were proper; but this very place is where. . .

THESEUS
Where you will do what thing? For I shall not obstruct.

OEDIPUS
. . . where I shall overpower the ones who cast me out.

THESEUS
The gift you promise through your staying would be great.

OEDIPUS
It will be, if you really carry out the things you've said.

THESEUS
You may be sure for my part. I'll not let you down.

OEDIPUS
I shall not tie you with an oath, as though untrustworthy.   650

THESEUS
You would gain nothing further than my word.

OEDIPUS (*with fear*)
What will you *do*, then?

THESEUS
What is it that you fear especially?

OEDIPUS
　Some men will come. . .

THESEUS (*indicating the Chorus*)
　Well then, these men will see to them.

OEDIPUS
　Be careful. If you let me down. . .

THESEUS
　Don't lecture me on what to do.

OEDIPUS
　There is strong cause to dread. . .

THESEUS
　My heart does not know dread.

OEDIPUS
　You do not know what threats. . .

THESEUS
　What I do know is this: no man is going to drag you off
　from here by using force against my will.
　°[Angry threats have often poured out angry words;
　but when the thinking mind exerts control,
　the threats evaporate.]　　　　　　　　　　　　　660
　As for those men, they may have been emboldened
　to big talk about abducting you;
　but, take my word, they'll find that sea
　too wide to cross and hard to sail.
　So I would urge you to stay confident:
　even without my firm intent, you should be so,
　provided that Apollo has directed you.
　Yet still I'm sure that, in my absence, just my name
　will shelter you against maltreatment.

Exit Theseus with his attendants towards the city.

CHORAL SONG

CHORUS
　　　°This country, guest, is good for horses;
　　　you've arrived at its best place,
　　　the gleaming landscape of Colonus.　　　　　670

Here the nightingale's clear voice
is often heard beneath the bushes,
trilling in dark ivy shade
and foliage of the gods,° untrodden,
berried thick with fruit kept safe
from heat of sun and every tempest.
Here Dionysus moves and dances,
in step with the Nymphs his nurses.   680

Narcissus clusters bloom in beauty,
fed by dewdrops from the skies
perennially, the ancient garland
for the two great goddesses;°
and crocus radiates all golden.
Rivulets run day and night,
fed by Cephisus,° our river,
never failing, spreading out
perennially about the hillocks   690
of the tender-breasted earth,
nursing unpolluted growth.
The Muses favour this Colonus
with poetry and song and dances°—
and Aphrodite's golden harness.°

°There is a thing
I have never heard of sprouting in Asian land,
nor the mighty isle of Pelops;° not raised by hand,
self-perpetuating, feared by attackers' spear,°
flourishing with special strength in our country here: 700
groves of grey-green olive that help our children grow.
No one old or young can kill it, no one destroy,
as the eye of Zeus unsleeping keeps constant watch;
as does our grey-eyed Athena's protective touch.

And I can boast
yet another strength of Athens: Poseidon's hand
gave us strongest grounds for claiming to be the land   710
good for horses, good for ponies, good for seas.
It was you, Poseidon, founded this special praise,
when you first taught skill of riding here on these roads,
with the bridle that soothes horses. And the oar-blades,
fitting hands, goes leaping swiftly across the waves,
following the fifty Nereids° who skim with ease.

SCENE 5

Creon approaches with military henchmen from the 'abroad' direction.

ANTIGONE

Colonus, place so lavishly adorned with eulogies,   720
now is the time to show them true indeed.

OEDIPUS

My child, what is this new alarm?

ANTIGONE

I can see Creon nearing us, and with an escort too.

OEDIPUS

Old men, my friends, now is the chance for you
to make my rescue finally secure.

CHORUS-LEADER

Take heart, it shall be yours. I may be old myself,
but still our country keeps its vigour young.

CREON

Old gentlemen, you leading people of this place,
I can see clearly from your eyes
that you are feeling rising fear at my approach.   730
But do not be alarmed, and speak no adverse word;
I am not here with any thought of drastic deeds,
for I am old, and well aware this city
is as strong as anywhere in Greece.
But, aged though I am, it is my mission to persuade
this man to come with me to Thebes,
not on the prompting of one man,
but by authority of all the citizens.
It is through kinship° that it falls to me to feel,
of anyone in Thebes, most grief concerning him.
(turns to Oedipus.)
Come, Oedipus, unfortunate,
pay heed to me and come back home!   740
The entire Theban people calls for you, and rightly so,
and I especially—or I would be the lowest of the low—
I feel especial pain at your misfortunes,
seeing you the wretched foreigner,

forever wandering without the bare necessities of life,
with just one female helper to attend on you.
And her I never thought would fall
to such humiliating depths, poor girl,
reduced to looking after you, and living like a beggar—   750
at her age, with no experience of marriage,
at the mercy of whatever man might cross her path.
This is a pitiful reproach I've laid on you
and me and all our family, is it not?
It is impossible to hide what's in the open view;
so now, by our ancestral gods, please, Oedipus,
give in to my persuasion and conceal the shame
by coming to the home and city of your ancestors.
Address this country here most gratefully, as it deserves:
but even more your native land.
[has more right for your respect, your nursery long ago.]°   760

OEDIPUS

You would try anything, and weave
a crafty artifice from any rightful argument.
Why are you trying once again to trap me,
and in ways I'd find most painful, once entrapped?
Back then when I was fevered with my private grief,
and would have gladly been cast out from Thebes,
you were not willing to bestow the favour I desired.
But once my passion was all spent,
and I was pleased to pass my days at home,
then you expelled me, threw me out. And all this talk   770
of kinship wasn't so important to you then!
And now once more, when you can see this city
and its people have accepted me with kindness,
now you try to drag me off,
and wrap harsh things in soothing words.
°(What is this great delight you have in pressing
friendship upon those who do not want it?
It is as though a person gave you nothing and no help
when you were begging for them, but once you'd had
your fill of what you craved, he gave it then,
just when the favour was no longer favourable.
Would this not be an empty pleasure that you got?   780
Well, that's the kind of thing you're offering me,

all fine in word, but foul in deed.)
And I'll explain to these men here,
so as to show you up as foul.
You've come to fetch me: not to take me home,
but so that you can settle me outside the yard,
and free your city of the danger from this land.
You won't get that, but shall get this:
my curse° shall dwell for ever in your country.
And this is how much soil my two sons shall inherit:
land enough to die in and no more.° 790
Well, am I better briefed than you concerning Thebes?
I am, because the sources that I hear are better:
Apollo and his father Zeus, no less!
You've come here with your artificial talk—
and you have done a lot of talking—
yet you'll gain from that more trouble than security.
I know I never can persuade you, though,
so go, and leave us to live here,
since we should not live badly, even in our present state,
as long as we're contented.

CREON

In this debate do you believe that I sustain more damage 800
from your attitude, or that you do more to yourself?

OEDIPUS

I'll be best pleased if you are no more able
to persuade these people here than you can me.

CREON

Poor man, shall you appear no wiser with the years,
but stay afflicted with a blight in your old age?

OEDIPUS

You are a formidable orator, but there is no just man I know
can speak with skill on every cause.

CREON

To speak at length is not the same as speaking to the point.

OEDIPUS

You're telling me your words are few and to the point?

CREON

Not so to someone with a mind that's on your petty scale. 810

OEDIPUS

Now go away—I speak for all these men as well—
and do not keep patrolling me,
here where I have to live.

CREON

I call these men, not you, to witness
how you've answered me, your kin.
But if I once can get a grip on you. . .

OEDIPUS

But who could capture me by force despite my allies here?

CREON (*with menace*)

You'll still have cause, apart from that, to wince with pain.

OEDIPUS

What action gives you grounds to threaten in that tone?

CREON

I have just caught and bundled off
one of your pair of daughters.
And right now I'll take the other.

OEDIPUS

No, no!

CREON

You'll soon have yet more reason to cry 'no'!   820

OEDIPUS

You've got my daughter?

CREON

And in a minute I'll have this one too.

OEDIPUS (*to Chorus*)

My friends, what are you going to do?
Don't fail me: drive the godless creature from this land!

CHORUS-LEADER

Leave, stranger. Quick, get out of here.
What you are doing now is wrong,
and so is what you've done before.

CREON (*to his henchmen*)

It's time for you to take this girl away—
by force, if she does not agree to go.

ANTIGONE
  Oh help! Where can I run?
  What gods will help me? Or what people?

CHORUS
  What do you think you're doing, stranger?

CREON
  I'll lay no finger on this man—only on what is mine.°   830

ANTIGONE
  Lords of this land!

CHORUS
  You're doing wrong here, stranger. . .

CREON
  No. Right!

CHORUS
  In what way right?

CREON
  Because I'm taking what belongs to me.

Creon's men grab Antigone and prepare to drag her off.

°LYRIC DIALOGUE SEQUENCE

OEDIPUS
      Help, Athens, I call on you.

CHORUS
      Don't do this. Let go of her.
      You'll soon test this out by force.

CREON
      Keep off me!

CHORUS
      No. Not while you set this course.

CREON
      My city will go to war
      if you do me any hurt.

OEDIPUS
      There, did I not tell you so?

CHORUS
      Let go of the girl—and fast!

CREON
> Don't order where you've no power.

CHORUS
> I tell you, let go of her.   840

CREON
> I tell you, be off, away!

CHORUS
> Here, help us! Come to our side;
> you men of Colonus, help!
> Now Athens, our city, ours,
> is being vandalized
> by force. Help us! here!

ANTIGONE
> I'm being hauled away. Friends, help me, friends!

OEDIPUS
> Where are you, child?

ANTIGONE
> I'm being forced to go.

OEDIPUS
> Reach out your hands to me.

ANTIGONE
> I can't, I'm held by force

CREON
> Get her away from here.

Creon's men take Antigone off.

OEDIPUS
> Ah ah, what misery!

CREON
> So, you'll no longer have this pair of crutches°
> to support you on your way.
> But, since you are so keen to be victorious   850
> over your country and your kin—
> at their command I do this, though myself a lord—
> enjoy your victory.
> In time, I'm sure, you'll come to realize your acts
> have done yourself no good, not now, nor in the past,
> whenever, in defiance of your friends, you give in

to your temper: it's that has always damaged you.

Creon begins to go, but the Chorus obstruct him.

CHORUS-LEADER
    Stop, stranger, stay right where you are.

CREON
    Let go of me, I tell you.

CHORUS-LEADER
    I shall not, not as long as you detain these girls.

CREON
    Then soon you shall repay my city at an even higher price;
    for it's not only them I'll drag away.

CHORUS-LEADER
    What are you threatening?

CREON (*moving towards Oedipus*)
    I'm going to seize and take this man.   860

CHORUS-LEADER
    That is a dreadful claim!

CREON
    And it's as good as done—
    unless the ruler of this land is going to try to stop me!°

OEDIPUS
    You have no shame in your big talk:
    you wouldn't really lay your hands on me.

CREON
    Stay quiet, I tell you!

OEDIPUS
    I shall not. Let these goddesses no longer
    keep unspoken this my curse on you, you filth,
    you who have violently plucked out my eyes again,
    just as I lost my eyes before.
    That's why I call on the all-seeing sun
    to grant to you and all your race
    an old age like my own.   870

CREON
    You witness this, you men of this locality?

OEDIPUS

They see both me and you, and understand
that, while I've suffered from your acts,
I still defend myself with words.

CREON

No longer can I hold my anger back.
I'm going to take him off by force,
no matter if I am alone and slowed by age.

Creon goes to Oedipus and grabs hold of him; the Chorus move to block him.

OEDIPUS

Oh, horror!

CHORUS

You've come with such arrogance,
if, stranger, you think you can
go on and see this through.

CREON

I think so.

CHORUS

Then this wouldn't be a city.

CREON

With justice, the little one
can conquer the greater power.   880

OEDIPUS

You hear that, the things he says?

CHORUS

<But Zeus knows>° he'll not succeed.

CREON

Zeus might know, but you do not.

CHORUS

This insolence without shame!

CREON

It's insolence you must bear.

CHORUS

You people, all come and help!
You lords of this land, come too!

Come quickly, we need you now!
These men here are trying to
make their escape.

SCENE 6

Enter Theseus with attendants from the 'city' side.

THESEUS

Whatever is this call for help? What's happening?
I was just sacrificing at the altar of the sea-god,
guardian of Colonus here. What fear
has made you interrupt like this? Explain it all to me:
why have I had to hurry here too quick for comfort?   890

OEDIPUS

Good friend, I recognize your voice.
I have been grossly treated by this person here.

THESEUS

What's this? Who has maltreated you?

OEDIPUS

It's Creon here, the man you see.
He has abducted my loyal pair of daughters.

THESEUS

What's this you say?

OEDIPUS

You've heard it all, my plight.

THESEUS

One of my men, run urgently towards the altar here;
make everyone who's there go from the sacrifice,
and hurry off on foot or galloping by horse   900
to where the two highroads to Thebes converge.°
That will ensure the girls do not get taken past that place,
which would make me ridiculous before this stranger,
humiliated by brute force,
Go as I say immediately.

An attendant departs.

As for this man, if I had shown the anger he deserves,

I'd not have left him physically unscathed:
but as it is, he shall be regulated
by the self-same rules as he has introduced himself.
(*to Creon*) This means you'll never leave this land
until you have returned those girls,
and set them here before my eyes.   910
You have behaved unworthily of me,
and of your birth, and of your country.
You travelled to a place that cultivates the ways
of justice, and which settles everything
in keeping with the law; and there you have discarded
all that land's authority by mounting this intrusion,
so as to take whatever you might want,
and make expropriations using force.
You must have thought my city
was devoid of men, or else enslaved,
and must have rated me at next to nothing.
°And yet it is not Thebans has trained you in bad ways:
the thebans don't encourage men to be corrupt,   920
and they would not approve if they found out
how you are looting what belongs to me—
and to the gods, by dragging off their helpless suppliants.
I never would intrude into your land,
however just the cause,
without permission from whoever was your lord,°
and I would never grab and snatch,
because I am aware of how a stranger should
behave towards the local citizens.
But you are a disgrace to your own well-deserving city;
and advancing years are making you   930
both senile and devoid of common sense.
So as I said, and now repeat: have those two girls
returned back here at once,
unless you want to be detained
as an unwilling immigrant in this land here.
I mean all this; I'm not just saying it.

CHORUS-LEADER
Look where you've got to, stranger.
You may seem honest from your ancestry,
but you've been shown as rotten in your deeds.

CREON

I do not, Theseus, claim this city is devoid of men,
nor have I set about this act unthinkingly,   940
as you suppose. But I assumed that no one here
would be so far devoted to my own blood-relatives
as to take care of them against my will.
And I was sure that no one would embrace a man
polluted by the murder of his father,
one with children who have been exposed
as products of an impious marriage-bed.
I knew the Areopagus° within this land to be responsible:
it would not suffer vagrants such as these
to settle in this city here.
It was secure in this belief that I reclaimed this quarry.   950
And, what's more, I never would have done this thing,
if he had not been raining acrid curses down on me and mine.
I thought it only proper to retaliate for this ordeal.
[For anger has no ageing, only death;
the dead alone are left untouched by pain.]°
At present you can do whatever you desire,
however just my claim, because my isolation
makes me weak. Yet I, though old, will do my utmost
to retaliate against these deeds of yours.

OEDIPUS

You have no sense of decency!   960
Which old man do you think you are humiliating,
me, or you yourself?
You spout out talk of murders,
incest-unions, and catastrophes,
yet I've not willed these impositions for myself:
it was the gods who wanted this to be,
perhaps arising from some ancient wrath against my line.
Because, for me in my own right, you'd not be able
to discover any wrong that's damnable,
which would explain why I did wrong
against myself and my own family.
Now tell me: if an oracle arrived and told my father
that he would be killed by his own child,   970
how could you fairly reckon me to blame for that,
when I had not yet been begotten by a father,

nor been sown within a mother, but was still unborn?
And if, once brought into this world, poor wretch,
as happened, I then came to blows with my own father
and so killed him, yet was unaware of what I did,
and who I did it to, how could you reasonably condemn
this act, when it was done in ignorance?
As for my mother, you should be ashamed
to make me speak about my union with her—
she was your sister after all.
But now I shall tell all, keep nothing back,   980
since you have gone this far with your obscenities.
She gave me birth, yes, to my sorrow gave me birth;
but she did not know me, nor I know her,
when she who gave me birth then, horribly,
got children by my seed.
But I am sure of this: that you are knowingly
abusing me and her; while I unknowingly
was joined with her, and now unwillingly speak out.
In any case, I'll never be convicted
as a bad man in this marriage,
nor the killing of my father,
the act you're always citing bitterly against me.   990
So answer me one question: if someone came along
right now and tried to kill you, you the righteous one,
would you investigate and check if the assassin
was your father, or would you retaliate immediately?
I have no doubt that you, as you love life,
would strike back at the guilty man,
not cast around to check legality.
Well, I walked into troubles of that kind, led by the gods.
So even if my father's spirit were to come to life,
I don't believe that he would speak against my case.
But you, who have no sense of what is just,   1000
and think it fine to say just anything—
what may be spoken and what ought to stay unsaid—
you dare accuse me in this style in front of these men here.
And you are pleased to flatter Theseus' name,
and Athens, and how well she is administered.
Yet in this lavish praise, you are forgetting this:
if any land knows how to pay the gods due honour,
this is the one that's best at that.

Yet it's from here you're stealing me,
the suppliant of the god, and have attempted
to lay hands on me, and have abducted my two girls.
It is because of these things that I now   1010
make imprecation to these goddesses,
and charge them with my prayers to come and help,
and fight for me. So may you learn
what sort of men this city keeps as guardians.

CHORUS-LEADER

My lord, the stranger's virtuous.
Although the story of his life has been so terrible,
he still deserves our help.

THESEUS

Enough of words. While the abductors
hasten on their way, we passively stay here.

CREON

Then what are you commanding me to do? I'm weak.

THESEUS

You must direct the way, and I'll accompany you.
Then, if you are detaining the two girls in this vicinity,   1020
you can reveal them to me for yourself.
But if their captors are now on the run,
then that's no trouble either: there are others
who can hurry after them and make damn sure
they never thank the gods for helping them
to get home from this land.
Come on then, on our way!
The catcher's caught, and fate has trapped the hunter, you,
since gains obtained by unjust tricks can never be retained.
°You won't have anybody else to help in this.
For I know well you never would have set about   1030
so bold an outrage without men and arms:
there must be someone you are banking on
in undertaking this. I must take care of that,
and so make sure this city does not prove inferior
to a single man. You understand?
Or are these things I've said to you
no more significant than when
you first set out upon this plot?

CREON

As long as you are here by me I'll treat your words
as unimpeachable. But once I am back home,
I too shall know what we have got to do.

THESEUS

Threats, threats! Now march!
You, Oedipus, stay calmly here, sure in this trust:
as long as I'm not killed before, I never shall give up   1040
until I have restored your daughters to your care.

OEDIPUS

God bless you, Theseus, for your noble stand,
and for your just concern on my behalf.

Exit Theseus and attendants, with Creon, in the 'foreign' direction.

°CHORAL SONG

CHORUS

°I wish I were where
the enemy force
must turn round and face
the bronze battle-cry,
near the Pythian place,
or shores where the lights
illumine the rites
that the Goddesses nurse: 1050
Eleusis shrine where
initiates act
the Mysteries kept
in silence secure.
And Theseus shall save
the unravished pair,
with battle-cry there
triumphant and brave.

Or they may have reached
the pasture beyond
the snowy high-ground°   1060
with horses full stretch.
For sure he'll be caught.
Our locals are fierce,
and Theseus' own force,

their harness all bright,
will spur every horse,
°all those who revere
Poseidon's great power,
and Athena's resource.

Are they fighting, or about to clash?
Intuition has me prophesy
that the girls, who've suffered terribly,
will be rescued. Zeus brings this to pass.
I'm a prophet of our victory.
If I could only as a rock-dove fly,
riding storm-clouds, strong and wild,
I'd peer downward from the airy cloud
to watch the struggle on the battlefield.°

Zeus, supreme of the divinities,
Zeus, all-seeing, let the champions
of our country end victorious,
catch the quarry in their ambushes;
and your daughter Athena Pallas.
And I call on you, Apollo, please,
hunter, and your sister Artemis,
who tracks dappled deer, two saviours:
come and help our land and citizens.

1070

1080

1090

SCENE 7

CHORUS-LEADER
My wanderer friend, you'll have no cause
to call your watchers faulty prophets.°
I can see your daughters
and their escort here approaching us.

OEDIPUS
Where, where? What are you telling me?

Enter Theseus with Antigone and Ismene from the 'abroad' direction.

ANTIGONE
O father, father, how I wish some god
would let you look upon this best of men:
he is the one who has conveyed us safely here to you.

1100

OEDIPUS
　My child, you're really there?

ANTIGONE
　We are, thanks to the strength
　of Theseus and his trusty guard.

OEDIPUS
　Come to your father, child.
　Let me embrace you,
　whom I never dared to hope I'd hold again.

ANTIGONE
　Your wish is granted; this is the gift that we desire as well.

OEDIPUS
　Where are you, where?

ANTIGONE
　Here we approach you, both of us.

All three embrace.

OEDIPUS
　My dearest flowers!

ANTIGONE
　How a father finds all dear!

OEDIPUS
　You are this old man's crutches. . .

ANTIGONE
　. . . poor crutches for a poor old man.

OEDIPUS
　I hold what's dearest to me;   1110
　and I would not call myself unfortunate
　were I to die right now, with you beside me.
　Embrace me close on either side; cling to your father
　and so give some peace and respite to this man,
　left desolate by wretched wandering.
　Now tell me all that happened, briefly,
　because brevity is right for those your age.

ANTIGONE
　This is the man who rescued us.
　It's right for you to hear the story from the one
　who put it into action. There, that's brevity from me.

OEDIPUS (*to Theseus*)

   My friend, don't be surprised
   I've eagerly devoted time to welcoming my children,
   whom I had not thought to see again.   1120
   I'm well aware that all my joy in them
   has reached me, thanks to no one else but you,
   for it was you recovered them and you alone.
   So may the gods reward you as I wish,
   both you and this your country,
   since alone of all mankind
   among your people I've discovered piety,
   a sense of fairness, and refusal to speak false.
   I know full well what I'm saluting with these words,
   because I have the things I have
   through you and no one else.
   Then reach your hand to me, so I may grasp it,   1130
   and, if permissible, may kiss your cheek.

Oedipus moves towards Theseus, then halts.

   But stop!° What am I saying?
   How could I want you to touch a man
   who's host to every noxious stain!
   I cannot, nor would I permit you.
   For only those who have lived through these things
   can share the dreadful burden.
   And so I greet you, where you're standing,
   and I ask you to continue treating me
   with justice, as you have up to this time.

THESEUS

   That you have talked at length, delighting in your girls,   1140
   does not affront me, nor the way you spoke
   with them before you turned to me.
   I do not take offence at things like this,
   because I've always tried
   to make my life shine brightly
   not through words so much as deeds.
   And here's a proof of this: I have not failed
   in anything I promised you.
   I've brought them here to you alive and well,
   unscathed by all those threats.
   And as to how the fight was won, why should I idly boast

when you will hear it for yourself from them?
But please advise me on a new concern   1150
which has been raised with me as I was on my way back here.
It's nothing much to speak of, yet it is surprising;
and there's nothing that a human
should dismiss as worthy of no notice.

OEDIPUS

What is it, Theseus? Please explain,
as I know nothing about what you're asking me.

THESEUS

They tell me that a man, not from your city, yet a relative,
has somehow claimed a suppliant place
upon the altar of Poseidon,° the one where I
was holding sacrifice before I came back here.

OEDIPUS

Where is he from? What is he seeking from this gesture?   1160

THESEUS

All that I know is this: they say he's asking
for a little word with you, but nothing burdensome.

OEDIPUS

What sort of word? A suppliant's position is not trivial.

THESEUS

They say he simply wants to come and speak with you,
and then return back safely from his mission here.

OEDIPUS

This man who's seated as a suppliant: who can he be?

THESEUS

Think whether you have any relative at Argos,°
one who might request this thing of you.

OEDIPUS

Good friend, stop there!

THESEUS

Why, what's the matter?

OEDIPUS

Do not request this thing of me. . .   1170

THESEUS

What thing is that? Explain.

OEDIPUS

From what I've heard from them, I realize who he is.

THESEUS

And who is this, that I should disapprove of him?

OEDIPUS

My son, my hateful son:
and I would find his words more torture-pain
to hear than those of any other man alive.

THESEUS

What? Why not hear him?
You still don't have to do a thing that you don't want.
Why should it be so painful just to listen to this man?

OEDIPUS

That voice, my lord, has come to sound
most loathsome in his father's ears.
Do not insist and force me to give way in this.

THESEUS

But think hard if his suppliant state requires you to;
think if your duty to the god should be maintained.   1180

ANTIGONE

Father, I may be young to give advice, yet listen.
Allow this gentleman to satisfy his own best judgement;
and to grant the god the favour that he wishes.
And give in to us by letting our own brother visit here;
since you may rest assured that nothing
he may say that is against your interests
can wrench you from your own resolve.
What harm can come from simply hearing him?
Those actions that are ill-conceived
are tested out by being put in words.
You are his father, which means that no matter
how appallingly he has behaved to you,   1190
it still would not be true and right
for you to wrong him in return;
and so allow him here.
Others have wicked children, and a pointed temper too,
yet they accept advice, and are alleviated
by the charms and coaxing of their friends.
Think back to your past sufferings,

deriving from your father and your mother,
not the present ones. If you consider those,
I'm sure you'll recognize how bad the end can be
that follows from a violent temper.
You have strong reason to be well aware of this,
reminded by your blinded, sightless eyes.   1200
Give in to me. It cannot be correct
if those who ask for justice
need to be reduced to pleading;
nor that someone who's been treated well,
should still not know the way
to pay the kindness back

OEDIPUS
My child, this pleasure that you win from me
is hard to bear. And yet so be it as you wish.
But, Theseus, if that person comes,
do not let anyone acquire the power to control my life.

THESEUS
I do not need to hear such words a second time,
old man. I have no wish to boast,
but rest assured that you are safe,
so long as there's a god preserving me.   1210

Theseus goes off in the 'city' direction.

CHORAL SONG

CHORUS
Whoever longs for life
beyond the measured lot
is clearly in my eyes
an idiot.
The stacks of days pile up
so much encroaching toil,
while where your pleasures lie
is hard to tell.
The helper° levels all   1220
when Hades' endgame shows:
no tune, no dance, no wedding march:°
death at the close.

Not to be born is best
by far: the next-best course,
once born, is double-quick
return to source.
Once days of youth have spent
their thoughts as light as air,   1230
no blow is kept at bay,
grief's everywhere.
Resentment, killings, strife,°
then, waiting at the end,
old-age, no strength, no warmth,
no friend retained.°

In this I'm not alone:
this man is also stricken,
like some north-facing cape   1240
with waves from all directions
lashed by winter gusts.
Like that, unceasing breakers,
ranks of crisis crest
upon his grizzled foreland,
some from sunset west,
some from the sunrise dawning,
some from noonday light,
some from howling arctic night.°

SCENE 8

°*Polynices approaches from the 'city' direction.*

ANTIGONE
Here is that stranger, so it seems;
without attendants, father, but with eyes   1250
all brimming full of tears as he approaches.

OEDIPUS
Who do you mean?

ANTIGONE
The man we have been all concerned about—
yes, Polynices has arrived.

POLYNICES

>What should I do?
>Weep first for my own sufferings, sisters?
>or for those of my old father, now I see them?
>I find him here with you, an outcast in an alien land,
>and in this shabby kind of clothing.
>Ancient filth is clinging to his ancient body,   1260
>fouling his whole frame;
>and on his head, above his empty eyes,
>his hair uncombed is ruffled in the wind;
>the bag of food he carries is in keeping too,
>with scraps to feed his hungry stomach.
>(*to Oedipus*) Too late I've come to realize this:
>I can bear witness that I've proved
>disgracefully neglectful in my care of you.
>I myself admit my faults: no need to hear from others.
>Yet Zeus has Mercy throned by him° in all affairs;
>so, father, let her take her place beside you too.
>There may be healing of past wrongs,
>though no undoing them.°   1270

Oedipus does not respond.

>Say something, father; do not turn your back on me.
>Will you give no response, and pack me off
>humiliated? Not a word?
>Not even telling me your grounds for wrath?
>(*to his sisters*) You, then, his children, sisters,
>please will you attempt to break our father's silence,
>so unapproachable, implacable.
>Don't let him cast me off, a suppliant of the god,
>disdained like this, without a single syllable.

ANTIGONE

>Speak, my poor brother, tell him for yourself   1280
>what you have come for. Full explanations,
>by inspiring pleasure, or hard feelings, or compassion,
>can unlock the voice of someone shut in muteness.

POLYNICES

>Well then, I'll speak: yes, your advice is good.
>And first I claim the god himself as helper:
>it was from his altar that the ruler of this land

encouraged me to rise and come like this,
and gave me confidence to speak, to hear,
and to depart unscathed. And I trust, strangers,
I shall be received that way by you,
and by my sisters here, and by my father too.　　　　　　1290
So, father, now I want to tell you why I'm here.
I have been driven from my fatherland an exile,
because I thought it only right that, as the elder son,
I should be seated on your throne in sovereign power.
But in response Eteocles, the younger born, ejected me;
not triumphing in argument, or putting things to any test
of hand or strength, but winning round the populace.
I reckon that the cause of this must be your curse°—
I've also gathered this from certain prophets.　　　　　　1300
For when I got to Argos, I became the son-in-law
to King Adrastos; and I forged a sworn alliance
with those men who are regarded
as the leading warriors of the Peloponnese.°
And with their help I've mobilized
a sevenfold command° to march on Thebes,
so that I either perish in a cause that's wholly just,
or banish from the land of Thebes
the perpetrators of these wrongs.
Well, what's my reason for arriving here and now?
The answer is to beg you as your suppliant,
both for myself, and for my allies,　　　　　　1310
who are now encamped all round the plain of Thebes
in seven companies with seven spears in front of them.
°[They comprise: first, valiant Amphiaraus,
best at fighting and at augury from birds;
then number two is Tydeus, the Aetolian son of Oeneus;
three, Eteoclus the Argive; fourth Hippomedon,
who has been sent off by his father Talaus;
the fifth is Capaneus, who claims he'll make
the town of Thebes come crashing down in flames;
sixth comes Parthenopaeus, named after Atalanta,　　　　　　1320
virgin, who at last begot and gave him birth.
And then there's me, your son—
or if not yours, the son of vicious fortune,
yet called yours in name at least—the leader
of this fearless Argive expedition versus Thebes.]

We all beseech you, father, by your daughters here,
by your own life, that you relent from your grim wrath
against me, as I march to take revenge upon
the brother who has thrust me out
and stripped me of my homeland.   1330
For if there's any credibility in oracles,
they say that power will tip
towards whichever side you join.
So by the springs and godheads of our race,
I beg you to agree and to give way.
Look, I'm a beggar and a foreigner, the same as you;
we live by asking charity from others, you and I,
both of us allocated matching fates.
Meanwhile that despot back at home
luxuriates in scoffing at the pair of us.
If you will join me in my cause, I'm sure   1340
to shatter him with ease, and quickly too.
Then I shall take you and establish you in your own house°—
myself as well, once I have forced him out.
If you will join me in these purposes,
then I'll make good these claims:
without you, though, I've not the strength to save my life.

CHORUS-LEADER
    For Theseus' sake, who authorized the man's approach,
    reply whatever seems appropriate and send him back.

OEDIPUS
    (*to Chorus*) You elders of this land, if Theseus
    had not brought him here, believing it was justified
    that I should listen to his speech,   1350
    he never would have heard my voice direct.
    But now he has this privilege, he'll make his journey
    after he has heard me utter things
    that shall by no means make his life the happier.
    (*to Polynices*) You lowest dregs, when you possessed the throne
    and sceptre that your brother now controls in Thebes,
    you drove me out, yes, your own father;
    and you made me stateless, made me wear these tatters,
    which you weep at now that you have fallen
    into troubles comparable to mine.
    These things are not for weeping: 1360

but for me, I have to bear the memory,
so long as I shall live, of you as murderer.
Yes, it was you who made me live a life of misery like this;
you pushed me out, you made me vagrant
and reduced to begging others for my daily bread.
Had I not borne these daughters, who have cared for me,
I'd be long dead, so far as you're concerned.
These girls have rescued me, and they take care of me;
they are the men who share the painful work: while you,
you are the sons of someone else, not mine.
And so the god° has got his eye firm fixed on you,   1370
although not yet the way that it shall be, the day
these troops of yours move into their assault on Thebes.
Because you never shall destroy that place:
before that you will fall, defiled in blood-pollution,
and your brother just the same.
I've uttered curses such as these against you in the past:
and now I summon them to come and battle on my side.
And that will teach you to respect
and not disdain your parents;
even though the man who got such sons is blind,
these girls have not behaved like that.
And so these curses overbid this suppliancy of yours   1380
and all your thrones of power,
if venerable Justice takes her seat°
alongside Zeus according to the ways of old.
And so to hell with you, spat out by me,
defathered, lowest of the low.
And take with you these curses that I now call down:
I pray you never overcome your native land by force,
nor ever go back homeward to the plain of Argos:
but I pray you perish at your brother's hands,
and also slaughter him, the one who drove you out.
Such are my curses. And I call upon
the loathsome gloom of Tartarus° to house you now;   1390
I also call upon these Goddesses, and call on Ares
who implanted this harsh hatred in the two of you.
Now that you've heard this message, go,
relay it to the Thebans all, and to your trusty allies.
Tell them all about the privileges Oedipus
has portioned out between his sons.

CHORUS-LEADER

    I take no pleasure, Polynices, in the paths
    that you have taken in the past.
    And now go back with all the haste you can.

POLYNICES

    Disaster for my mission, and my futile efforts,
    and my friends in arms. What a conclusion   1400
    for the expedition we have launched from Argos,
    an outcome such that I can't even speak of it
    to my companions, nor turn them around.
    No, I must go and meet this fate without a word.
    But, sisters, you his daughters,
    now you hear these fatal curses from our father,
    for gods' sake don't, if these damnations are fulfilled,
    and if you find your way back home,
    don't let me lie dishonoured,
    but ensure me burial with proper funeral rites.°   1410
    Then, to the praise that you are winning now
    from caring for this man, you'll add yet more,
    and just as great, in recognition
    of your services on my behalf.

ANTIGONE

    °I beg you, Polynices, follow my advice in this.

POLYNICES

    What do you mean, my dear Antigone?

ANTIGONE

    Turn back your troops to Argos, and at once;
    do not go on to crush yourself and Thebes as well.

POLYNICES

    Impossible. How could I ever lead these men again,
    if I'd once given up in fright?°

ANTIGONE

    But why should you become provoked again?   1420
    What gain is there for you in wrecking your own fatherland?

POLYNICES

    It is disgrace to run away;
    and for the elder brother to be mocked like this.

ANTIGONE

    But can't you see how you're precisely

bringing to fulfilment his predictions,
since he's declared you each shall kill the other?

POLYNICES
Yes. That is what he wills. Must we not go along with it?

ANTIGONE
But who will dare to follow you, once they have heard
the things this man has prophesied?

POLYNICES
I'll not pass on bad news. A good commander
should convey the better things, and not the weaknesses.   1430

ANTIGONE
So you're determined on this course?

POLYNICES
I am, so do not hinder me.
This expedition shall be my concern,
although it's driven to misfortune
by my father here and his avenging demons.°
But for you two, I pray that Zeus will make
your journeys prosper, provided that you carry out
those things for me when I am dead,
since you can do no more for me in life.
So now let go of me, and let us say farewell,
because you'll never more set eyes on me alive.

ANTIGONE
What misery!

POLYNICES
Do not cry out for me.

ANTIGONE
But who could help lamenting for you, brother,
when you're setting off for certain death?   1440

POLYNICES
If needs be, I shall die.

ANTIGONE
But don't. Take my advice.

POLYNICES
Don't plead for what you should not.

ANTIGONE
Then I am truly wretched, if I am to be bereft of you.

POLYNICES

  Well, that rests with the god, to turn out one way or the other.
  But I still pray that you two never meet with harm,
  because you least of all deserve unhappy lives.

Exit Polynices in the 'abroad' direction towards Thebes.

°CHORAL SONG

CHORUS

          Grave new troubles from the sightless
          stranger come accumulated,
          unless this is somehow fated: 1450
          never call the gods' will pointless.
          Time sees everything, and fully;
          Time sees all, some things depressing,
          other things in turn increasing
          up again, continually.
          °(*thunder*)
                  Thunder from the sky!
                  Help us, Zeus on high!

OEDIPUS

  My daughters, daughters, if there's anyone about,
  please have them fetch here Theseus, best of men.

ANTIGONE

  What is the reason, father? Why call out for him?

OEDIPUS

  This winging thunderbolt of Zeus will lead me very soon   1460
  to Hades. Therefore send, and quick.

CHORUS

  (*thunder*)
          Look, look! How the mighty thunder
          crashes, Zeus-sent, beyond speaking,
          standing hair on end; I'm quaking
          as my spirit cowers in wonder.
          (*thunder*)
          Once again the lightning flashes:
          what conclusion does it portend?
          I am fearful: for this portent
          must mean something, bode some crisis.   1470

(*thunder*)
>   O you mighty sky!
>   Help us, Zeus on high!

OEDIPUS

My children, now the ending of my life, as prophesied,
approaches. There is no postponing any more.

ANTIGONE

How can you know? What token do you have for this?

OEDIPUS

I know it well enough. Now someone go at once
to fetch me here the ruler of this land.

CHORUS

(*thunder*)
>   There, there, oh see! Once again
>   piercing crashes crack all round.
>   Kindly, kindly, O you gods,   1480
>   if you bring our motherland
>   some sort of impending dark.
>   May I find you well disposed;
>   don't turn that favour into cost
>   with no gain, because we've looked
>   upon a person who's accursed.
>   Hear us, mighty Zeus!

OEDIPUS

Has he got close? Is he, my children, going to find me
still alive, and in control of my right mind?

ANTIGONE

What is the pledge you wish to keep firm in your mind?

OEDIPUS

I want to grant in full the favour, as I promised
at the time, in recompense for being treated well.   1490

CHORUS

>   Come, my son, come quick, my prince;
>   if you're deep in that recess°
>   at Poseidon's altar where
>   you make oxen-sacrifice
>   to the sea god, come back here!
>   For the stranger values you
>   as worthy, and our friends and town,

to be offered favour due
in return for favours done
    Run, lord, come in haste!

SCENE 9

Enter Theseus from the 'city' side.

THESEUS

What is this shouting that rings clearly,   1500
both from you the locals and the stranger?
Has there been a Zeus-sent thunderbolt,
or a hail-shower rattling down?
When there's a god-raised thunderstorm
as great as this, one might guess anything.

OEDIPUS

Good king, your being here is what I longed for;
it is a god has granted you the fortune of this journey.

THESEUS

What is this new event then, son of Laius?

OEDIPUS

The pivot of my life.
And I don't want to die without first making good
the promises I pledged you and this land.

THESEUS

What token do you take to signify your death?   1510

OEDIPUS

The gods themselves make their announcement to me,
true to all the signs foretold.

THESEUS

And how have these been manifest, you say?

OEDIPUS

The rolling thunder and the many lightning-bolts
hurled down from Zeus' unconquerable hand.

THESEUS

I take your word. I've seen you making many prophesies,
and never false. So tell me what to do.

OEDIPUS

I shall instruct you, Theseus, in the things that lie in prospect
for this city, things immune from age.
I shall myself soon guide you, with no helping hand,   1520
towards the place where I must die.
You must not ever speak about this spot to anyone:
not where it is concealed, not even whereabouts it is.
This way it shall provide you with protection
stronger than the ranks of shields or allied neighbours' spears.
And you yourself, when you come there—alone—
shall learn of the taboos and mysteries
not right to be disturbed in words,
as I would never tell them to these citizens,
not even to my daughters, dearly though I love them.
No, keep them safely to yourself,   1530
and when you near the ending of your life,
entrust them to your closest heir alone;
and let him pass them to successors down through time.
This way you'll build this city safe
against the soldiers sown from teeth.°
So many cities, though they're ordered well,
turn lightly towards reckless violence;
and though the gods may take their time,
they note it well when anyone abandons piety
and turns to madness in their ways.
Don't let that ever be the case with you,
good son of Aegeus. But I am instructing you
in matters that you know full well.
Now for the place.
the prompting of the god is urging me,   1540
so let us make our way, no longer hesitate.

Oedipus begins to move on his way, without any help.

My children, follow me; I have emerged anew
so as to be your guide, as you have been to me.
Come on, but do not touch me.
Let me discover for myself the sacred grave
where it is fated that this man
should be kept hidden in this land.
This way. . . here. . . come. . .

this is the way that guiding Hermes
and the Goddess of the Underworld are leading me.°
O light of day—no light to me, though once you were—
my body now is warmed by you this one last time.   1550
I'm moving now towards chill Hades
where I'll hide away the ending of my life.
(*to Theseus*) My dearest friend, I wish that you and this your land,
and all who follow you, may prosper well.
Remember me, though dead, in your prosperity.

°*Oedipus makes his way off into the sacred grove, followed by his daughters
and by Theseus and his attendants.*

CHORAL SONG

CHORUS

     If I may frame my prayer
     to the Goddess unseen,
     and to you, Aidoneus,°   1560
     lord of the world of night,
     then I make this request:
     please let our stranger-guest
     reach the enclosing plains,
     where all the dead lie hid,°
     without hurt or anguish.
     After much pointless pain,
     a righteous god would then
     have raised him high again.

     °Goddesses under ground,
     and beast with your kennel
     by the frequented gate   1570
     of Hades, where you growl,
     untameable sentinel,
     as all the stories say;
     and you please do your best,
     Earth-son of Tartarus,
     to help and clear the way,
     when he, our stranger-guest,
     treads the darkening plains:
     long Sleep, to you I pray.

SCENE 10

Enter Attendant of Theseus from the grove.

ATTENDANT OF THESEUS
My fellow-citizens, the most concise account
I have to give is this, that Oedipus is dead.   1580
But there's no hasty way to tell of what transpired;
nor were the things done there achieved in haste.

CHORUS-LEADER
So he is dead, poor man?

ATTENDANT OF THESEUS
He has departed from this life; that is for sure.

CHORUS-LEADER
But how? By some fate sent by god and free from toil?

ATTENDANT OF THESEUS
That is indeed the most amazing thing.
As you were here yourselves, you know how he departed
from this place without a guiding hand from anyone,
with him directing all of us instead.
°Well, when he came to that sheer threshold   1590
rooted in the earth with steps of bronze,
he paused on one among the many paths
that branch from there, close to the hollow basin,
token of the pact perpetual between Peirithous and Theseus.
Midway between that place and the Thorician stone,
he stopped, and on the marble tomb
beside the hollow pear-tree took his seat,
and then undid his filthy rags.
Next thing he called his daughters and instructed them
to fetch him water from a flowing stream
for washing and for pouring out an offering.
They went to the green hillock that was visible,   1600
sacred to Demeter. In a little time
they had completed all their father's wishes,
washing him and clothing him in customary robes.°
When he had had full satisfaction from these rites,
and none of his requests was left undone,
then Zeus beneath the earth° made thunder sound.

His daughters trembled as they heard;
they knelt beside their father and they wept,
and beat unceasingly upon their breasts
with long lamenting cries.
And when he heard this bitter burst of grief,   1610
he wrapped them in his arms and said:
'My children, on this day your father is no more.
My life is wholly finished now,
and you no longer need to bear
the weary task of looking after me.
It has been harsh, I know, my girls,
but there is one small word°
redeems these many sufferings:
you never could have had a *love*
more full than from this heart of mine.
But now henceforth you'll live a life devoid of me.'
Entwined within each others' arms they all wept deeply.   1620
When their lament had reached completion,
and their crying had subsided,
there was stillness.
Suddenly a voice cried out for him,
and made our hair stand up in fear:
[because the god repeatedly and variously called out to him:]°
'You, Oedipus, yes you, what's keeping us from going?
Too long you have been dragging out delay.'
When once he realized the god was calling him,
he told King Theseus to approach.   1630
When near, he said: 'Dear friend, please take
my daughters by the hand and give your solemn pledge;
and you, girls, do the same.
Now promise that you never will betray them purposely,
but always will in kindness do what's best for them.'
And Theseus, nobly and without lament,
swore on his oath he would do this for him.
With that completed, Oedipus reached out
and held his girls with his unseeing hands, and said:
'My daughters, you must raise the strength of will   1640
to move away from this place here,
and not expect to look upon the things you should not,
nor to hear what's spoken next. So quickly go.
No one except the master, Theseus,

should stand near, and learn what now is done.'
All of us heard him say these words,
and made our way beside the girls, lamenting tearfully.
We had not walked for long before we turned around:
we could no longer see him anywhere, the man.
But Theseus stood there still, his hand held up   1650
before his face to shield his eyes,
as if some awesome thing had come in sight,
something unbearable to look upon.
Then after a brief quiet we saw him
paying homage down towards the earth
and up to the Olympian gods above,
both at one time.°
What sort of death he met, that man,
there is no human but for Theseus who can say.
There was no fiery thunderbolt that ended him,
nor any whirlwind swirling off the sea.   1660
Either some herald came down from the gods,
or else the basis of the earth, the world below,
in favour to him opened painlessly.
He was sent on without distress,
not by disease, no cries of pain,
but in a way, for any human, wonderful.
And if I seem to some to speak of things
that make no sense, I do not care to win them round.

CHORUS-LEADER
Where are the daughters and the men who went with them?

ATTENDANT OF THESEUS
Not far away. The sounds of their lamenting
make it clear that they are coming near.

°SCENE 11—LYRIC DIALOGUE

Enter Antigone and Ismene from the grove.

ANTIGONE
It's left for us to mourn   1670
in one way or another
accursed blood inborn

deriving from our father.
For him we have endured
unending pain and anguish;
and at the end, strange things
we've had to bear and witness

CHORUS

What was done?

ANTIGONE

We can't be sure.

CHORUS

Has he gone?

ANTIGONE

As anyone might wish:
for sure, it was not warfare
destroyed him, nor did sea
engulf him with salt water.   1680
The darkening plains have cloaked
him with mysterious binding;
while we can only see
a fatal gloom descending.
For how on earth are we
to find a life through wandering
across some far-off land
or over waves unending?

ISMENE

I cannot tell. I wish
Hades would hold me under   1690
with his deadly grasp,
to die with my old father.
For I can see no life
worth living in the future.

CHORUS

You daughters, best of all,
bear what the gods have brought him.
And do not burn too fierce;
your course can not be faulted.

ANTIGONE

So even dreadful things,
once gone, can stir up longing:

unloveliness was loved
while in my arms belonging.
My father, O my dear,   1700
though darkness is your covering
for ever, even there
you still shall find us loving.

CHORUS

He achieved. . .

ANTIGONE

. . . the thing he wished.

CHORUS

How is that?

ANTIGONE

He ended as he chose:
beneath a soil that's foreign
he has eternal rest
with shadows soft upon him;
and he has left behind
a grief with tears unceasing.
O father, these my eyes
still flow for you with weeping;   1710
I have no way to drown
this grief. A soil that's alien
provides the death you wished,
but death leaves me forsaken.

ISMENE

Dear sister, now what fate
can there be waiting for us,
now that our father has
forsaken us as orphans?
°. . .

CHORUS

He reached an end that's blest,   1720
so now let go this mourning.
There's nobody who is
immune against misfortune.

ANTIGONE

Let's hurry back again.

ISMENE

What could we do?

ANTIGONE

Such a longing seizes me. . .

ISMENE

What for?

ANTIGONE

Gazing at the home beneath. . .

ISMENE

Whose home?

ANTIGONE

Our own father's.

ISMENE

That would be impure
for us. You must see that.   1730

ANTIGONE

Why this reproach?

ISMENE

Yet there is this. . .

ANTIGONE

What's this as well?

ISMENE

. . . he fell unburied, all alone.

ANTIGONE

Take me there, and kill me too.
°. . .

ISMENE

Where shall I turn, abandoned now?
Where can my pathless life-steps go?

CHORUS

Do not be frightened, girls.

ANTIGONE

Where can I run?

CHORUS

You already have escaped. . .

ANTIGONE

How so?

CHORUS
>from the troubles threatening you.

ANTIGONE
>   I mean. . .   1740

CHORUS
>What is your thought?

ANTIGONE
>   . . . that I cannot see
>how we can get back home.

CHORUS
>Make no attempt.

ANTIGONE
>   Troubles grip us.

CHORUS
>They did before.

ANTIGONE
>Desperate back then: now even more.

CHORUS
>Your share of pains would fill a sea.

ANTIGONE
>That's true, too true.

CHORUS
>I must agree

ANTIGONE
>O Zeus, which way are we to take?
>What future hope can drive my fate?   1750

°SCENE 12

Enter Theseus with attendants, from the grove.

THESEUS
>Stop this lamentation, children.
>When the common good is stored in
>earth to bless us as a favour,

it's not right to go on grieving:
that might draw divine resentment.

ANTIGONE

Son of Aegeus, we implore you.

THESEUS

Tell me what you want to happen.

ANTIGONE

We ourselves would like to look on
where our father has been buried.

THESEUS

It's forbidden to approach there.

ANTIGONE

Why declare that, lord of Athens?

THESEUS

He himself decreed it, daughters;   1760
ordered me to stop all mortals
from approaching that location,
nor to let them raise their voices
near the sacred place he's settled.
He assured me, if I did this,
I would keep this country ever
free from menace. And our god here°
heard me, so did Zeus' attendant,
god of Oath, who always hears us.

ANTIGONE

Well, if that was his intention,
that will have to close the issue.
Please, though, help us make our way to
ancient Thebes, to see if we can   1770
somehow try to stop the slaughter
that's advancing on our brothers.

THESEUS

I shall do that, and whatever
other favour I can offer
to assist you, and respect the
one below, the new-departed.
I must not let up my efforts.

CHORUS
> Well, no more sound,
> raise no more lamenting:
> these things are bound
> firmly to this ending.

°*Antigone and Ismene, accompanied by Theseus and his attendants, depart in the 'foreign' direction, towards Thebes. The Chorus go in the other direction.*

EXPLANATORY NOTES

NOTE that line numbers refer to the standard numbering of the Greek texts, not to the lines of this translation.

OEDIPUS THE KING

1 *ancient land of Thebes*: the powerful city of Thebes, with its ancient walls and their celebrated seven gates, was conspicuous in the plain near the southern edge of the large, relatively fertile area called Boeotia (see Map 1). In tragedy it is often called 'the city of Cadmus', as it is here in the Greek, after its legendary founder some four generations earlier.

3 *suppliant branches*: leafy branches tied round with bands of wool were often carried as a token of the ritual, when suppliants put themselves at the mercy of a person, or more often at the altar of a god.

5 *Paean*: this was a title of Apollo, in his role as a god of healing. Some songs in honour of Apollo were known as 'Paeans'.

20–2 *before the double temple . . . of Apollo*: literally 'the double-temples of Pallas [Athena] and the prophetic embers of Ismenus'. Ismenus (probably more correctly Hismenus) was a special Theban cult-title of Apollo, and was also the name of the river that flowed past one side of the city. These lines may suggest a certain fascination with real Theban institutions.

30 *a profiteer in groans and tears*: Hades, the god of the Underworld, was sometimes known as 'Ploutos', which means 'Wealth', so this is a kind of word-play.

36 *that cruel singing lynx*: here and several times elsewhere the Sphinx is alluded to by a riddling phrase, as though it might be bad luck to speak her name. The only time she is directly named is by Creon at 130.

56–7 *A city's like a ship . . . but a hulk*: I agree with those scholars who argue that these two rather leaden lines have been added to Sophocles' text.

70–1 *Creon, brother of my wife, to Delphi*: the father of both Iocasta and Creon was Menoeceus, who was, like Laius, a descendent of Cadmus. Thebes was nearer to Delphi and its famous pan-Hellenic oracle than most Greek cities, but it still involved some difficult terrain round the southern flank of Mt Parnassus (see Map 1). (In 71 the oracle is given the grand periphrasis of 'the Pythian house of Phoebus'.)

103 *Laius*: this is the first allusion to Laius in the play, and his name will be heard again and again before it is finally found to be that of Oedipus' father. In this translation, as in Greek, Laius has three syllables, not two (as is often mispronounced in English): more or less '*La*-ee-us'.

122–3 *He said . . . many hands*: this surviving eyewitness is the old slave of Laius, who will later be summoned. His false account of the number of those who killed Laius will prove crucial to the difficulties of reconstructing the past.

124–5 *how could any bandit . . . here?*: highway robbery was not a widespread phenomenon in ancient Greece, and Oedipus thinks first of a politically motivated payment, as he will later with Tiresias.

150–1 [SD] *The Priest and young people . . . from the city*: as the Priest and suppliants depart, the Chorus of Theban elders arrive and embark on their long opening song (the technical term "parodos" is sometimes applied). They are in effect the response to Oedipus' summons in 144, even though they have gathered unrealistically quickly. A similar choral licence allows them to have heard already that there has been an oracle from Delphi, although they do not know what it says.

151–8 *What are you . . . and let me hear*: the first stanza (strophe) is addressed to Apollo, mainly through the device of addressing the voice of his oracle. At 153 he is called Paean (see note on 5) with the epithet "Delian" because he was born on the small Aegean island of Delos.

159–67 *First I summon . . . now come*: the second stanza (antistrophe) calls on Athena and Artemis as well as Apollo. As often in Greek prayers, help is asked for now on the precedent of previous favours. The Greek includes further elaborations of cult: Artemis has a "circular throne" in the centre (*agora*) of Thebes, and Apollo is given an epic epithet thought to mean "who shoots from far off" (omitted in the translation).

190–201 *Ares, war god . . . thunder blows*: Ares is usually the god of war, and a patron of Thebes; but here, although it is not explained, he is portrayed as the alien and hostile plague- god. They want him to be banished either to "the great hall of Amphitrite", an ornate way of referring to the Atlantic in the far west, or to the dangerous Thracian Sea, which probably means the Black Sea to the east. The words of 198–9 ("Anything surviving . . . set to right."), though plain, remain mysterious.

203–8 *Arrows from your golden bow . . . in her hands*: in the Greek Apollo is called "Lycian" and Artemis is said to leap through "the mountains of Lycia", so the association seems to be with their cults in Asia Minor. I have omitted both these ornamental flourishes.

209–15 *Come too . . . every other god*: finally the chorus calls on Dionysus (here called "Bacchos" in the Greek) to help against the plague god. Dionysus, son of Zeus, was born at Thebes to Semele, daughter of Cadmus; the chorus even say he "shares his name" with Thebes. He is here, as often, associated with wine and with torchlight rites accompanied by his possessed Maenads.

216 ff. *At prayer . . .* : Oedipus' abrupt intervention may make him seem almost godlike; but, taken in context, this is more likely a sign of his absolute authority rather than any more-than-human presumption. His proclamation echoes several features of Athenian murder investigation and prosecution. In Athens it was the task of blood-kin to pursue the judicial procedures; and this gives a special irony—characteristic of this play, of course—to Oedipus' making himself out to be the surrogate son of Laius (264).

222–3 *it's only later I've become a citizen*: Oedipus' emphasis on not being a native citizen, but a late arrival, will turn out to be ironically false. The same point is implied by Tiresias at 452–4.

246–51 *I pray the guilty party . . . down on them*: I agree with editors who have cut these lines out as a weaker duplication of the preceding curse in 236–43 and a diminishing addition to Sophocles' text. They may well have been added by an actor who wrongly thought that the curse was only on people who concealed the culprit and not on the actual agent. In these added lines the irony about Oedipus' own household is too heavy-handed and is exploited too early in the play.

267–8 *Laius. . . . Agenor long ago*: this solemn genealogy makes Oedipus seem like some kind of honorary successor to the royal line; he will in fact he turn out to be the direct blood-successor.

300 ff. *Tiresias . . .* : the blind prophet, affiliated to Apollo (see 284–5), was an awesome figure in several Theban myths. Oedipus is characteristically impatient in demanding a response from Tiresias, and addresses him on his arrival without giving him space to exchange courtesies. Throughout their whole confrontation Oedipus speaks in public terms, insistently invoking "the city" *(polis)*, while Tiresias speaks in private, spiritual terms.

324 *thought*: I have translated a variant text rather than the more usually accepted "speech".

337–8 *You criticize. . . . your life with you*: the first riddling phrases from Tiresias. The word translated as "temperament" *(orge)* means passion, temper, disposition; and in a way, it is Oedipus' passionate temper that has led to his living in his incestuous house.

376 ff. *Creon! . . .* : it seems to be Tiresias' use of the word "fall" which sets Oedipus thinking in terms of a political coup plotted by Creon. It is a characteristic of Oedipus to work out alternative explanations; and here he turns to his strong sense of political insecurity.

413 ff. *you have your sight . . .* : it is with this speech that Tiresias gets into his full prophetic stride. And there is a shift of enigmatic gear at 417 ff., where the curse that will dog Oedipus is called *deinopous*, "fearful-footed". This surely plays with the name Oidipous ("swollen-footed"). For further word-play with Oedipus' name, see p. 5.

420–3 *There is no anchorage . . . voyage fair*: Cithaeron is the long mountain range some 15 km to the south of Thebes (see Map 1), and it will prove to have an important place in Oedipus' life-story. But at this first naming it is wrapped up as part of Tiresias' strange, riddling prophesy of the terrible things that will be discovered before the end of this play. These four particularly strange and haunting lines interweave three threads: (i) entering the harbour, which hints at Oedipus entering his marriage-bed and his own mother's womb (see on 1207–10); (ii) Oedipus' cries of distress when he discovers the truth, cries which will be a distortion of his wedding-song; (iii) the mountain whose harbour-like hollows will echo with lamentation.

425 *crush*: an editorial conjecture which makes stronger sense than the verb in the manuscripts, which means "level".

447–62 *I'll go then once I've had my say . . .* : some scholars, especially Bernard Knox, have made much of there being no response from Oedipus at the end of this powerful and intriguing speech, and of the way that he does not come to the "obvious" conclusion that it is all about him. They have even proposed that Sophocles had Oedipus exit after line 446, leaving the blind Tiresias pontificating to thin air. But this is to miss the point that it is all in the form of *riddles*—at 456 even echoing the riddle of the Sphinx ("probing for his footsteps with a stick"). Oedipus does not realize that these are also literal facts; that while the answer to the Sphinx's riddle was "mankind", the answer to Tiresias' is "you, Oedipus, but literally, not figuratively". His silent departure shows that he is, for now, unable to meet Tiresias' challenge to "go inside and work that out".

458–60　*And he shall be revealed . . . who begot him*: in these three lines Tiresias sets up a kind of incantation: each contains a riddling pair of nouns: [he shall be revealed as] "both *a* and *b*", and in each the second term is a two-syllable word beginning in Greek with a *p*.

463–82　*Who has the chanting crag . . . tormenting flies*: the first pair of stanzas dwell on the oracle and the unidentified murderer, who is envisaged as a desperate fugitive. There are several high-flown poetic allusions: "chanting crag" (463) because Delphi is perched high on the southern flank of Mt Parnassus (see also 475); "Zeus' own son" (470) meaning Apollo, who can deploy his father's armoury; "Earth's primordial navel" (480) alluding to the sacred "omphalos" stone at Delphi which was held to be the navel of the world.

483–512　*How shaken I am . . . evil by my mind*: in the second pair the chorus is deeply disturbed over how to interpret Tiresias' personal attacks on Oedipus. They know of no reason why he should have wanted to kill Laius ("the royal line of Labdacus", 489). In view of Oedipus' great benefit to Thebes in confronting the Sphinx ("the feathered girl", 508), they are more inclined to doubt the authority of Tiresias, since seers are not necessarily infallible.

490　*Polybus*: the king of Corinth, believed to be the father of Oedipus, will have his place in the story explained at lines 774 ff. and later. It is difficult to know whether this allusion to him here is because he was already well known from previous versions of the myth, or if it is merely a circumstantial detail in preparation for a new version of Oedipus' early life. The point is that the chorus believe that Oedipus' ancestry had no connection with Labdacus, the father of Laius.

600　*A mind . . . corrupt*: it is widely agreed that this line is a sententious addition to Sophocles' text.

624–5　*Now you have shown . . . when I see one.>*: something has gone wrong with the text here, and there must be at least one line missing; but there is no agreed solution among editors. I have given two consecutive lines to Creon, and then made up a line of my own for Oedipus, but this is mere guesswork.

649–97　*[Lyric Dialogue]*: the emotional atmosphere becomes so tense that Oedipus and the chorus break into a stanza in lyric dialogue in 649–68 (see p. xvii on this kind of mode). Then, after a few lines of spoken dialogue, ending with the departure of Creon, there is a matching lyric stanza in 678–97, but with Iocasta replacing the lines of Oedipus. This unusual sequence of dramatic technique marks the important transition between the Creon part and the Iocasta part in the middle of this very long act, which lasts from 513 to 862. With this the whole emphasis turns from the problems of the city (636 is the last allusion to the plague) to the reconstruction of Oedipus' personal past.

716 *where three wagon-tracks converge*: the reported detail of the three wagon-tracks, dropped in circumstantially, turns out to be true (unlike the plural "bandits"), and to be a crucial piece of the jigsaw. The exact location will soon be pinpointed: see note on 733–4. It is important to be aware that in the mountainous terrain of Greece (as opposed to the fertile plains), tracks that could be managed by wagons were quite few and far between. They needed to have negotiable gradients, and were often engineered with ruts in the rock.

733–4 *The country is called Phocis . . . from Daulia*: this locates a specific place on the route over the mountains between Thebes and Delphi (see Map 1). About 25 km east of Delphi at the bottom of a long ravine descending from the Delphi direction lies a small upland plain, where one valley heads north to the town of Daulis, and another continues east towards the plain of Boeotia. Every traveller between Thebes and Delphi (in modern no less than ancient times) had to go past that junction, the "split road"- it became a site for tourists. Any Athenian pilgrim to Delphi travelling along this route, called a "Sacred Way", would know this spot, an ominous place where the world of myth and the present world of the audience eerily brush by each other.

758–64 I *know he's not* . . . : the old eyewitness was so keen to be far from the city because of his guilty secret: he knows the new king is the very man who murdered Laius. He also gives the deliberately false information that there were several robbers, not just a single man. His complicity and his lying, however well meant, are crucial to the misinformation on which the whole tragedy is built.

774–5 *Polybus . . . Merope*: Corinth (see Map 1) was an ancient and wealthy city, located at the trading "crossroads" of the isthmus which joins mainland Greece with the Peloponnese. Polybus may be an invention of Sophocles—it was a common mythological name—but he has been already mentioned at 490 (see note). It is implied that he is the chief power at Corinth rather than a hereditary king. Merope may also be invented for this play, and it is not clear what it means that she is said to be "from Doris".

780 *not my father's true-born son*: the insult slurs his paternity; it does not imply, let alone allege, that Merope is not his mother.

788 *to Delphi*: it is only a short voyage down the Gulf of Corinth to the port below Delphi (see Map 1).

794–7 *On hearing this . . . oracle fulfilled*: Oedipus is keen to make sure he never again goes anywhere near Corinth. His random route takes him north-eastward round the southern flank of Parnassus through Phocis (see Map 1).

811 *my stick*: the Greek word *skeptron* is used both of rough sticks and of formal regal sceptres (long staffs, often with an eagle on top). There is no explicit indication that Oedipus was holding one in this play, but if he was, then the *skeptron* wielded "by this hand of mine" becomes that much more vivid.

821–2 *with these same hands*: this physicality of the hands that killed Laius being the same hands that make love to Iocasta anticipates the almost macabre details of incest that will be explored later (see notes on 1208–13, 1403–9).

842 ff. *You said he witnessed . . .* : the plot is suspended on the single thread of the evidence as reported by the eyewitness about numbers (see note on 758–64). It never gets spelled out, however, that he told a direct lie; and the murder of Laius is not revisited, because from now on all attention is going to be focused on the earliest days of Oedipus' life.

863–910 [*Choral Song*]: in this grand and difficult choral song it is the task of the chorus not to draw authoritative morals but to attempt to make some sort of sense of what it witnesses in the tragedy (see p. xvii on the role of the chorus). Far from linear philosophical reasoning, it produces a tortuous, sometimes contradictory sequence of intuitions and protestations. So what this song does is attempt to make sense of the ways that Iocasta's scepticism about prophesy is sensible yet at the same time irreligious; and that Oedipus is a great ruler yet at the same time possibly the polluter of Thebes.

867 *Olympus*: from being simply the mountain-home of the gods, Olympus comes to mean the higher cosmic world.

873–83 *Proud arrogance . . . strong shield*: the chorus turns in the second stanza to human behaviour and its dangers. They start from the idea of *hybris*, a word which signifies a range of wrong behaviour allied to presumptuous bullying, here translated as "proud arrogance". After exploring the idea that *hybris* leads to a fall, it seems that in the closing lines they hope to exempt Oedipus from that implication: he is the beneficial champion-wrestler, not the bully.

873 *Proud arrogance begets bad kings*: the opening three words in Greek say "*hybris* begets a *tyrannos*", which I have translated as 'Proud arrogance begets bad kings'. This is problematic, however. First, *tyrannos* and related words are generally in this play used of a sole ruler in a politically neutral way. So to take the step of giving it a bad sense here, i.e. dictator/tyrant, while not impossible in the Greek of this period, goes against its usage elsewhere in the play. Secondly, the phrase seems bound to be referring to Oedipus; yet, however dubious some of his behaviour towards Tiresias and Creon, the chorus stays loyal and favourable to him: so neither *hybris* nor *tyrannos* (in the bad sense) seem to fit their view of him. A change of punctuation and of one letter would produce the more sententious meaning: "Proud arrogance begets proud arrogance as a tyrant." This is quite an attractive emendation, and would reduce the apparent application to Oedipus personally. I have stuck with the usually accepted reading, but without confidence.

896 *why should I dance and sing in the sacred chorus?*: this stanza has been largely spent on trying to establish some firm ground in the sphere of divine sanctions. *If* people behave appallingly, then surely, the chorus claims, they should incur punishment. And *if* such actions thrive, they conclude, "why should I participate in choruses?" The self-referentiality of the chorus-members questioning whether what they are doing at that very moment is justified has appealed to modern sensibilities. But, while that level of reference is surely there, it is clear in the context that participating in a chorus is thought of as primarily a pious religious observance. And there were other forms of

choral participation that are more obviously religious, e.g. hymns, processions, dithyrambs, and paeans.

897–910 *If these signposts . . . and religion's going*: the fourth and final stanza is even less confident. The first part is covered by a conditional *if:* if oracles are not true, people will no longer have good reason to go to Delphi ("navel" of the earth—see note on 463–82), nor Abai, an oracle not far from Thebes, nor the great sanctuary of Zeus and Hera at Olympia. But towards the end they suspect unconditionally that the oracles concerning Laius and his family are proving false. And in that case, they conclude with the ominous fear that the significance of the divine is fading away—which it is not, of course, because the oracles will turn out to be true.

919 *Apollo . . . house*: there was probably a sacred stone of Apollo actually represented on-stage. Iocasta prays to him as "closest", which has an ominous further significance.

924 ff. *[SD] Enter the Old Corinthian . . .* : this new character has been conventionally known as the 'Messenger', but, since he does not even deliver a standard eyewitness report (unlike the proper Messenger at 1223 ff.), this label is more than usually unhelpful. He seems to be a welcome "answer" to Iocasta's prayers, but in fact he supplies knowledge which precipitates horrible recognitions of the past. It is not an absurd coincidence or stroke of Fate that the shepherd who gave the baby Oedipus to Polybus at Corinth should be the one who some thirty years later hurries to Thebes with the news that Polybus is dead, and that Oedipus has been proclaimed the new king. He has a personal interest in Oedipus; he is familiar with the drove-road over the mountains (see note on 1026); and he hopes for a reward in return for what he takes to be good news (explicit at 1006). Nor is it is implausible that Oedipus should become king of Corinth (the word used in line 939 is *tyrannos*): nearly everyone at Corinth and everyone at Thebes believes Polybus to have been his father.

924–6 *where . . . where*: the old man is also misleadingly amusing, at least at first. His opening three lines all end with the syllable *pou*, and exploit the wordplay on the way that the name of *Oidipous* is close to *oid- pou*, "know where"—see p. 5.

969–70 *unless perhaps . . . because of me*: the idea that Polybus might have died from missing Oedipus is not merely frivolous, since oracles were sometimes believed to have symbolic rather than literal applications. It also shows Oedipus' characteristic ability in finding ways of explaining away unwelcome evidence.

977–83 *Why should we humans . . . life most easily*: Iocasta's almost jubilant speech verges on a kind of anarchic creed of living in a haphazard, day-by-day fashion. Her claim is that men dreaming of sex with their mothers is as unimportant and random as oracles, and this is made to seem sensible. Yet it was these very lines that Freud made central to his *Interpretation of Dreams* (1900). The suggestion that it is good psychology to come to terms with this fantasy has an ironic resemblance to Freud's own ideas about therapy.

1022 *these hands of mine*: there is emphasis throughout the play on hands and exchanges between hands, and I have hazarded the conjecture of adding one letter to the Greek—from *ton emon* to *tond' emon*—so that it comes to mean "from these hands of mine" instead of simply "my hands".

1026 *forest glens of Mount Cithaeron*: this is only the second time that the mountain has been named in the play (see note on 420–3), but from now on it will become a more and more significant location. Corinth is a good distance away, some 50 km over harsh terrain across Mt Geranos, but there is archaeological evidence that Corinthians actually did take their transhumant flocks to Cithaeron for summer grazing in the upland valleys, and that there was an ancient track over the mountains. This route was intrepidly traced on foot by N. G. L. Hammond in 1953: the modern journey by road, via Eleusis, is about double the distance.

1034 *take your name from that misfortune*: the derivation of the name *Oidipous* from words meaning "swell" and "foot" is evidently taken as familiar here. But not a lot is made of this in the play as a whole.

1042 *the slave of Laius*: Iocasta has been standing by in silence ever since the Old Corinthian intervened at 989 ff. At some stage during this dialogue she must be supposed to have realized the whole terrible truth. It is impossible for us to pin down a precise moment: perhaps the mention of the ankles at 1032 ff.; or perhaps here, when the slave who took the baby to the mountain is identified. Iocasta knows well the trusted man who was given that task (left vague at 719). A much-reproduced vase from Sicily painted about 100 years later captures this moment in her silent gesture as she raises her robe to her face—whether or not this is how Sophocles himself staged it.

1062–3 *Take heart . . . lowly born*: Oedipus supposes that Iocasta is trying to put him off searching further because she is ashamed of his humble origins. He unwittingly twists the knife, because she knows well that, far from his having a slave for a mother, she is herself his mother.

1080–3 *But I regard myself as born . . . as great*: in rather exhilarated and high-flown terms Oedipus claims that, contrary to Iocasta's snobbish prejudices, he is not ashamed of his origins, because he is "the child of Fortune (*Tyche*)". Metaphorically this rings true; but while Oedipus talks of Fortune "with her generosity" (literally, "who gives well"), he is actually the child of Fortune who is malign. He then goes on, because Fortune changes with time, to invoke the Months as his close relations, who have raised him from humble origins to greatness: in truth time will, in the course of this play, have reduced him the other way round, from the highest to the lowest.

1084–5 *other than I am*: I have translated the transmitted text. An emendation (*atimos* instead of *pot'allos*) would produce the arguably stronger sense: "I'll never shall turn out dishonoured, and never rest . . ."

1086–97 *If I trust my intuition . . . healing god, we sing*: in this jubilant and fanciful song, a false celebration before the full horror strikes, the chorus take their cue from Oedipus' final speech of proud assertion. As they try to make sense of the new revelations, they move in completely the wrong direction, hoping that Oedipus' mysterious origins will be a matter of wonder, and even of divine birth. They pin their optimism on the local mountain of Cithaeron, where Oedipus was handed over as a baby. In the first stanza they envisage that it will become the site of future religious cult, instituted to celebrate its place in his story. Choral singing and dance during the night of a full moon (1090) was a common occasion for Greek cult celebrations. In the Greek at the end of the stanza, they call on Apollo with the epithet *ieie* (four syllables), an invocation which seems to be associated with his role as Paean.

1098–1109 *Oedipus, who was your mother . . . company for play*: in the second stanza the unsubstantiated exhilaration becomes even more fanciful. With a strange blend of high-flown cult-titles and rather explicit sexual language, the chorus speculate that Oedipus might be the fruit of a union between a named male god and an anonymous mountain-nymph. They think of Pan (who lived in the wild and was apt to rape); Apollo (Loxias); Hermes, called "Lord of Cyllene", the mountain in the Peloponnese where he was born; and finally "the Bacchic god". While regularly accompanied by nymphs on the mountains, Dionysus is not usually portrayed as fathering children with them.

1108 *with sparkling eye*: the reading in our manuscripts describes the nymphs as "of Mount Helicon". Since Helicon is in a different part of Boeotia and completely distinct from Cithaeron, and since this whole song is so centrally focused on Cithaeron, this word cannot be right. Fortunately the great scholar Wilamowitz hit on the emendation to an epic poetic epithet meaning something like "with glancing eyes".

1110 ff. [*SD*] *Old Slave of Laius*: this old man has usually been known as "Herdsman" or "Servant", but the defining role of his life was to have been a close and loyal slave to Laius. This is why he was given the sensitive task of exposing the royal baby; and he was one of the small band who accompanied Laius on his fatal trip to Delphi. Since then he has tried to live securely and quietly, away from the city, and from the king whom he alone knows was the killer of Laius.

1145 *he is the man who was that little babe*: the old Corinthian is rather pleased to recall that event so many years ago: as Oedipus stands between the two old shepherds it is a kind of re-enactment. Yet it turns out to be the last line spoken by this character. Far from being a source of pleasure, it is enough to make the old slave of Laius realize the truth about Oedipus' life-story, that the baby he gave away on Cithaeron has grown up to be the same man whom he saw kill Laius at the place where three roads meet.

1154 *when you're in pain*: it was standard practice in ancient Greece to interrogate slaves under torture. This is what Oedipus unhesitatingly threatens as he senses he is getting near the truth.

1171–2 *But she inside . . . your wife*: in the Greek word-order the old slave says "the woman inside . . .", and then adds ". . . your wife", knowing full well that she was also the wife of Laius.

1186–96 *Human generations . . . human blest*: the word *broton*, which comes in the opening and closing words of this powerfully sombre stanza, covers all of humanity and is not gendered. The chorus take Oedipus as their paradigm (the Greek word used in 1193 actually is *paradeigma*) for the "moral" that nothing human can aspire to a blessed state, which is secure only for the gods.

1208–13 *you have made the voyage twice . . . crying out aloud?*: here the chorus
confront in lyric expression the sexual implications of Oedipus' incest, tap-
ping metaphors which verge on the lurid. First they figure Iocasta's womb as
a "harbour" (foreshadowed by Tiresias—see 420–3), twice visited by Oedipus, because this is where he was gestated as a baby and where he "plunged"
as an adult. They then switch from sea to land, and invoke the image of the
wife's womb as fertile furrows, a metaphor used in the ancient Greek for-
mulae of marriage. They suggest, however, that Iocasta's womb should have
screamed out rather than endure such horrible abuse. I have tried not to cloak
these rather macabre expressions in euphemisms.

1209 *as a husband*: I have accepted the textual change from "father" (*patri*) to
"husband" (*posei*), since this makes stronger sense.

1227 *the mighty river Danube or the Dnieper*: the Istros (modern Danube) and Pha-
sis (modern Rioni) are two of the great rivers that flow into the Black Sea and
from there into the Mediterranean. For the latter I have substituted the more
familiar river Dnieper.

1258–60 *And as he raged . . . some guide*: although there is very little suggestion
in *OT* of any direct intervention by a superhuman power (see pp. 6–8), the
messenger makes it clear here twice that, in his perception, there was some
strange external agent leading Oedipus on (the word used in 1258 is *daimon*,
which is less distinct than "god").

1260–2 *he hurled himself . . . into the room*: it is hardly a heady excursion into
Freudian symbolism to recognize in this narrative a re-enactment of Oedipus'
incestuous displacement of his father. He forcefully breaks the closed doors
of his parents' marital bedroom, and "plunges in"—the same image as was
recently used at 1210 by the chorus of his entering his mother's "harbour".
Also note the same "mother-soil" image at 1257 as the chorus had used at
1212 of his "father's furrows".

1278–9 *and kept on spattering . . . thick as hail*: these two lines are rejected by
the Oxford Classical Text edition (OCT) on the grounds that this goriness is
over-the-top, the kind of thing a fourth-century ham actor might have added.
But there is no shortage of gory passages in fifth-century tragedy, and no
evidence of a special taste for it in the fourth century. There are undeniably,
however, textual uncertainties in all three lines, 1278–80.

1295 *watchers of a spectacle*: the Greek word for "spectacle" is *theama*, which is
closely related to *theatron* and *theatai*, spectators. So these lines come close to
a theatrical, or metatheatrical, allusion: the doors are to be opened to reveal
"to you as well . . ." (1294). The messenger's mixture of revulsion with sympathetic emotion is quintessential of tragedy. The chorus also capture this
contradictory state at 1303–6: they cannot bear to look, and yet they are eager
to find out and even to see ("much to observe").

1297 ff. [*SD*] *Oedipus emerges . . .* : some have thought that the *ekkyklema* was used
here (see p. xix); but Oedipus is not merely revealed, he is groping his way
for himself, even though, as is emphasized, he has no one to guide him. The
emotion and horror are too much to be contained in iambic speech, and
in 1297–1311 both the chorus and Oedipus use anapaests, a chant-metre,

somewhere between speech and song. After that, between lines 1313 and 1366, Oedipus expresses himself in song with the chorus responding with occasional spoken lines.

1329 ff. *Apollo, friends, Apollo . . .* : on the allocation of responsibility, see pp. 7–8. While Apollo has, in the long view, brought Oedipus' life-story to this horrible shape, it was his own decision to blind himself. He also goes on to explain why in his speech at 1379 ff.

1372 *down in Hades*: Oedipus supposes that he will take his blindness with him after death. But in general the Greeks had indistinct ideas about the physicality of the dead in the underworld.

1380 *though raised . . . in Thebes*: this intrusive line was probably added by someone else: Oedipus had, after all, been brought up in Corinth, not in Thebes.

1389–90 *both blind . . . beyond the reach of pain*: it is probable that these two lines were added later to Sophocles' text. They do not add much—nothing, after all, can be "sweet" now to Oedipus—and they weaken the conclusion of this part of his self-hating speech.

1391–1403 *O Mount Cithaeron . . .* : Oedipus constructs a kind of mental map of his life-story, and revisits the key places in it: Cithaeron; Corinth: the place in Phocis where the three roads meet, where further detail about its narrowness and oppressive vegetation give it an extra sinister quality. Finally Thebes is not named, but simply reached as "here". For the locations see Map 1.

1403–9 *O wedding, joining . . . wrong to act in deeds*: the Greek *o gamoi, gamoi* is conventionally translated "marriage, marriage". But this too polite: *gam*-words are associated with sex, and are, indeed, used of sex in non-marital contexts. The whole emphasis in these lines is on actions; and those actions are not celebrating weddings, but having sex. I have tried to reflect this explicitness. There seems to be a certain relish in the expression of these incest-distortions, including the recurrent motif about Oedipus' "seed" being sown in his mother's "field" (see note on 1261–2). This almost prurient explicitness may be one of the factors that drew Freud so powerfully to Sophocles' play: the suppressed fascination of son–mother incest is made explicit in words.

1411–12 *throw me . . . or hide me*: the transmitted text has "hide me outside . . . or throw me in the sea . . ."; I have followed some editors in reversing these two verbs.

1416 ff. [*Scene 11 to end*]: there is quite a concentration of problematic passages of one sort or another in the final 100 lines of the play. So much so that one scholar (R. Dawe) has recently argued that nearly all of this entire section is not by Sophocles, and that it replaces the original ending. This is, in my opinion, too drastic a solution, and it condemns much that is fully worthy of Sophocles. But, at the same time, it should not be denied that there are some real questions to be raised: see the notes on 1424–9, 1457, 1463–5, 1485 (on 1482–5), 1510, 1515–23, 1524–30.

1424–9 <*Yet I am shocked . . . inside the house immediately*: there is a substantial problem with the text at this point. The verbs in these lines are plural ("even if you've lost your sense of shame. . . ." etc.), and so cannot be addressed to Oedipus alone. Most scholars have supposed that Creon is addressing some attendants that he has just brought on with him. But this cannot be right: who are these anonymous lackeys that they should be addressed in such portentous and reproachful terms? It is most likely that the lines are addressed to the chorus, and, in view of the reproach, to Oedipus himself as well. But if this is right then there must have been some lost transitional lines in between lines 1422 and 1423, bringing the chorus into the picture. For the sake of completeness I have made up a couple of lines. The command at 1429 ("accompany him inside") might then be addressed to the trusted elders of the chorus, or to a couple of personal attendants.

1451–4 *No, let me go and live . . . meant to kill me*: these lines are the culmination of the Cithaeron motif. The mountain exerts a kind of magnetic pull on Oedipus, and the idea that he should end his days where his parents meant him to die as a baby is so powerful that in some ways the postponement of his departure there is a disappointment (see further on pp. 11–12). And there is another level to this invocation of the mountain which is not commonly appreciated. Oedipus calls it "my Cithaeron" and says that it is "called" that: the Greek word even implies that it is "famed" as that. But it has only been a very short while since it was discovered, thanks to the old Corinthian shepherd, that Cithaeron had played any part at all in his life-story. Within the time of the play it cannot yet be famous, strictly speaking, for its connection with Oedipus (the deluded song at 1086 ff. is not enough for that). It is, rather, through mythical narratives that the connection between Oedipus and Cithaeron became celebrated. So a kind of complicity is set up between Oedipus and the *audience of the play*. It is for the public of future story-telling that Cithaeron becomes known as "Oedipus Mountain", so to speak.

1457 *some fearsome doom*: Oedipus asserts that he has somehow been preserved from death for some reason. But what is this? His actual words say merely ". . . for some terrible evil". These plain words are enigmatic, to say the least. Most critics have taken this as a prophetic forward-reference to his future sufferings, ending with his redemptive death and hero-cult at Colonus, as dramatized by Sophocles many years later in *Oedipus at Colonus*. But how is that invoked by "some terrible evil"? The vague phrase seems to be an inexplicable and disappointing anti-climax. It is not impossible, I think, that it may have been corrupted and/or shortened in its textual transmission, conceivably from something about the fate of a lonely death on the mountain.

1459 *the males*: the way that Oedipus' two sons, Eteocles and Polynices, quarrelled with each other, and brought down curses from their father, was an essential and well-known part of the whole myth. These future conflicts are, however, only lightly hinted at here.

1462 *But for my girls . . .* : the two daughters, Antigone and Ismene (neither actually named in this play), are still little, too young to understand according to Oedipus at line 1511. Their fame, especially that of Antigone, may well have been largely the invention of Sophocles himself through the impact of his "hit" tragedy *Antigone*, and of this very scene here. He also makes them important in *Oedipus at Colonus*. Fourth-century sources take them for granted as integral; and that includes, interestingly, the Sicilian vase-painting (see on 1042), where their presence even acts as a kind of identifying signal for this play.

1463–5 *(whose dinner-table . . . put my hands to)*: these three lines on how insepa-
rable Oedipus has been from his daughters at mealtimes seems rather over-
emphasized, and, assuming they are by Sophocles, they may be textually
corrupted.

1485 *ploughman*: this word *(aroter)* is an excellent emendation of the manuscripts,
that merely repeat "father" *(pater)*. There is, however, some strange wording throughout lines 1482–5: and in 1482 I have omitted the baffling epithet
"gardening" from before "father's eyes".

1510 [*SD*] *Creon does so*: it only makes sense for Oedipus to continue his speech
if and when Creon agrees; and this must be done in a way that he, though
blind, can register. This means Creon must put his hand on Oedipus, not the
girls (the Greek could mean either). But it is strange that this gesture is not
expressly acknowledged.

1515–23 *That is long enough . . . life through*: the metre changes to "recitative"
trochaics, and most of the lines are divided between Oedipus and Creon. This
is peculiar technique but would not in itself be good reason doubt the author-
ship of this dialogue. But there are also undeniable problems in content and
expression. Except for the last two lines, they are disappointingly thin and
awkward for such a climactic context. And four out of the eight lines are spent
on pointlessly going over the same ground as has already been more clearly
dealt with at 1434–45. It is hard to believe that Sophocles is responsible for
this scrappy dialogue. But supposing that someone has added these inferior
lines, then why? The best answer would seem to be to ensure that at the end
of the play Oedipus goes into the house. (A possible motive for this might be
to square the ending of this play with *Oedipus at Colonus*—see note on *OC*
433–40.) But does that suggest that in Sophocles' original play Oedipus did
not go into the house, but went off into exile? This is discussed further in the
Introduction, pp. 12–13.

1523 [*SD*] *An attendant . . . city*: assuming that Oedipus goes into the house,
helped by an attendant, as expressly indicated by Creon at 1515 ("time to go
inside the palace"), this leaves a difficult problem for the staging of the end
of the play. Since Creon has now taken over the rule of the country, and since
he is now responsible for the children, it might be expected that he would
go with them into the background building, the royal palace of Thebes. But
this is surely out of the question: it would make terrible theatre for them to
go off the same way as Oedipus, whether in front of him or behind. So the
best that can be salvaged is for Creon to take them off by a side-road, presumably towards his own house. All this is, however, poorly indicated, which is
not at all the way that Sophocles usually manages significant stage-action. If
Sophocles had his original play end with Oedipus' departure into exile, in
the direction of Cithaeron, then Creon and the girls would simply have gone
into the palace: for the attractions and drawbacks of this radical solution, see
pp. 12–13.

1524–30 *Look at this, my fellow-Thebans . . . without disaster*: it is highly unusual
to have the chorus-leader address the rest of the chorus in this way, yet is
out of the question that the lines should be spoken by Oedipus himself (as
has sometimes been supposed). Most modern editors are agreed that these

closing lines are not by Sophocles, and that they have displaced his ending, which was probably in anapaests not trochaics. The two main arguments raised against them are: (i) that some of the lines are found in Euripides, suggesting that they somehow existed independently; and (ii) that the text is heavily corrupted—the translation given here requires at least two substantial emendations. At the same time, it has to be said that the lines are a good deal better (or less bad) than the preceding lines 1515–23. The sentiments are generally appropriate to the play, and are less trite than the closing lines of many other Greek tragedies. If they replace genuine Sophoclean lines, they may still have been based on them.

AIAS

1 [SD] *Odysseus comes on . . . watching*: the setting is usually described as Aias' "tent", but it is clear that the quarters where he (like the other Greek leaders) has been living for the last nine years are envisaged as more substantial than that.

There has been much dispute over how Athena was presented in this scene, mainly because of the phrase "even if you are invisible" in line 15. But if it once recognized that the point of that wording there is to emphasize how intimate Odysseus is in his relationship with the goddess, and not her visibility or invisibility, then it seems far the most likely staging is that she was simply on the ground close to him. It may still be, though, that Odysseus is supposed to be unable to see her. Or perhaps he does not even need to turn round in order to recognize her?

4 *at the fringes of the fleet*: this picks up an account of the layout of the Greek camp in the *Iliad* 11. The two most powerful heroes, Achilles and Aias, are allocated the end positions because those are the sectors which are most vulnerable to attack, and so need the strongest defenders. Those who know something of Troy and the entrance to the Dardanelles (Hellespont—see Map 3) would be aware that Achilles' famous tomb was at the western end of the shore, clearly implying that Aias was encamped at the eastern end.

17 *trumpet's brazen mouth*: the trumpet was for the Greeks primarily a battlefield instrument. It is the given epithet "Etruscan" here (its invention was often attributed to them), omitted in the translation.

19 *the famous shield*: Aias' huge and uniquely tower-like shield is prominent in the *Iliad*.

26 *all our captured flocks*: all the livestock that had been captured to provision the besieging army was evidently penned under some communal guard.

41 *Achilles' armour*: this is the first allusion to the competition mounted for possession of the god-made armour of Achilles after his death. This is taken as the already-known background to the play.

49 *the twin command*: the two Sons of Atreus, Agamemnon and Menelaus, are often spoken of a pair.

97 *all bloody*: I have adopted a conjecture that, by changing two letters, produces "bloodied your hand" rather than "armed your hand".

110 *I'll lash*: there is no sign that Sophocles had Aias bring the whip on in this scene. But at some stage in the performance history, probably during the fourth century BC, it became customary for Aias to appear here carrying one. The play even acquired the subtitle *"carrying a whip"*.

118–31 *You see, Odysseus . . .* : this key dialogue conveys vividly the unbridgeable divide between gods and humans. Set beside the immortals, humans, however great and powerful in their own microcosm, are puny and ephemeral. This may make Athena appear rather impersonal and sententious in human terms (and her words in 132–3 are scarcely the "moral" of the play), but the point is that the gods are not to be understood in human terms. Odysseus, by contrast, comes across as relatively magnanimous in his pity for Aias and his realization of the changeability of human fortune; although he makes it clear that this sympathy is not because he has any love for the man but because he feels his own vulnerability. At the same time Odysseus' insight here prepares for the importantly humane role he will play in the final scene of the play (see further p. 80).

133 [*SD*] *Athena and Odysseus . . . of the camp*: it is an interesting (but unanswerable) question whether Sophocles had Athena and Odysseus depart together, which would show Athena's closeness to the man, or separately, emphasizing the chasm between gods and humans that has opened up in the closing dialogue. Odysseus presumably departed towards the camp.

[*Choral Entry Recitative*]: for nearly forty lines (until line 171) the men deliver anapaests, a chanted metre, before they embark on the lyric part of their first contribution.

134–5 *son of Telamon . . . wave-surrounded Salamis*: the chorus immediately introduce two crucial names. Telemon, Aias' father, was an important old warrior, and he looms continually in the background of this play, as a figure of emulation and fear to both Aias and Teucros. Salamis is Aias' island, close to the coast of Attica (see Map 2). It is important in the play, both as the location of home and for its close relationship with Athens – see pp. 84–5 and note on 861.

172 *Artemis*: in their first lyric stanza the chorus search for an explanation for Aias' alleged strange behaviour; they suspect that a god has been acting out a grudge against him, but do not rightly guess which. Their first shot is Artemis, called "Tauropolos" (omitted in the translation). She was given this strange cult-title ('connected with bulls'?) in several sanctuaries.

179 *bronze Ares*: the Greek says "Enyalios with the bronze breastplate". Enyalios is often equated with Ares, but sometimes treated as a separate god.

189 *bastard brat / of low Sisyphus*: detractors of Odysseus liked to bring up to the allegation that his mother was already pregnant before she married Laertes of Ithaca. The rumour was that his real father was Sisyphus, king of Corinth, who was celebrated as the greatest trickster of all time.

201 [*SD*] *Tecmessa*: the chorus have called on Aias to respond, but it is his "war-wife" Tecmessa who comes to the door. The emotional tension is such that she chants in anapaests, rather than speaking iambics; the chorus also chant in reply at first, but then at 221 ff. become so upset that they sing. The relative calm of sustained speech is not reached until lines 263 ff.

202 *earthborn stock of Athens*: the high-style periphrasis used here says literally "from the race of the earth-born descendants of Erechtheus". Erechtheus was a founding king of the city, who was claimed to have no human parentage. People from Salamis were not, strictly speaking, Athenians, but in this play the distinction becomes blurred.

209 *night . . . daytime*: a couple of words must be missing from the text, but this reconstruction is probably along the right lines.

210 *child of Phrygian Teleutas*: Aias captured Tecmessa when fighting against the Phrygians, Trojan allies to the south, where Teleutas was presumably king. Aias evidently lives monogamously with her as his "concubine", and would

officially marry her if they ever were to get home to Salamis. There is some discussion later by Teucros about the status of such wives, at 1288 ff.

237 *two white rams*: if these two animals are to be equated with anyone in particular, they would seem to refer to Agamemnon and Odysseus.

245 ff. *Now it is high time . . .* : the chorus are so closely associated with Aias that they fear that they will share his punishment; and they foresee a danger of communal stoning. Their first priority is to get safely home from the war (see further note on 900).

301–4 *Then finally he darted . . . their insults*: it is strange but rather effective narrative technique to have Tecmessa give her inside perspective on the scene that we, the audience, have witnessed outside in the prologue. Thus, while she is baffled, we know that what she regards as an inexplicable "shadow" was in fact Athena. There was no indication of Aias' mad laughter during the prologue, and it is an interesting question whether he did (in Sophocles' production) laugh at the time, or whether this is a slightly inconsistent new twist to the narrative.

314 *and also asked . . . in this*: most editors reject this line as a dilute addition to the original Sophocles, but I do not consider the case for this is strong.

327 *as that is what . . . portend*: most editors reject this dragging line, with good reason in this case.

340 *Eurysaces*: this is the first allusion in the play to the son that Aias has with Tecmessa. He will later be brought on stage at 545 ff. (see note). On the hero-cult of Eurysaces at Athens, see p. 84.

342 *Teucros*: this is the first allusion to Aias' half-brother, who will have an important role to play later. It is conveyed without exposition that he is away attacking some neighbour or ally of Troy in order to acquire booty.

348–429 [SD] *Aias is revealed . . .* : this is clearly an occasion for the use of the stage-machinery known as the *ekkyklema*, the "roll-out" (see p. xix). The macabre scene that is revealed, of Aias sitting blood-spattered among the slaughtered animals, has been fully prepared for by Tecmessa's description.

In the heat of his distress Aias expresses himself in lyric. There are three pairs of stanzas interspersed with spoken—hence calmer—lines from Tecmessa and the chorus-leader. The first pair (348–55) is brief and simple; the second (356–93) is a more complex dialogue with Aias' lyric divided into three parts in each stanza (I have attributed all the spoken lines to Tecmessa, whereas most editions give some to the chorus). Finally, in 394–429, Aias has a longer lyric, almost an "aria", followed by a spoken couplet.

379 *hear*: this small emendation, made in the OCT, improves on the transmitted "always".

387–91 *Ancestor Zeus . . .* : Zeus was claimed to be the great-grandfather of Aias. I have tried in these lines (and at 380) to bring out the strange and virulent invective of Aias against Odysseus (to promote this I have omitted "and the twin-ruling kings" from lines 389–90 of the Greek).

395 *underworld*: the Greek has *Erebos*, another name, particularly associated with darkness, for the realm of Hades.

401–2 *The daughter of Zeus*: the chorus did not know which god had thwarted Aias, but he is well aware that it is Athena.

405–6 *So if . . . to dust*: the text is badly corrupted here, but this may give the gist of what it said.

412–13 *Tracks . . . by the brine*: I have taken these "tracks" to be on land rather than in the sea, in which case all of these three locations refer to the shoreline. This is where Aias will go to his death.

418–20 *Scamander's streams*: one of the two rivers which flow across the plain of Troy and into the sea at the mouth of the Dardanelles (see Map 3). It is "kindly to the Greeks" because it keeps them supplied with fresh water. This appreciation of the Trojan landscape is in keeping with the fine preceding lines—see further p. 79. (The OCT makes the false step of changing "kindly" to "unkindly".)

421–6 *no longer . . . come from Greece*: in making this boast he is guilty of some self-aggrandizement, since it was well known that Aias was the second-best in the Greek army, second only to Achilles, as is expressly said in the *Iliad* (and by Odysseus at 1341).

430–2 *Aiai . . . redoubled*: aiai is a common interjection of grief in Greek. Aias dwells on the way it fits his name to his sad state (the same name-play recurs at 904). This is far from a joke: the Greeks often took seriously such word-plays with names.

433 *and tripled . . . that I'm in*: this weakening line was surely added by an actor wanting to pile on the agony.

435–6 *prize for highest bravery*: this is an allusion to Telamon's winning Hesione, princess of Troy. She was the mother of Teucros—see further the note on 1302.

476 *a move . . . and now away*: the image may be of life as a board-game.

485–524 *Aias, my lord . . .* : the whole speech is pervaded by echoes of that which Andromache makes to Hector in *Iliad* 6 while they dandle their young son. In several ways the *Iliad* situation is very different—Hector is a much-loved leader, not a humiliated outsider—but there are two important links: Hector, like Aias, is doomed to an early death; and Andromache, like Tecmessa, is totally dependent on her strong-willed husband. The affinity is particularly close in lines 500–4, where demeaning words are put into the mouth of a future observer, gloating over the woman who has fallen from prosperity into drudgery.

545 *[SD] Eurysaces is led on by an attendant*: scenes involving children (usually not speaking parts) are not rare in Greek tragedy. It is likely, but not certain, that they were played by real children. It is not clear what age Eurysaces is supposed to be—perhaps between three and five, since he is neither a baby nor yet fully aware. "Lift him" in 545 suggests that he is actually lifted up and put on to the *ekkyklema* beside Aias.

555 *for being . . . ill*: this line, which seems to be an empty duplicate of 554, is omitted in all editions. But it is hard to see how it got added, and it might be the vestige of more serious textual disruption.

571 *until . . . the god below*: most editors insist that this line has been added to the Sophoclean original, but for no adequate reason that I can see.

573 *and not . . . ruined me*: text and sense unfortunately not clear.

574–6 *the armour that explains . . . Eurysaces* : the name means "broad shield". Since Aias' famous shield was enormous, it seems most unlikely that he literally handed it over on stage.

595 *[SD] Aias is shut inside . . . taken away*: it is unclear what Tecmessa should do. She is on-stage in the next scene (see 652), and yet it seems unlikely that she should go inside with Aias, not after this closing dialogue with his determination on suicide and his rejection of her pleas.

601 *under Ida*: the mountain range of Ida was closely associated with Troy. It is nine years now since the chorus knew the comfort of house and home.

627–31 *cry ailinon . . . piteous trill*: the lament of Procne, who was turned into the nightingale, crying for her dead son, was often cited as the poetic archetype of mourning in song. Some editors claim that the text contrasts the song of the nightingale with the screeching cries of Aias' mother, but the quotation of the lament-motif *ailinon, ailinon* would surely not be included in order to be *not* applicable.

645 *your high stock*: the Greek says "one of the descendants of Aeacus". Aeacus was the legendary father of Telemon, and son of the nymph of the island of Aegina. He is alluded to only here in this play, where Aias is connected with Salamis rather than Aegina.

646–92 *Long and incalculable time . . .* : the previous scene clearly raised the expectation that Aias was about to kill himself inside amid the carnage of the animals. So it is a dramatic surprise when he re-emerges, delivers a long and complex speech—the so-called 'deception speech'—and then sets off elsewhere by himself. The interpretation of this speech is one of the greatest challenges of Sophoclean criticism. For a brief discussion see pp. 80–1.

651–2 *but now . . . this woman here*: the awareness of Tecmessa's presence shows that this is not a totally self-absorbed soliloquy. The word in 651 translated as "edge" also means "mouth", an ambiguity hard to convey.

658 *this sword of mine*: the first time in the play that attention is drawn directly to this significant object—see further p. 78. Aias might, however, have been holding it already during the scene with the slaughtered animals at 359 ff., foreshadowing its later use. He goes on in the following lines to recall that it was a gift from Hector, a touch derived from their inconclusive duel in *Iliad* 7, which ended with the chivalrous exchange of gifts.

667 *to bow before the Sons of Atreus*: it is hard to see how this rather extravagant turn of phrase can be delivered without some sarcasm; the verb translated as "bow before" could even mean "revere".

670 *proper place*: the Greek word, which is *timai*, has a wide range of meanings circulating around the notion of "honour", "authority". This passage is remarkably like Ulysses' discourse on "degree" in Shakespeare's *Troilus and Cressida*.

695 *Arcadia*: the Greek specifies Cyllene, a mountain in Arcadia in the central Peloponnese, associated with Hermes, father of the wild god Pan.

699–70 *steps that you have found*: the dance-steps are specified as "Mysian and Cnossian", but the significance of these epithets remains uncertain.

720 *Mysia*: an area in northern Asia Minor, traditionally allied to Troy.

746 *Calchas*: the much-respected seer who accompanied the Greek expedition to Troy.

756 *this single day alone*: it might be objected that, to be strictly realistic, if Aias had stayed inside he would already have killed himself by now. The main point of this time-limitation on the danger to a single day seems to be to inject an extra, futile, urgency into the imminence of Aias' death.

805 *the bays . . . others to the east*: this east–west alignment of the camp and the shore, reiterated by the chorus when they return at 874–8, maps onto the actual topography of Troy: see Map 3 and p. 83.

812 *not if we want . . . hastening to death*: most editors believe that this line has been added, but the arguments seem to me far from conclusive.

814 [SD] *Exit Teucros' man . . .* : this clearing of the scene, with the chorus leaving the stage in mid-play, is extremely unusual technique for Greek tragedy. It clearly signals that something very extraordinary is about to happen: this turns out to be the solo suicide scene of Aias. It is also very unusual for the chorus to divide into two parts like this. This both creates a sense of urgency, and makes it clear that the empty stage marks a change of scene to the place where Aias has gone after his exit at 692: "along the shore to where the meadow washing-places are . . ." The change of scene may have been reinforced by some change of setting or of scene-painting; this is a subject we know little about. One obvious move would have been to fix the stage-building doors open to signify that they no longer represent a habitation.

815 [SD] *Aias enters . . .* : the staging of Aias' death and of the subsequent display of his body is a complicated problem and much disputed. Many scholars have insisted on observing the convention that the display of violent death in view of the audience is to be avoided in Greek tragedy. As a consequence they have to maintain that the sword, and hence Aias' fatal fall on to it, must have been out of sight, either behind a stage screen or inside the door of the stage-building. They also argue that, since the actor of Aias is needed to play other parts later in the play, his substitution could be more easily managed this way; but there are other solutions to this bit of stage-management (see note on 916), and such a small practicality should not dictate such an important piece of theatre.

   I maintain that, on the contrary, Sophocles has employed highly unconventional dramatic techniques here precisely in order that Aias can be seen falling on his sword in view of the audience (of course, some sort of illusion, such as a collapsible blade, would have to be devised). It seems to me essential that the sword itself, which is so repeatedly emphasized, should be fully visible to the audience (and indeed, this was already an emblematic fixture in earlier iconography). The sword would need, in that case, to be planted towards the back of the stage-area, near the door of the *skene*, because the body is first found by Tecmessa, who emerges from "this copse nearby" (892). Also, when the chorus first re-enter they do not see the body: if they were at the front of the acting-area this would be no problem to stage convincingly.

It is possible that the sword was already fixed in the ground "behind the scenes", and that it was somehow revealed by the removal of a screen or something of that sort. It would, however, make far stronger theatre if Aias fixed the weapon with his own hands, even though that requires a "dumb-show". Most scholars have advocated that he must have made his entrance from the *skene* door, which then will turn out to represent the "copse", in order to keep the "dumb-show" as brief as possible. I believe it is important, however, that Aias should enter from the side of the camp in order to convey his journey eastward along the shore. This would call, then, for some very unusual dramatic action: Aias enters, crosses the stage, and fixes the sword in the ground, all done in silence without any accompanying words of explanation. This would admittedly be highly exceptional stage-technique, but on any account Sophocles has done something very unconventional in changing the scene at this "hinge" in the middle of the play. The re-entry of Aias on to an empty scene is already so exceptional that the extended action without words is all part of this unique *coup-de-theatre*.

816 *if there is . . . calculate*: this rather pedestrian line is probably a later addition. The celebrated death speech appears to have been a favourite for expansion by actors: see also notes on 839–44, 855–8.

832 *Hermes*: Hermes, the *psychopompos*, was the god who escorted the spirits of the newly dead to the underworld.

837 *Erinyes*: the Erinyes (four syllables, something like "e-**reen**-you-ess") were primeval non-Olympian goddesses (often Englished as "Furies" through their Latin translation as *Furiae*). They were especially associated with cosmic order, punishment, and revenge (see also 1389–92). Their naming is often held up until towards the end of the sentence, as if there was some reluctance to utter these dangerous sounds.

839–44 *And may they . . . dearest offspring*: these four lines are rightly regarded by most editors as a later addition. As well as containing some awkward turns of phrase, they dilute the powerful invocation of the Erinyes by over-prolonging it.

846 *the whole damned army*: Aias curses them all because they have in effect supported the Sons of Atreus by not protesting against them. Achilles takes a similar stance in the *Iliad*.

855–8 *and yet I'll meet . . . more again*: editors are surely right to cut out these four lines as overblown padding contributed by an actor; they are repetitious, and contradict Aias' determination to be quick. Many also exclude line 854 ("Now, death . . . tend to me"), but this is not so obviously weak (contrast 855!).

861 *glorious Athens*: Aias lays special emphasis on the close connection between his ancestral home and Athens. For the island of Salamis, and the assimilation of Aias into the Athenian social fabric, see pp. 84–5.

879–973 *[Lyric Dialogue]*: this elaborate lyric dialogue structure, during which Tecmessa always speaks and the chorus mostly sings, is ordered in two long corresponding "stanzas": (a) 879–924 and (b) 925–73.

884 *Bosphorus*: given the setting of the play, this must refer to the Dardanelles (Hellespont), not the straits at present-day Istanbul. The mountain in the previous line is called "Olympus", and this must refer to a range near Troy, not the mountain of the gods in northern Greece.

890 *whose mind is mad*: most manuscripts have an archaic word which means "feeble", but I have preferred this alternative text.

900 *my journey home*: there is a poignant realism about the way that the chorus' first thought is for their own future. Because they are his dependants, Aias' death means disaster for them too—unless he can somehow be rehabilitated.

915–16 *I shall . . . this enfolding cloak*: this explicit covering of the dead man (already represented on an earlier vase-painting), and the subsequent uncovering by Teucros at 1003 ff., are further indications that the body was visible to the audience. I go along with those who surmise that, under cover of the cloak, the actor of Aias gets off (to play other parts), and is replaced by another man costumed to look as similar as possible.

956 *much-enduring*: this epithet (*polytlas*) is frequently used of Odysseus in the *Odyssey*, and is all that is needed to invoke him. While it is a word of praise in the epic, its use here implies ruthlessness.

966–73 *For me his death's . . . and of tears*: editors have found various problems in the expression of several of these eight lines (the OCT cuts 969, "Why . . . laughing over him?"). For myself, I have doubts about the authenticity of 971–3 ("So let Odysseus . . . and of tears"). The lines make a weaker ending to Tecmessa's last contribution than line 970, and they disrupt the symmetry between this speech and 915–24.

1013 *the bastard-son*: Teucros' mother was Hesione, a captured Trojan princess, as is more fully set out later at 1299 ff.

1019 *cast out from my land*: Teucros's lengthy anticipation of his father's hostile response on his return home (1008–20) culminates in his prediction that he will be expelled in exile. There was indeed a tradition that this is what eventually happened, and that Teucros went off and founded a city in Cyprus, a second Salamis.

1028–39 *Consider, by the gods . . . keep these*: the OCT (followed by Finglass) is firmly of the opinion that this entire twelve-line passage consists of later additions, and is none of it by Sophocles. But without some further closing lines after 1027 Teucros's speech as a whole would be over-dominated by the passage about Telemon; some lines are needed in order to bring full attention back to Aias and his fate. Apart from minor complaints about some expressions, the cutting editors maintain that the bombast of these lines is characteristic of later ham actors and not of Sophocles. Since this comes down to a matter of aesthetic taste, I feel, on the contrary, that there is some strikingly artful and unpredictable language here that cannot be plausibly attributed to anyone other than a highly practised poet. The padding which is characteristic of line-swelling actors is much more the kind of verbiage that is found in the last two lines (1038–9). The previous two lines (1036–7) are also pretty banal. I am, therefore, inclined to believe that the last four lines are not by Sophocles. In that case, Teucros' speech would have ended with the rather grand couplet about the Erinys and Hades (1034–5), a much stronger ending than line 1027.

1102 *king of Sparta*: this is the only time the great city of the Peloponnese, and authoritarian antithesis to Athens, is explicitly named in the play. Menelaus' discourse on the rule of fear (1173–86) might, however, be regarded as typically Spartan.

1105–6 *You sailed here . . .* : these two lines, which do not fit well in the argument, were probably interpolated.

1111–17 *It wasn't for . . . kind of man you are*: there are some incoherences in these seven lines, and some editors go so far as to cut them. But Teucros is expressing fierce anger, and there are good, authentic-sounding touches. Furthermore, his speech would be too short without them. The "oath" in 1113 alludes to a traditional story that all the suitors for the hand of Helen (including Aias) swore to stand by the successful one.

1020 *bow-and-arrow-man*: Teucros is already portrayed as an archer in the *Iliad*. The Greeks, who fought mainly with spear and sword, were often ambivalent about the use of bow and arrow.

1135 *the crooked vote*: the rights and wrongs of the vote over the arms of Achilles are never explored in the play.

1142–58 *One day I saw . . . the moral of my fable clear?*: Menelaus tells a kind of fable, and Teucros improvises one in return. Such moral tales, best known to us from Aesop, were familiar in Greek culture, but they were rather too "folksy" to occur much in tragedy. Once Menelaus has come down to this level, Teucros' response is rather closer to a description than a fable.

1163–7 *There is bound . . . mortals evermore*: these lines are delivered in the anapaestic metre, possibly chanted, marking the change in tone. They include two small but telling indicators of what is at stake in the issue of whether or not Aias is buried: the Iliadic resonance of the phrase "hollow grave-trench" (repeated at 1403), and the bearing of "memorial for mortals evermore" on future hero-cult are both discussed on pp. 83–4.

1171–81 *My boy, come here . . . and hold tight*: Teucros spends some time solemnly setting up a tableau with the boy and his mother sitting beside the corpse. This will be held still for more than 200 lines until the final procession at 1402 ff. It is explicitly given symbolic significance, since the corpse is assigned the kind of sacred power of protection that would be normally the property of a tomb or an altar. The language of ritual supplication is repeated three times in the four lines 1172–5. Also Teucros utters a solemn ritual curse (1175–9) on anyone who does not respect the power of asylum that the body supplies, praying they may be cut down as he cuts his hair. This reinforces the sense that the dead Aias will have more-than-human powers.

1184 *[SD] Exit Teucros . . .* : since it is the direction of the camp that threatens danger, Teucros must surely set off in the other, eastwards. This means that, when he returns at 1223, he must be supposed to have seen Agamemnon in the distance, across the stage-space, so to speak. It does not make theatrical sense for him to go in search of a suitable burial-place in the same direction as Menelaus' departure and Agamemnon's approach.

1220 *Sounion's headland*: the first mainland approached by anyone sailing to Athens across the Aegean from the east was (and is) the headland of Sounion, crowned with the celebrated temple of Poseidon (see Map 2). It was, therefore, the token "gateway" to Athens (and it is said that from there sailors could sometimes see the tip of the spear of the huge statue of Athena on the Acropolis, created in about 450 BC). Here, then, the Salaminian chorus in their despairing nostalgia reassert their close affiliation with Athens – see p. 84.

1273–9 *Can you really . . . reach the hulls?*: this exploit of Aias corresponds broadly, but not exactly, with the battle narrated towards the end of book 15 and beginning of book 16 of the *Iliad*. There, if Hector could manage to set fire to the ships, the Greeks would be deprived of their only means of escape; but Aias almost single-handedly manages to fend off the Trojan attack.

1283–7 *Another time . . . the helmet's bowl*: this account of single combat against Hector is also based broadly on an episode in the *Iliad*, this time in book 7. Several potential champions put lots into a helmet, and, when the helmet is shaken, the one selected is the man whose lot is the first to jump out. There is, however, no suggestion in Homer that anyone cheated by putting in a sticky clod of earth.

1291–7 *You must be well aware . . . by the hungry fish*: Teucros has plenty of invective material, since the saga of Agamemnon's family included no shortage of unsavoury elements. His grandfather, Pelops, father of Atreus and Thyestes, came from Asia Minor, and was sometimes denigrated for barbarian practices. Thyestes committed adultery with Aerope, his brother's wife, and in revenge Atreus served him the "Thyestean feast" of his own children cooked in a pie. Aerope was herself promiscuous even before marriage; her father condemned her to be drowned at sea, but she survived to be mother to Agamemnon and Menelaus.

1302 *the daughter of Laomedon*: Hesione was awarded to Telamon as a kind of trophy, a practice also found in the *Iliad*: it is by implication the case with Tecmessa also. The story alludes to the relatively little-known earlier expedition against Troy, led by Heracles.

1311–12 *your woman . . . your brother's*: there seems to be an innuendo here, implying that Agamemnon had had some dalliance with Helen. It is not, in that case, a familiar myth, and is pretty low invective.

1366 *works for himself*: the shallowness of Agamemnon is made especially clear by his inability to see that Odysseus is speaking about universal patterns of changeability in human life, and not merely out of self-interest.

1402 ff. *That's enough . . .*: the metre changes to anapaests, probably chanted rather than spoken, to mark a turn toward action, and to signal the imminent ending of the play. Teucros now organizes the funeral procession which will betoken the restitution of Aias' honour. He had gone off earlier (1184) to organize a burial place (note "hollow grave-trench" in 1403, as in 1165). This will been further along the shore, away from the main encampment; and the audience might well think of the famous tomb near Rhoeteum – see also pp. 83–4. Teucros gives a series of instructions in 1402–8. It is possible that members of the chorus carried these out, but it is more likely that there were extras available for this. Then the chorus could, as most appropriate, form part of the final, solemn procession.

1411–13 *livid fluid*: some have thought that this detail of still-flowing blood, which is not physiologically realistic, is somehow significant. But in context it seems to be nothing more than a reason for lifting the body carefully.

1416–17 *No one . . . I assert that*: these two lines are either so corrupted as to be beyond correction, or, more likely, they are incompetent additions.

1418–20 *After they've seen . . . can forecast*: many tragedies end with choral words of this sort, not specific to the particular play. They serve as a kind of frame, marking a move from the world of the play to the world of the audience. Scholars who have supposed that they are banal later additions have failed to appreciate their function.

The final procession means not only an honourable burial for Aias, it also stands for the future security of his dependants. Throughout the play there have been fears for the safety of Tecmessa, the boy, Teucros, and the chorus; their participation in this procession signifies their survival and a secure future. On the suggestion that they are in effect inaugurating a hero-cult, see pp. 83–4.

PHILOCTETES

1–3 *Lemnos isle*: Lemnos (in Greek the 'e' is a long vowel, and the 'o' short) is quite a large island with the best harbour in the northern Aegean, an important port on the trade-route between Greece and the Dardanelles (see Map 4). It featured in various myths (e.g. Jason and the Argonauts), and is alluded to as a supply-source in the *Iliad*. So it is inconceivable (to my mind) that Sophocles could, as is usually supposed, be asking his audience to think of the whole island as uninhabited. It is this remote "shore" that is an uninhabited part of the island. Since he is marooned there, and unable to move far because of his infirmity (see 41–2), the island as known by Philoctetes is, in effect, uninhabited.

4 *son of Achilles*: his father's name is placed before that of Neoptolemus himself; it will recur some twenty times in the play, an index of how this association with his father is crucial for his role.

4–5 *the man from Malis, son of Poias*: Philoctetes is not actually named here (not until 54); his homeland comes prominently first, and then his father Poias, a relatively minor hero. Malis and Trachis form the area around the gulf to the south of Thessaly (see Map 4), homeland of several Homeric heroes, including Achilles. The river Spercheius flows into the Aegean here, and the dominant mountain of the area is Oeta, the site of the funeral pyre of Heracles. These significant localities are "name-checked" at 490–2 and 724–9 (see notes).

6–19 *double-entrance cave*: this detail about two entrances is alluded to again, and it may have some special significance which is lost on us. The main point may simply be that, as explained, this makes for an unusually "commodious" cave, which stays ventilated in the heat, and has places to sit facing both east and west to catch the sun in winter. It seems unlikely that both entrances were made visible in the stage-setting. Similarly, while it is hard to say just what the actor of Neoptolemus did during the following lines, especially as we know so little about set construction and painting back at the time of Sophocles, I think it unlikely that the references to "higher" and "lower" were translated into actual stage movement, rather than left to the audience's imagination.

29 *footprints at the entrance*: the text accepted by most editors says "and there is no sound of a footstep". But this seems inappropriate to the context: what is called for is some evidence that he has found the right cave. A nineteenth-century scholar took out two letters to produce a reading which means "and there is the imprint of footsteps on the threshold". This makes such appropriate sense that I have accepted it.

68–9 *if that man's bow is not acquired*: the spiel that Odysseus' has spun for Neoptolemus is a characteristic mixture of falsehood and truth; most notably, the Greeks really did award him the unique armour of Achilles. There is an important uncertainty lurking in these two lines: is it only the bow that is needed, and is it Neoptolemus alone who will take the credit for the sack of Troy? See further p. 146.

72–3 *you were not bound by oath*: the leaders of the expedition had (except for

Achilles) taken an oath when they were suitors for Helen's hand. Odysseus tried to evade this, but was still made to go.

102   *persuasion*: Neoptolemus raises the third "option" after force and deceit. It will recur.

114   *as you have claimed*: Odysseus had evidently been economical with the truth when he got Neoptolemus to come along with him in the first place.

126–31   *and if I think . . . leaving things to you*: rather elaborate preparation for the so-called "false merchant scene", which is put into effect at 539–628. (I have some sympathy with editors who cut out line 128 as too laboured.)

134   *also Athena . . . keeps me safe*: it is very likely that this line is an addition to Sophocles, probably to make Odysseus' prayer seem a bit less unscrupulous. It is not only that Athena is given two distinct cult-titles together, and that one of these (Polias, "of the city") was specifically and irrelevantly Athenian, it is even more that the previous line makes such a strong and appropriate ending to the scene, implicating both Odysseus and Neoptolemus under the banner of Hermes, the god who is patron of trickery.

135–218   [*Choral Entry with Lyric Dialogue*]: instead of being purely choral, this entrance-song, consisting of three pairs of stanzas, is interspersed with responses from Neoptolemus in chanted anapaests. Similar dialogue structures, though unusual, are found in the entrance-songs of other plays (including *OC*). While this reduces the autonomous detachment of the chorus, it does, on the other hand, integrate them in the action and emphasizes their role as followers of Neoptolemus.

147   *comes back here*: the Greek includes the additional phrase "from [or "of"] these halls" which I have omitted as it does not seem to fit the context at all. It may be corrupt, or possibly added in a mistaken attempt to clarify.

176   *O gods*: I have here followed the widely accepted emendation of "humans" to "gods", but without feeling sure that this change is justified.

194   *Chryse's raw cruelty*: this is the first allusion in the play to the cause of Philoctetes' malady, which is, in fact, never fully explained—see also p. 145. It transpires that the sanctuary of the Nymph of the island Chryse was guarded by a snake, which had bitten Philoctetes. It is possible that the story was well known and taken for granted.

201–18   *Hush, keep quiet . . .* : throughout this last pair of stanzas Philoctetes' cries of pain get nearer and nearer. He is probably coming into sight for some time before he speaks at 219.

217–18   *maybe he hates . . . no boats*: rather obscure: maybe they think how bitterly Philoctetes must lament when for so long he has seen no ships by his shore.

219   [*SD*] *Philoctetes has been slowly . . .* : there has been much dispute over the staging of Philoctetes' entry here. Most scholars think that a sudden entry from the central door, i.e. the cave, would be most dramatic; and in support they cite the words in 211 (here translated as "not so far away, he sounds closer by'). I believe, however, that a long, slow, increasingly visible entry from the side-entrance would be far more effective. If so, this would be the one and only time that the "wild" path is used in the entire play. That direction stands

for Philoctetes' way of life on the island, while the other pulls towards the ship and departure.

220 *and from what land* : this is the text in all the important manuscripts. Because the same phrase is repeated two lines later, almost all editors accept a variant, "with your sailors' oars', which is found in some late manuscripts. I find the repeated question rather effective, however, in bringing out Philoctetes' anxiousness and loneliness.

225–30 [*SD*] *(silence)* . . . : there are occasions where the wording of tragedies clearly indicates a silence; and this is particularly frequent in this play. Here the silence betokens shock at Philoctetes' appearance, but also Neoptolemus' reluctance to embark on the planned deceit. There was probably also a silence at 225 (as indicated in my stage-direction), and it may be there should also be one after line 221 (i.e. after "no inhabitants").

239–41 *I am from Skyros . . . everything*: Neoptolemus' speech blurts out four short sentences, the first and third true, the second and fourth false (Philoctetes certainly does not know everything!) The island of Scyros is midway between Lemnos and Achilles' homeland in Thessaly (see Map 4). Achilles was sent there by his mother Thetis to keep him out of harm's way; while there, he married the mother of Neoptolemus, Deidameia, daughter of the king, Lycomedes (named in 243).

261–2 *this bow of Heracles*: Philoctetes identifies himself through the crucial bow before he even gives his own name. This is the first reference to the emblematic object, which he has been carrying ever since his entrance. I have taken the liberty of making a small change from the standard transmitted text, which says "the bow of Heracles" (*ton Herakleion . . . hoplon*), to the deictic word *tond(e)*, drawing direct attention to the bow, "*this* bow". Otherwise there would be no focus on it until 654 (see note on 668). It might be argued that this delay in its identification is effective; but, since it is referred to as "this bow" at 288, it is preferable to have Philoctetes hold up his special token at this point.

264 *lord of Ithaca*: the Greek text calls Odysseus "king of the Cephalonians", the people of the larger island next to Ithaca (cf. similar phrase at 791). The pair of generals are (as usual) Agamemnon and Menelaus.

304 *No people . . . voyages here*: some editors have felt that this line piles on the agony too far and have rejected it as an interpolation, possibly rightly.

314 *Odysseus*: here and in some other places Sophocles uses an old epic formula meaning literally "the strength of Odysseus". This suggests "strong Odysseus", but clearly praise is not implied here, and I can find no good way of reflecting this idiom.

321 *from the . . . Odysseus*: this repetition is so heavy-handed that we might well suspect that the line is added.

325 *Mycene . . . and Sparta too*: the powerful home cities of Agamemnon and Menelaus.

331 *Achilles' death*: although it is his own father's death he is "playing with", Neoptolemus cleverly speaks as though it is common knowledge. It was, but it is still news to Philoctetes.

334–5 *arrow of a god, Apollo*: the standard story was that Paris, with the help of Apollo, shot Achilles with an arrow in his vulnerable heel. This may be left vague here because it will be revealed later that Philoctetes will kill Paris (see 1426–7).

344 *Phoenix*: traditionally Achilles' "pedagogue", the male equivalent of a nurse. (It is possible that this line has been added to the Sophocles.)

355 *Sigeion*: the place at the southern entrance to the Dardanelles which was the site of Achilles' burial-mound – see Map 4.

363 ff. *But their response . . .* : up till this point there is nothing patently false in Neoptolemus' story. But in the matter of Achilles' armour Sophocles cleverly plays on the uncertainty of how much is true and how much fabricated: if Neoptolemus really had already been refused the privilege, as he narrates, it would surely be implausible that he should be helping Odysseus like this?

384 *bastard of the low*: an allusion to disparaging tales about Odysseus' legitimacy – see note on 417. At 64–6 Odysseus' explicitly gave Neoptolemus permission to be as abusive about him as he wished.

385–8 *And yet I don't . . . from their leaders*: the OCT is surely right to reject these four sententious lines as an addition. There is no good reason why Neoptolemus, who is in full flow with his abuse of Odysseus, should suddenly start letting him off the hook. In any case, Odysseus is one of "those in charge", and hardly needs any "teaching" from the less intelligent Sons of Atreus. The lines may well be transplanted from some other context.

391–402 *All-feeding Mother Earth . . .* : the extremely long spoken scene between Neoptolemus and Philoctetes, lasting all the way from 219 to 538, is given some variety by two emotional lyric outbursts from the chorus, first here and then in the corresponding stanza at 507–18. They seem to be so passionately caught up in Neoptolemus' story that they recall—or pretend to recall—the indignation they felt back at Troy. The chorus call on the Great Mother: this is Cybele, a special divinity in Asia Minor, and sometimes (as here) identified wirth Rhea, mother of Zeus.

394 *Pactolus*: the river runs through Lydia past the city of Sardis; it was famous for carrying gold-dust.

410–11 *the greater Aias*: the catalogue of the good old-type heroes who are now past and gone is inaugurated with Aias, who, as told in Sophocles' own play, killed himself at Troy. He is here called "the greater Aias" to distinguish him from another, less noble warrior of the same name; in the *Iliad* they are sometimes "the pair of Aiantes".

416–17 *Sisyphus . . . Laertes*: Odysseus is contemptuously called the son of Sisyphus, a king of Corinth and the master-trickster of Greek mythology. The allegation was that he had made Anticleia pregnant and then somehow got Laertes to pay handsomely for the privilege of marrying her. Diomedes, called here "the son of Tydeus", was not a disreputable hero, but he was often partnered with Odysseus in exploits at Troy.

425 *Antilochus*: in the *Iliad* Antilochus is a noble young warrior, close to Achilles.

In the minor epic *Aethiopis* it was told how he was killed by Memnon while rescuing his old father.

442 *Thersites*: in the *Iliad* Thersites is a loud-mouthed commoner who irritates both Odysseus and Achilles. In the *Aethiopis* he was higher-born, but still provoked Achilles so badly that he killed him. Again, it remains unclear whether Neoptolemus is telling the truth or lying.

452 *when I investigate divinity*: the transmitted text says "when I praise divinity". I do not see how this could make good sense, and I have accepted a slight emendation. Philoctetes' cogent denunciation of the morality of the gods is left unanswered here. To some extent it is met by the final dispensation of Heracles, especially in 1418–22.

453 *Oeta*: this is the first time that Mt Oeta, Philoctetes' home territory, is named in the play (see Map 4). It will gather more significance, and its connection with the pyre of Heracles becomes a key motif.

480 *one whole day*: this is an optimistic calculation of the voyage time from Lemnos to Skyros, without even adding the second stage to Malis (see Map 4).

486 [*SD*] *Philoctetes kneels*: the usual ritual for a suppliant to another human was to kneel and grasp them by the knees and/or beard. This is physically difficult for the lame Philoctetes, as he says. It may well be that he stays on his knees until Neoptolemus agrees at 526 ff.

489 *Chalcedon's . . . Euboea*: presumably this kingdom was in the north of Euboea (see Map 4), and so a better stage en route to Oeta than Scyros would be. For the place-names registered in 490–2 see note on 5.

504–6 *A person needs . . . off his guard*: the previous lines have expressed a general sentiment about the changeability of human life, and this further moralizing is excessive for this emotional context. I think that recent editors are probably right to reject the lines as a part-swelling addition.

507–18 *Take pity on him . . . resentment from above*: this is the corresponding stanza to 391–402—see the note there. Once again the chorus so passionately support Neoptolemus' deceit that they might almost be sincere. It is notable that they call again on religious sanction in support of Philoctetes: by respecting the Zeus-supported suppliant and taking him home they should avoid divine resentment (the Greek word for "resentment" is *nemesis*). The implication is that if they do not take him home they may offend the gods. And yet Neoptolemus' real mission is to take him to Troy.

542 ff. [*SD*] *Enter attendant disguised . . .*: the "false merchant" scene. The arrival of the assistant disguised as a merchant skipper was elaborately prepared for by Odysseus at 126–31, where he also paves the way for the improvised role-playing that this will need. It is ironic that he arrives just as Neoptolemus is doing so well with his deceit. But the scene does still serve to cement the bond between him and Philoctetes yet more firmly, and to inject a new sense of urgency.

549 *Peparethos*: modern Skopelos; so a route from Troy via Lemnos is perfectly plausible.

562 *Phoenix and the sons of Theseus*: for Phoenix see note on 344; the sons of

Theseus seem to be arbitrary nominations, except possibly for an Athenian connection.

603–21 *Well, since you may not . . . get a move on quick*: the "merchant" says at the beginning and end of his speech that he is telling "everything". But he is not, of course; and—characteristically for this play—it is impossible to disentangle what is true and what false. The Trojan seer Helenus and his prophecies about the fall of Troy were a well-known story, but within this play it remains unknown, at this stage at least, whether he specified that Philoctetes was needed as well as the bow; whether he said "by power of persuasive words" (612); and whether Odysseus promised "against his will", if necessary. Helenus' prophesies are more seriously restated by Neoptolemus towards the end of the play at 1332 ff. See also p. 146.

607 *That man . . . reputation*: this over-the-top line may be an addition.

619 *cut off his head . . . succeed*: it is a nice touch that the unusual oath "cut off my head if not . . ." is used twice by Odysseus in Homer.

624–5 *like . . . Sisyphus*: Sisyphus (see note on 417) was said to have somehow tricked his way out of the underworld for a prolongation of his life.

637–8 *Come on then . . . once the work is done*: there has been no talk of exhaustion, and editors who think this couplet was added might be right.

660–1 *I long for that . . . then let it be*: the reply is rather abruptly phrased, either because Neoptolemus is so sincerely reverend, or because he is guiltily inarticulate—a nice critical divergence! The latter interpretation would be confirmed if it is Philoctetes, and not Neoptolemus, who speaks 671–4—see below.

668 *to give it back again*: this passing phrase foreshadows the events later at 924 ff., when Neoptolemus refuses to return the bow. Some have claimed that the bow is at this juncture briefly handed over and returned, but there is not enough indication in the wording for such a momentous event. Contrast 763–78, which clearly mark the crucial actions that are lightly prepared for here. These lines are, indeed, referred to as a "request" at 764.

670 *It was by . . . first came by it*: the bow was first introduced as "the bow of Heracles" at 262; but this is the first allusion to how it came to be passed on to Philoctetes. The story, as will be elaborated later (see 801–3), was that he was the one who agreed to light the pyre on Mt Oeta, even though Heracles was still alive, thus saving him from unending agony.

671–5 *I am so pleased . . . stand firm by my side*: I have accepted the usual division of these last five lines of the scene between the two of them, but this allocation is far from certain. If it were not for the apparent dialogue in the (textually uncertain) line 674 ("'Now go in.' 'And I shall take you in as well.'"), it might have made better sense for Philoctetes to continue after line 670 and thus speak all of 662–75. That would mean that Neoptolemus would remain awkwardly silent for all of the rest of the scene after his rather stammering words in 660–1. (There is a light word-play in 673, impossible to translate, between the name of Philoctetes and the words for "possession" (*ktematos*) and "friend" (*philos*).

676–85 *I've heard . . . so full of tears*: in this first stanza of the song the chorus try to think of someone who has suffered as grimly as Philoctetes. They hit upon the story of Ixion, who, as a punishment for attempting to rape Hera, even after Zeus had granted him a favour, was bound in the underworld to a perpetually turning wheel. They go on to recognize, however, that the treatment of Philoctetes is even worse, because he had led a morally unobjectionable life, and was guilty of no ingratitude or unjust offence. (This and the corresponding second stanza are full of textual problems, but their gist is clear.)

719–29 *Now by meeting . . . above Mount Oeta*: this fourth stanza is generally regarded as highly problematic, because the chorus seem to endorsing the deceit—that Philoctetes is about to be taken home—when there is no point in doing so because he is off-stage and inside the cave. Some scholars have even claimed that Philoctetes and Neoptolemus must have silently come back on stage after the third stanza: but this would be totally unlike the open dramaturgy of Greek tragedy. There may, I suggest, be a way out of this problem implicit in the phrase (722–3) "after many months of waiting". This is usually taken to refer simply to the long time Philoctetes has been away from home. But that has been years not months; and, since the chorus are interpreting the situation in the rosiest possible light for Philoctetes, it makes sense for this phrase to anticipate that he will eventually get home, even if only after the months that it will take to conquer Troy.

   In 724–9 Philoctetes' homeland is again evoked through place-names (see note on 5): the region (Malis), river (Spercheius), and mountain (Oeta). This time, however, Oeta is glorified in somewhat enigmatic terms as the site of Heracles' pyre: he ("the man with the bronze shield" in the Greek) was placed on the pyre, and, as he burned, was supernaturally fetched to join the gods on Olympus. The "nymphs of Malis" may suggest a story that the pyre was extinguished with water poured by the nymphs, and this water eventually re-emerged, still hot, as the sulphurous mineral springs at Thermopylae, another important landmark of this area.

730–820 [*SD*] *Philoctetes is in pain*: during ninety lines Philoctetes is in excruciating pain. The Greek text quite often spells out his cries of agony, sometimes containing them within the spoken metre, sometimes not. It is, however, quite possible that Sophocles meant these to be indications of even more and longer cries. I have not thought it helpful to transliterate the Greek interjections, and have indicated cries by stage-directions only where they are included or clearly indicated in the Greek text.

749 *do not hold back*: the transmitted text says "do not spare my life". But Philoctetes is begging for his ulcered limb to be cut off, not to be killed, so I have adopted a small emendation which means "do not spare any force".

776 *pray to keep resentment off*: at the very moment that the bow changes hands Philoctetes plants the notion that it is somehow dangerous for its possessor, that it might attract jealousy or resentment (the Greek word is *phthonos*). This might even come from the gods, because the supernatural weapon has more power than human goods should properly have. He and Heracles can both witness to this danger.

794 *you . . . instead of me*: this line looks very like a badly worded expansion, as the OCT and other editors have concluded.

800 *famous fire of Lemnos*: Lemnos is a volcanic island, and one of the active vents, possibly Mt Moschylus (now submerged?), was known as the "Lemnian Fire", which figured in both myth and ritual. Philoctetes must gesture towards this as he draws the parallel with the way that he set light to Heracles' pyre on Oeta (see notes on 670 and 724–9).

814–17 *Now take me there . . . touch will murder me*: strangely enigmatic and frantically broken-up lines. Where does Philoctetes want to be taken? Why does Neoptolemus refuse, at least until Philoctetes seems less delirious? Some have suggested that he wants to go to his cave, and some that he wants to throw himself off the rocks, but neither of those impulses would particularly fit the context. The most usual suggestion is that that he has a vision of flying up to the sky in death: but the Greeks generally thought of death as being a downward direction. If there is a specific reference at all, I suspect that that he is supposed to be looking up towards the volcano of Lemnos (see note on 800). In a brief fit he seems to think that he can somehow "fly" there, if only Neoptolemus' hand were not restraining him.

827–64 *Come . . . most powerful*: this choral song, which consists of one pair of stanzas and a free-standing third (epode), involves at least two very unusual dramatic techniques which contribute to its strangeness. First, instead of the conventional exit of a character before it and an entry after it, Philoctetes makes an "exit" and "re-entry" out of and back into consciousness. This means that it forms a continuation of the scene rather than a division between scenes. Secondly, there is a spoken (or chanted) intervention from Neoptolemus after the first stanza—see further note on 839–42.

827–38 *Come, Sleep . . .* : the song begins with a soothing invocation of sleep that may well draw on traditional lullaby, while also echoing the genre of paean. Then there is an abrupt change at 832 ("Think, son . . ."), as the chorus turn to Neoptolemus and urge him to take advantage of this opportunity. While the lullaby is more likely to be taken as calculating rather than sentimental, this is nonetheless a very sudden and rather shocking change of tone.

835 *Look, he is deeply asleep*: the transmitted text says "you see now". While this makes reasonable sense, the emendation is so attractive that I have incorporated it.

839–42 *His ears hear nothing . . . patched with lies*: Neoptolemus responds with four lines in which he rejects the chorus' urgent advice. But instead of these being in the usual spoken iambic metre they are in dactylic hexameters. These are, in fact, the only unmixed speech in this metre in the whole of surviving tragedy; and, whether they were spoken or chanted, this gives them a very different tone. The two main associations of the hexameter are epic (like Homer) and oracles, and it is primarily the oracular that is tapped into here. The impression is given that Neoptolemus is having some kind of "revelation", and newly sees the truth that the bow without the man is no good. "A god" said as much, he claims—possibly an oblique reference to Helenus? The chorus still respond, however, with a less scrupulous attitude.

849–54 *That thing . . . insoluble strains*: there are unfortunately several unsolved textual problems in these lines, so their sense remains pretty uncertain.

859 *forgetful*: a corrupt word here (*alees*) is usually emended to *adees*, meaning "without fear". But *adaes*, "forgetful" (the word also comes in the first line of the song at 827) makes even better sense.

895 *Ah, ah! What am I going to do? What next?*: the line begins with the interjection *papai*, a sound of pain which occurs several times during Philoctetes' agony in the previous scene. This suggest an affinity between the physical and mental pain. Neoptolemus' distress at betraying Philoctetes' trust, brought to a head by the physical contact, has reached the crisis, so that he does not know which way to turn, neither in his movements nor his words.

931–3 *By capturing . . . my bow, my life*: these lines exploit an ambiguity of the Greek word *bios*, which, with a slight difference of pronunciation, means both "life" and "bow". Philoctetes exploits this to make clear how essential the bow is to his whole existence. The word-play recurs at line 1282.

961–2 *To hell then . . . die in agony*: line 960 would make a strong ending to this powerful speech. These last two lines, with their rather laboured "no, not yet . . .", might possibly be a later addition by an actor wanting to keep the spotlight on himself for longer.

974 [*SD*] *Neoptolemus begins . . . behind Philoctetes*: the abruptness of Odysseus' intervention, just in the nick of time to stop the bow from being handed over, is emphasized by the extremely unusual device of his entering in the middle of a line (in the Greek). While the exact staging is bound to remain uncertain, it seems clear that at first Philoctetes cannot see Odysseus, perhaps because of the difficulty of his turning round; but he can still immediately recognize that hated voice after all these years.

987 *fire created by Hephaestus*: the god Hephaestus was connected with volcanic places like Lemnos. It was here that he landed when thrown off Olympus, as recalled in *Iliad* 1.

1000–2 *I'll throw myself . . .* : there is no way of knowing whether this suicidal threat was in any way conveyed by use of the stage space.

1011–12 *But now . . . my sufferings*: is Philoctetes referring back to Neoptolemus' crisis of conscience at 965 ff., before Odysseus intervened? Or does he mean that Neoptolemus is displaying silent signs of his regrets at this stage? Perhaps both.

1025 *a trick and force*: there were stories of how Odysseus tried to evade recruitment for the Trojan expedition but was tricked into compliance.

1034 *since that . . . me ashore*: the OCT regards this line as an interpolated addition, but for no good enough reason that I can see.

1057 *we have Teucros*: the half-brother of Aias, was celebrated in epic for his bowmanship (and taunted for it at *Aias* 1022). Odysseus' skill with the bow is, of course, crucial in the *Odyssey*.

1080 [*SD*] *Odysseus and Neoptolemus . . . depart together*: it is one of the greatest questions in the interpretation of this play whether this departure, leaving Philoctetes behind to rot on Lemnos, is supposed to be genuine or a bluff. See also the discussion on pp. 142–3. If it is a pretence, to play for time while some other way is contrived to lure Philoctetes, then Odysseus' sudden concession at 1053 ff. is false—that is easy to believe. And so too—less easy to believe—would be Neoptolemus' complicity with him in the final speech of the scene (1074–80). In favour of the belief that they genuinely intend to leave him, in the hope that the bow will be enough, and despite earlier indications to the contrary, it is notable that Neoptolemus does not address Philoctetes directly in that final speech. This mask of impersonality may indicate a suppressed discomfort. The great objection to regarding the desertion as a bluff is that, if the audience is made fully aware of this, it would bleed all the emotional power out of Philoctetes' lyrics in the following highly crafted and emotional scene.

1081 ff. [*Lyric Dialogue*]: in earlier tragedy there would have been a purely choral ode at this juncture, between the two "acts". In keeping with the way that later Sophocles diminishes the detachment of the chorus, while at the same time increasing its integration, there is here instead an exceptionally long lyric dialogue. The first two pairs of stanzas are dominated by Philoctetes, with tail-pieces sung by the chorus. In these Philoctetes descants in an almost delirious way on the obsessive motifs of his fate: his slow death in his cave; the reciprocity of his past food feeding on him; the degradation of his bow; the villainy of Odysseus. There is then a long, more quick-fire dialogue with no stanza structure, lasting all the way from 1169 to 1217.

1135 *man of many / devices* Philoctetes does not even need to name Odysseus during these invectives; the epithet here, *polymechanos*, is one of the standard terms beginning 'many-' (*poly-*) that are used of him in Homer.

1143–5 *That person . . . defended*: text and sense are unsure, but it seems that "that person" refers to Odysseus. Philoctetes pays no attention to the chorus' attempt to defend his hated enemy.

1181–3 *I call on . . . don't abuse*: it seems that Philoctetes calls so frantically on "Zeus of curses" that it alarms the chorus. He goes on to make a sort of apology in 1193–5.

1217 [*SD*] *Philoctetes goes into the cave*: on this as a possible, if dark, ending, see p. 147.

1218–21 *I would have long ago . . . towards us*: it is highly unlikely that these lines go back to Sophocles. There is no one on stage for them to be addressed to, and they are expressed in clumsy Greek. The transition between the exit of Philoctetes and the re-entry of Odysseus and Neoptolemus is exceptionally abrupt, and it looks as though some later performer wanted to buffer it with some lines of "filler".

1222 ff. *I'd be obliged . . .* : the wording of the opening speeches is made to suggest that this dialogue has already begun before they enter. This helps to convey what is an extremely daring and unusual occurrence in Greek tragedy: a major decision taken off-stage, unwitnessed by the audience.

1251–2 *I do not dread . . . threat of force.>*: it looks probable that a line spoken by Odysseus has dropped out of our transmitted text. The line given him here is a reconstruction of the kind of thing he is likely to have said.

1293 [*SD*] *Odysseus comes out . . . bow changes hands*: Neoptolemus stretches out his hand to return the bow, as he had done earlier at 974 (see note). But there he hesitated and Odysseus successfully intervened. This time he goes through with the action, and so Odysseus' attempt to stop him is in vain. For the staging of the ambush, it is notable that, as at 976–7, Philoctetes recognizes Odysseus by his voice even before he makes himself visible to him.

1327 *the guard of Chryse*: see note on 194.

1333 *Asclepius' sons*: the two sons of the semi-divine physician are warriors and healers in the *Iliad*.

1338 *Helenus*: the duplicitous "merchant" had already deployed his prophesies at 604 ff. Neoptolemus speaks with far more integrity, of course, but it remains necessarily impossible to sort out a definitive version of exactly what Helenus said—see also p. 146.

1365 *rating . . . your father's arms*: editors are agreed that this bit of story-filling was added and damagingly holds up the flow of Philoctetes' speech. Without this addition Philoctetes is referring back to the events as told by Neoptolemus at 360 ff.—an account of dubious truth, though never contradicted.

1367 *as you have promised me*: Philoctetes reiterates at 1398–9 this claim that Neoptolemus had sworn on oath that he would take him home. He had, in fact, never done so, but he did swear that he would stay with him (810 ff.). It seems that he accepts that he has, in moral effect, made this promise.

1395 *The time has come*: the transmitted text would mean "It is easiest . . .", this emendation makes stronger sense.

1402–8 *If you're certain . . .* : the metre changes from the usual iambics to more agitated trochaics, which indicate the initiation of movement. They are in long lines (in the Greek), each split between the two speakers.

1407–8 *Very well . . . this island*: unfortunately the text of these closing lines of the trochaic dialogue is seriously corrupted (but it is unlikely that there is interpolation as supposed by the OCT).

1409 [SD] *the vision of Heracles appears above them*: Heracles' epiphany is very sudden, and it is debatable whether he "flew" on with the crane-type machine (the *mechane* – see pp. xix–xx), or whether he simply stepped out onto the roof of the stage-building.

1409 ff. [*Scene 9*]: Heracles' first lines (1409–17) are in anapaests, possibly chanted; this metre often marks the move towards the end of a play. He then changes into standard spoken iambics at 1418, before the metre finally reverts to anapaests at 1445 ff. On this juncture as a fully fledged possible ending, see pp. 147–8.

1420 *immortal status*: there were conflicting accounts of what happened to Heracles after his death. While some said that he went as a mortal to Hades, it was by this time widely accepted that from his pyre on Oeta he was raised to immortality on Olympus (as celebrated by the chorus at lines 727–9). His supernatural epiphany here visibly confirms his apotheosis.

1426 *taking life away from Paris*: this particular achievement of Philoctetes at Troy has not been prophesied until this moment.

1432 *my pyre-mound*: throughout Classical times there was an annual festival at the huge mound of ashes which marked the site of the pyre of Heracles, and further offerings were added. It has been excavated not far from the modern village of Pavliani, at a height of 1800 m (see Map 4).

1437 *Asclepius*: Helenus had prophesied that the sons of Asclepius would heal Philoctetes (see 1333); but Heracles "trumps" that with the semi-divine father himself.

1439 *a second time*: this refers back to the less celebrated earlier expedition against Troy and its king, Laomedon, led by Heracles.

1440–1 *respect the province of the gods*: this closing advice to avoid sacrilege when sacking Troy is bound to bring to mind the notorious act of Neoptolemus: he slaughtered old King Priam, even though he had taken refuge at the altar of Zeus. Eventually he will be killed at Delphi as a punishment by Apollo. So, while Heracles brings a promise of glory and safe return home for Philoctetes, he lightly but unmistakably casts a shadow over the future of Neoptolemus. See further p. 144.

1443–4 *that's Zeus. . . . it's indestructible*: this couplet is so lame that it is hard to attribute it to Sophocles. It is impiety, not piety, that Heracles has been talking about, and all that this addition does is to weaken the telling allusion to Neoptolemus' ambivalent future.

1459 *Mount Hermaion*: probably the north-east cape of Lemnos.

1461 *Lycian well-head*: this spring, which might have been associated with Apollo Lycius, is not otherwise known. All the watery places alluded to in these lines are not inconsistent with Philoctetes' own poor sources of drink, if it is supposed that he knows about the rest of the island even though he has no way of ever reaching it himself.

1471 *back to home*: the Greek word *nostos* ("return home") in the last line of the play surely refers not to a safe return to Troy, as it has usually been taken, but back to Greece. The chorus have been sensitive to Philoctetes' longing to see his homeland and his old father again. And for themselves (like the chorus of *Aias*), it is the return home after the war that matters most.

OEDIPUS AT COLONUS

14–15 *quite far away*: Colonus was actually less than 2 km from Athens (see Map 2). The structures most visible from there would be those up on the Acropolis. There may have been some scene-painting—see p. xix.

16–18 *clearly sacred*: while the most obvious sign of a sacred place would be a temple, a flourishing yet uncultivated grove might also indicate a place set apart for divinities.

19 *unchiselled ledge of rock*: this "seat", presumably represented by a painted stage-prop, carries significance: it is a kind of landmark step on Oedipus' journey in between the human and the sacred.

42 *Eumenides . . . goddesses benign*: the cult-title here at Colonus was the euphemistic "Eumenides" (Benign Ones). (The third play of Aeschylus' *Oresteia* trilogy was also known by this title, but the word does not actually occur in our text of the tragedy.) They are equated with, or are at least closely associated with, the group of divinities most commonly known as "Erinyes" (cf. note on *Aias* 837), fearsome underworld goddesses of cosmic order, revenge, and punishment. That was, however, a name that people did not say lightly, and they were spoken of by several other, less sinister titles, including *Semnai* (Solemn Ones) and *Potniai* (Queenly Ones), as well as Eumenides.

46 *password of my destiny*: Oedipus will recount at 84 ff. how Apollo had prophesied that he would reach his final resting-place when he came to a sanctuary of goddesses such as these. So he recognizes their naming as a kind of "key", although enigmatic at this stage.

55–6 *Poseidon . . . Titan-god*: Poseidon was an important deity at Athens (see the song at 708 ff.); his nearby altar figures later in the play. Prometheus was a rebel Titan, not an Olympian: he was represented as holding a flare, the gift of fire that he gave humans. An annual torch-relay took this statue as its starting-point.

56–7 *bronze-stepped threshold* : evidently there was nearby a fissure in the earth which was believed to be one of the entries to the underworld. This place will figure again at lines 1590–1, when Oedipus is going to his death.

58–61 *this horse-rider Colonus*: Colonus was not a pan-Hellenic god, but a hero in the cultic sense (see p. 212), unique to this place. To judge from the deictic "this", it looks quite likely that a statue of him on horseback was actually represented on-stage; but possibly it was to be imagined as close by. Lines 62–3 offer a kind of "apology" for the relative obscurity of this figure and his story, but it is touchingly put in terms of local pride.

66–9 *The ruling power*: there is a monarchy, as usual in tragedy, not a democracy, even at Athens. It emerges, however, that some authority lies with the local elders.

89–90 *Solemn Goddesses*: Oedipus implies that this was the "password" that had been used by Apollo's oracle. This was one of the titles by which the Erinyes were known: see note on 42 above.

100 *no wine*: the Erinyes were never made offerings of wine; the austerity of Oedipus' life supplies an affinity with this.

116 [*SD*] *Antigone helps Oedipus hide* . . . : it is likely that the background skene building, with its doors left open, was taken to represent the sacred grove. In that case Oedipus and Antigone would move and hide just inside the doorway.

117–236 [*Choral Entrance-song, with Lyric Dialogue*]: this long first song, also known as the "parodos", starts with choral lyric, but soon becomes a lyric dialogue between the chorus and Oedipus (and occasionally Antigone). This means that the chorus does not really establish itself in the usual way before it becomes engaged with the action. With Oedipus' interruption at 138 the metre changes from sung lyric to chanted anapaests; and then returns to the matching stanza of lyric at 150 ff. Then at 207–36 the lyric dialogue, which includes many short-line exchanges, becomes "free-form", without any ordering into stanzas.

176–202 [*SD*] *During the following lyric* . . . : there is a slow and long-drawn-out stage movement during the course of this pair of stanzas. Oedipus moves laboriously from the entrance of the sacred grove to a seat in the "secular" world; and with this he moves from a kind of sanctuary into the ambit of social interaction, and of having to face questions.

183–4 [. . .]: because this stanza should be metrically matching with that at 192–206 there must have been around here some lines of sung dialogue between Oedipus and Antigone that are now missing. But their exact place in the exchange is not certain.

220 *son of Laius*: the notorious name of his father, Laius (three syllables), is enough to enable the chorus to identify Oedipus. The family was also often alluded to also by the name of Laius' father, Labdacus.

226 ff. *Go away. Leave my country!* . . . : as soon as the chorus realize Oedipus' identity they go back on the undertaking they made at 176–7, that no one would remove him against his will from this place of refuge. They go on to plead that they were deceived in the first place, and that this justifies their repudiation because, they imply, the presence of Oedipus would bring pollution on Colonus and Athens.

237–53 *Strangers, men of respect . . . break free*: the long lyric sequence is brought to a close by an unusual kind of "aria" sung by Antigone. It is full of tender pathos, and the young woman succeeds in restraining the first violent response of the chorus to her father's identity.

260–2 *Why bother . . . the persecuted stranger*: it was a conventional praise of Athens that she went to exceptional lengths to protect foreign suppliants. This is, indeed, sometimes exemplified in tragedy, e.g. Euripides' *Suppliants*.

278–9 *Don't grant the gods . . . benighted*. Text uncertain and disputed.

312–14 *pony . . . hat*: the specifications of horse and headgear are there simply to add convincing detail. Similarly, it is explained at 334 that she has one faithful attendant to protect her on her travels. Her travelling like this has called for bravery.

330 *kindred sisters*: there may be a hint of the incestuous kinship here.

337–41 *the way they do in Egypt*: this reversal of gender roles evidently featured in the Greek popular anthropology of Egypt. The account here is so close to that in Herodotus (2.35) that direct influence from the historian/ethnographer is quite likely.

367 *leave the throne for Creon*: I have adopted the most plausible emendation of a disputed text. Creon, first named here, seems to be regarded, as in *OT*, as the sensible older relation, by marriage, not by blood. But later in the play he will turn out to be a nasty piece of work.

371–2 *god . . . minds*: the way that the two brothers' fatal conflict is "doubly motivated" (see p. 7), both by a higher power and by their own flawed thinking, is made particularly explicit here.

374–6 *elder brother, Polynices*: in *OC* it is insisted that Polynices is older than Eteocles (see also 1292–8). In other versions it is the other way round; they agree to rule alternately, but Polynices reneges and goes off to recruit foreign support to invade Thebes. In both Aeschylus' *Seven against Thebes* and Sophocles' own *Antigone* Eteocles is regarded as the "good" brother, while in this play it is Polynices' case that is treated with relative sympathy—see further pp. 215–6.

381 *smoking to the sky*: the text and interpretation of this line is disputed.

411 *beside your tomb*: the danger that Oedipus' tomb threatens against the Thebans is vague at this stage. Oedipus will later spell it out more fully (see note on 607 ff.).

420 *bring this message*: this is an emendation of the transmitted text, which says "hear this message".

433–40 *Back on that day . . . by force*: this account of the past events recurs with variations in the play (see also 765–71 and 1354–64). This insistence on Oedipus not going into immediate exile fits with the final scenes of *OT* as we have them. Some scholars believe, however, that *OT* has been tampered with precisely to reconcile it with this account in the later play. See further p. 12 and note on *OT* 1515–23.

460 *this country's enemies*: this is an emendation of the transmitted text, which says "my enemies".

486 *name them 'Benign'*: for the Eumenides and their titles see note on 42.

510–48 *[Lyric Dialogue]*: at this juncture there would conventionally have been a fully choral song, in some way stepping back from the mainstream of the play. Here there is, instead, this highly charged, rapid lyric dialogue of two pairs of stanzas in which the chorus relentlessly interrogate Oedipus on his past story. So, while dividing two scenes, those of Ismene and of Theseus, this song is also part of the continuum of the plot.

521 ff. *Bad things I have endured . . .* : this exchange directly introduces an important motif (already raised in 240): Oedipus pleads (in contrast with *OT*) that he is not guilty, because his acts of parricide and incest were not deliberate. See also note on 960 ff.

521–2 *excessively*: the transmitted text has Oedipus say "I have endured against my will", but this must be corrupt, if only for metrical reasons, and I have adopted this emendation.

539–41 *I received . . . never won*: the text is uncertain, but it makes good sense for

Oedipus to reiterate that he did not choose Iocasta as his wife: she was the reward given him by Thebes for ridding them of the Sphinx.

547–8 *He tried . . . innocence*: the text here is most uncertain. I have followed the heavily emended solution favoured by Jebb (better than that in the OCT). Fortunately the important claim, "pure before the law . . . innocence", is not in dispute: Oedipus claims that in legal terms he is not guilty of murder.

554 *look at you*: this is an emendation of the transmitted "hearing you".

562–4 *I have in mind . . . as any man*: Theseus makes the most of the rather tenuous similarities in their life-stories. Although his father Aegeus was king of Athens, Theseus was brought up in Trozen, like (and unlike) the way Oedipus was brought up in Corinth. And he had a series of heroic adventures as he made his way to Athens and on his arrival there, like (and unlike) the way that Oedipus had adventures on his way between Corinth and Thebes.

607–28 *My dearest son of Aegeus* . . . : Oedipus' speech here unveils a scope and power that have been no more than glimpsed in the play so far. His sentiments on changeability and time are reminiscent of Aias in his "deception speech", and in a different way of Oedipus at *OT* 1076 ff. His predictions of future warfare, and of the Athenian defeat of Thebes with the help of his vengeful corpse, go far beyond anything communicated by Ismene: they verge on the autonomously prophetic.

658–60 *Angry threats . . . evaporate.*: these three lines do not seem particularly apposite here. It is probable, as is held by some editors, that they have been imported from another tragedy by a reader who was reminded of them by Oedipus' talk of "threats".

668–94 *This country, guest . . . with gold harness*: the first pair of stanzas of this first purely choral song of the play are devoted to praise of Colonus, where Oedipus has now been assured of his safe haven. Some of the features are typical of praise-poetry (such as the victory odes of Pindar): the locally special divinities, the unfailing rivers, and the fertile farmlands. Here there is also, however, an emphasis on the flora and fauna (nightingales, ivy, wild fruits, narcissus, crocus), creating an appealing kind of "nature poetry" which is quite rare in ancient Greek.

675 *of the gods*: the transmitted text has the singular "god", and this is usually taken to be Dionysus. But this does not fit with the way that he is freshly introduced in the following lines, so I have adopted the small change to plural; presumably this alludes to the Eumenides, whose sacred grove was introduced in similar terms by Antigone at 16–18.

683 *two great goddesses*: this refers to Demeter and her daughter Persephone (often known simply as *Kore*, 'Girl').

687 *Cephisus*: this was one of the two main rivers near Athens, flowing to the north-west and west of the city, not much further out than Colonus. (It is now covered and channeled, and far from "unpolluted"!) The wording seems to allude to agricultural irrigation.

691–3 *The Muses . . . song and dances*: I have slightly expanded the original, which says literally, "And the Muses' choruses do not abhor it [the place]". There were many kinds of choral dance-song (*choroi*), not least tragedy. Sophocles of Colonus has, it appears, worked in a touch of self-praise.

693   *Aphrodite's golden harness*: Aphrodite is similarly associated with the river Cephisus in the song in praise of Athens at Euripides' *Medea* 835–6. Her golden harness can tie humans, no less than the birds of her conventional chariot.

695–719   *There is a thing . . . skim with ease*: the second pair of stanzas turn from Colonus to Athens and Attica as a whole. Behind them lies the mythical contest between Athena and Poseidon over who should be the city's patron god. This was eventually won by Athena, who gave the olive, over Poseidon, who gave the horse. But, rather than the competition, Sophocles emphasizes the favours granted by both gods. So the first stanza is devoted to the olive and its protection in Attica by Zeus, the second to the horse and to seafaring.

695–8   *Asian land . . . isle of Pelops*: the point is not that olives do not grow in Asia Minor or the Peloponnese (they do, of course), but that the original sacred olive grew spontaneously at Athens. Indeed, its descendant was still to be seen on the Acropolis.

699   *feared by attackers' spear*: the allusion is probably to certain sacred olive trees that were protected by the gods.

719   *Nereids*: the sea-nymph daughters of Nereus were often envisaged as gambolling alongside ships. (The text here is disputed, but the general picture is clear enough.)

738   *through kinship*: Creon was the brother of Iocasta, and hence uncle to her two sons with Oedipus. It transpires, however, that he is in effect the agent of Eteocles, the one who has seized the throne.

760   *has more . . . long ago*: this line surely does not go back to Sophocles. Thebes was not Oedipus' "nursery", since he was sent off to be exposed when three days old; even Creon could not have got away with such a distortion. It was probably added to fill out the rather elliptical previous line.

775–82   *(What is this great delight . . . foul in deed.)*: these lines seem uncharacteristically rambling, and it might be felt that the play would not suffer harm if they were not included. (Perhaps Sophocles died before he had purged them in revision!)

788   *my curse*: the Greek word, *alastor*, is something like a spirit of vengeance.

789–90   *land enough . . . no more*: Oedipus' curse on his two sons, as reflected in Aeschylus' *Seven against Thebes* for example, was that they should be granted enough earth to be buried in.

830   *what is mine*: Creon claims that he is responsible, legally speaking, for his nieces, since their father has no civic rights.

834–86   [*Lyric Dialogue Sequence*]: as Antigone is being actually manhandled, the emotional pitch reaches the point where an exchange in lyric, instead of spoken dialogue, breaks out. This is matched, after more spoken lines, by a second stanza of emotional lyric dialogue at 876–86.

848   *crutches*: the same Greek word, *skeptron*, means both a sceptre, symbol of

power, and a staff to support weak limbs. Sophocles plays on this ambiguity and the way that one sense applies to the sons of Oedipus, the other to his daughters.

862   *unless . . . to stop me!*: this line, if spoken by Creon, must be sarcastic; but it is possible that, with the alteration of just one letter, it should be spoken by the chorus, and should say ". . . is going stop you".

882   *<But Zeus knows>*: there is a small gap in the text, and this is a plausible guess at the missing words.

900–1   *two highroads to Thebes converge*: it is not clear exactly where Theseus means, but it is clearly a strategic point on the way to Thebes, perhaps the dip in the hills between Athens and Eleusis (modern Daphni)—see Map 2.

919 ff.   *And yet it is not Thebes . . .* : on the portrayal of Thebes in *OC* see pp. 218–9.

926   *without . . . your lord*: this rather pointless line might be an addition.

947–9   *Areopagus*: a hill sacred to Ares, near the Acropolis, which was the meeting-place of an ancient Athenian court. Creon uses Athenian patriotic cliché as part of his polemic.

954–5   *For anger . . . by pain*: this banal and inapposite couplet is rightly regarded as an interpolation by some editors, including the OCT.

1028–33   *You won't have . . . to a single man*: in these lines Theseus makes it clear that he is aware that Creon must have further forces in reserve, possibly corrupt Athenians; but he will make sure that these are overpowered. "You won't have anybody else to help . . ." is a rather odd way of introducing this, but not odd enough to justify the compex reordering of lines adopted in the OCT.

1044 ff.   *[Choral Song]*: instead of a messenger-speech describing the victory of Theseus' men over Creon and his forces (it is left vague whether they are Theban or treacherous Athenians), the battle is imaginatively envisaged by the chorus in this song of two pairs of stanzas. This device also has the advantage of covering the considerable period that the pursuit and battle would have taken in "real time". There are, unfortunately, several places where the text is very unsure, e.g. 1068–9, 1076–8.

1044–58   *I wish I were . . . triumphant and brave*: in the first two stanzas the chorus envisage where the clash might be happening and how the battle might be fought. In this stanza it is imagined as happening in the area of the coast around Eleusis, where the route from Athens towards Thebes first heads before turning north across the mountains (see Map 2). The topography is given an ornate dressing of high poetry. The "Pythian" location (1048–9) must refer to a shrine of Apollo, probably halfway to Eleusis near modern Daphni (see also note on 900–1). Eleusis is invoked through the celebrated Mystery rites of Demeter and Kore ("the Goddesses"). Initiates were bound to secrecy, and the cult was officiated by an Athenian priestly family; this is elaborated in the original (not translated in full) as, "on whose tongues is set the golden key of the attendant Eumolpid family".

1059–61   *the snowy high-ground*: the topography of this stanza is more debatable. The text as transmitted refers to "west of the snowy rock in the region of Oea [or Oe]". This might suggest a less obvious alternative route towards

Thebes, which would go north and then east without going down to the coast at Eleusis. But there is no reason why this should be near a landmark called "snowy". This epithet would be more appropriately used of the high pass between Attica and Boeotia at Oenoe (see Map 2), which leads me to take seriously the change of *Oiatidos* (of Oea) in 1061 to *Oinatidos*, meaning "of Oenoe". In that case they envisage a mountain skirmish at a strategic spot considerably further away from Athens and nearer to Thebes.

1070–3 *all those . . . resource*: this simplifies the more elaborate original, which says literally, "who revere the horse-goddess Athena and the marine, earth-holding, dear son of Rhea". In theogonies Rhea was the mother of Poseidon as well as Zeus, Hera, and Hades.

1081–4 *If I could only . . . the battlefield*: by wishing they could have a dove's-eye view, the chorus can diminish the time and distance that would be covered in real time and place, while also stimulating the mental vision of the audience.

1096–7 *faulty prophets*: the chorus are pleased that they (Oedipus' "watchers") have proved right in their lyric prophesying at 1075 ff.

1132 ff. *But stop! . . .* : the Greeks had a strong sense of pollution, although it was often treated as intuitive rather than objective. In this case Theseus does not dispute that he should avoid physical contact with Oedipus.

1156–9 *the altar of Poseidon*: Polynices is first introduced here as a suppliant, like Oedipus himself. And he has placed himself at an altar which is an important local cult-site, as Theseus will emphasize at 1179–80. The ethical assessment of Polynices is far from simple—see pp. 215–6.

1167 *at Argos*: this is enough to identify Polynices: Ismene had told at 373–81 how he went there in exile and set about building up alliances.

1220 *The helper*: this is not a standard title of Hades, but is, rather, a riddling way of referring to Death.

1221–2 *no tune, no dance, no wedding march*: the piled-up negatives come back in 1236–7 as well. There is similar phrasing in Antigone's farewell lament at *Antigone* 876. They might be a feature of poetic laments.

1234–5 *Resentment, killings, strife*: in the Greek there are five nouns, not three: resentment, factions, conflict, battles, and killings.

1236–8 *no friend retained*: after this the Greek adds "where all evils of evils live together", omitted for the sake of concision.

1245–8 *some . . . arctic night*: after three fairly straightforward indications of west, east, and south, the last is the more oblique: literally "from Rhipae covered in night". Rhipae was a semi-legendary mountain range in remote northern Scythia.

1249 *[SD] Polynices approaches from the 'city' direction*: it is carefully indicated that Polynices comes from the local altar of Poseidon. This was where Theseus was sacrificing before he came to the rescue at 887, and so it must lie in the unthreatening "home" direction of Athens. So Polynices comes from the opposite direction to that used by Creon. Also, the approach of Polynices, in sorrow and by himself ("without attendants", 1250), contrasts with the bold approach of Creon and his henchmen ("with an escort", 723) – see further p. 216.

Does Antigone go over and embrace her brother, or does she stay by Oedipus' side? It seems impossible to be sure which way Sophocles staged it, but the decision of staging would make a considerable difference to the emotional dynamics of the whole scene. If Antigone does stand beside Polynices then she will remain there all the time until he detaches himself from her clinging at 1432 ff., and she would probably return to Oedipus only when he calls on his daughters at 1457. If, on the other hand, she stays with her father this creates a kind of distancing of Polynices.

1268 *But Zeus has Mercy throned by him*: in reply to this appeal by Polynices to *Aidos*, ("Mercy"), Oedipus will counterclaim that Zeus has *Dike* ('Justice') sitting by him (1381–2). *Aidos* (often translated as "shame") is, at root, a sense of restraint or compunction that stops people from behaving in ways that they know are wrong: in this context "Mercy" probably best reflects this. Throughout this speech Polynices' language has been high-flown and vivid, even when sordid. Some critics consider this to be a sign of his self-indulgent fraudulence; others see it as evidence that his regret is keen and sincere. It is, at least, to his credit that he sees the state of things for himself, and that he unreservedly admits his own neglect and guilt.

1270 *though no undoing them*: the transmitted Greek text says, "though no increasing them". I find it hard to see what this is supposed to mean, and have adopted a slight emendation.

1299 *your curse*: the Greek word is " Erinys" (on the Erinyes, cf. note on 42). At this stage Polynices may be alluding to the curse on Oedipus' whole life and family, rather than his paternal curse on his sons, since he has yet to hear that. Alternatively, he is leading up to Oedipus' potential demonic power over the outcome of the war, made explicit at 1331–2. It may be that the next line, 1300, is an addition, as accepted in the OCT. It is also possible, however, that the textual problems are more complex, since the connection between Oedipus' curse in 1299 and the narrative in 1301 ff. is not at all clear.

1304 *the Peloponnese*: in the Greek this is given the circumlocution "the land of Apis", after a mythical early king.

1305 *sevenfold command*: the numeral "seven" is by itself enough to bring to the foreground the ill-fated expedition of the "Seven against Thebes". Six commanders, plus Polynices as the seventh, set themselves to attack the legendary seven-gated walls of Thebes.

1313–25 *They comprise . . . versus Thebes*: this ten-line catalogue enumerates the six allied leaders, before devoting three lines to Polynices himself. It is a kind of potted lecture on the Seven, touching on the most familiar mythical details: Amphiaraus was a prophet; Capaneus boasted about burning Thebes; Parthenopaeus was so called because his mother Atalanta had done her utmost to remain a virgin (*parthenos*), etc. Reeve has argued, mainly from some clumsiness of expression, that this whole passage is an intrusion into the Sophocles, perhaps added by an actor to swell the role. This bold conjecture seems to me very plausible: the numeral sequence is pedantically laboured, and the catalogue is easily detachable. This is an issue of considerable consequence for the interpretation of Polynices. If the lines are authentic they portray him as a conceited power-broker, insensitive to Oedipus' situation: for why should Oedipus give damn about these alien military leaders? If the lines are added, however, then Polynices' plea remains much more personal and, arguably, more honest.

1342　*establish you in your own house*: is this a lie? Creon had no intention, of course, of taking the polluted Oedipus back to Thebes: but is Polynices equally duplicitous? When Ismene reported the determination to keep Oedipus out of the city at 396 ff., she specified Creon and the Thebans. Polynices' sincerity may, then, remain an open question. Oedipus does not, however, recognize any mitigating considerations.

1370　*the god*: Oedipus does not say which god (the Greek has *daimon*, which is not specific), but he presumably implies that it is his avenging Erinys, which is a superhuman power, supported by the sanction of Zeus.

1381–2　*if venerable Justice takes her seat*: Oedipus sets up *Dike* in direct opposition to Polynices' appeal to *Aidos*—see note on 1268.

1389–90　*Tartarus*: thought of as the punitive "dungeon" of the underworld. (I have omitted the epithet "paternal" which the Greek text gives it here, since I can make no sense of it.)

1410　*proper funeral rites*: the story of how Antigone chose death in order to give Polynices proper burial was immortalized in Sophocles' own earlier *Antigone*—indeed, it is likely that he invented the story. The play was such a huge success that he is able to allude to it and take it for granted that the irony would not be lost. In a sense he, the playwright, is responsible for granting Antigone her double "praise" (1411), both as the companion of Oedipus in exile and as the champion of her brother to the death.

1414–46　*I beg you, Polynices . . .* : in the dialogue that follows the workings of double motivation (see p. 7) are particularly clear; it may be influenced by a similar situation, on a greater scale, with Eteocles in Aeschylus' *Seven against Thebes*. Polynices is doomed to death by the supernatural power of Oedipus' curse; at the same time he is determined to go and fight at Thebes of his own volition. He has an understandable motive, because he feels he cannot let down the allied expedition that he has started.

1418–19　*lead these men again . . . fright?*: Polynices' argument here is particularly weak: since he is doomed to die, there can be no future opportunities. He seems to betray a forlorn hope that Oedipus' curse might not actually be fulfilled (cf. "that rests with the god . . ." in 1443–4).

1434　*avenging demons*: in the Greek, Oedipus' Erinyes.

1447　ff. [*Choral Song*]: the unusual context produces unusual technique: in between each of the four stanzas of choral lyric there are five spoken lines, in the pattern Oedipus (2), Antigone (1), Oedipus (2). The first stanza embarks on the usual kind of choral conceptualizing, but as soon as thunder begins to sound (see note on 1456), the song changes to matter closely consequential on the immediate situation.

1456　[*SD*] (*thunder*): suddenly, with no warning, there is thunder; the noise is not (of course) marked by a stage-direction in the Greek text (see p. xxxii). We do not know whether a special thunder-machine had been developed this early in the history of the Greek theatre, but clearly there must have been some sort of sound-effect. It is repeated several times in the following scene. Oedipus recognizes it straightaway as the promised signal that his end is near, as predicted back at 94–5.

1492–3 *in that recess*: the text is unfortunately corrupt, but it seems to refer to a vale where the local Colonus altar of Poseidon was located.

1534 *soldiers sown from teeth*: this alludes to the myth that when Cadmus founded Thebes he sowed the teeth of the dragon he killed, and that the Theban warrior-elite were descended from the five survivors of the warriors that grew from these. The following lines insist that Thebes, although friendly at this mythical time, may turn hostile, as expounded at 607 ff. (see note).

1547–8 *Hermes . . . leading me*: Hermes *psychopompos* escorted newly dead souls to the underworld, whose goddess was Persephone, wife of Hades.

1555 *[SD] Oedipus makes his way off . . . Theseus and his attendants*: where within the stage-space does this extraordinary procession go as it follows behind Oedipus' lead? If it were to depart by one of the side-entrances it would have be the one in the direction of Athens, since this is a deeply Athenian event. But it would, in my opinion, be much more effective for it to depart into the sacred grove which forms the background to the setting. This would then be the first time in the entire play that this route has been taken (though Oedipus and Antigone probably hid there—see note on 114–16). This sacred "path" will lead, as is narrated by messenger at 1586 ff., to various special and numinous locations on the way to the mysterious disappearance of Oedipus. Some scholars have objected to this staging because so much has been said in the early scenes of the play about the grove being ground that should be untrodden by any human foot. But that then becomes part of the point about the supernatural strangeness of Oedipus' departure: this not a chosen route, but one he is led on by the gods, as he fully expounds in lines 1544–8. All those who follow him into the sacred grove also have a kind of special dispensation because they are with him.

1556–60 *Goddess . . . Aidoneus*: the chorus invoke Persephone and Hades, who is here given the rarer alternative name "Aidoneus" (duplicated in the invocatory Greek).

1564 *dead lie hid*: the Greek has in addition, "and the Stygian home", derived from the underworld river, Styx.

1568–78 *Goddesses . . . to you I pray*: the invocations in this second stanza are not easy to disentangle. First, it is not obvious what goddesses are meant here at the beginning—maybe the Erinyes. There is then a surprisingly elaborate invocation of Cerberus, the guard-dog who allowed only the new dead in through the doors of Hades, and would let none out. After that, in 1574–8, it is something of an enigma which underworld god is being called on. He is addressed as son of Earth and Tartarus (so it is not Hades), and as "the eversleep" (here "long Sleep): the answer may be simply Thanatos, Death.

1590–7 *Well, when he came . . . took his seat*: these lines specify a whole series of landmarks, giving the impression that they were familiar, even though we know of no reference to them anywhere else, except for the cleft in the earth with bronze steps, already been singled out by the local man at 56–8. The "basin" is a memorial to Peirithous and Theseus, who went down to Hades together: this emphasizes Theseus' reputation for reliability. The epithet "Thorician", used of a certain rock in 1595, is obscure and may be corrupted. I do not consider it by any means inconceivable that these numinous-sounding spots (and even the hill of Demeter at 1600–1) were fictions created to lend appropriate atmosphere for this mythopoeic occasion.

1603   *customary robes*: this must mean that, while still alive, Oedipus was clothed in the white robes that were traditionally put on corpses before burial.

1606   *Zeus beneath the earth*: this epithet (*Zeus Chthonios*) is occasionally used of Hades, brother of the Zeus above on Olympus. Here it may prepare for the way that Oedipus' passing is somehow shared between the two, cf. 1653–62.

1615–18   *one small word*: this word is *philein*, "to love". It is tempting to nudge these beautiful lines towards some universal doctrine of the redemptive power of Love, but, in context the sentiment is strictly personal. (A possible change of one letter, from *taut'* to *tout'*, would slightly shift the sense to "but there's this one small word / redeems all of the sufferings".)

1626   *because . . . called out to him*: I agree with those who think that this rather heavy line is a histrionic addition: the call is supposed to be urgent!

1654–5   *we saw him . . . both at one time*: the Greeks directed their worship either down towards the powers of earth and underworld or upwards towards the canonical gods. So this simultaneous combination is indicative of the exceptional mystery of Oedipus' end.

1670–1750   [*Scene 10—Lyric Dialogue*]: the first two stanzas (1670–1723) of this extended lamentation are dominated by Antigone, with contributions from Ismene and the chorus. The briefer second pair (1724–50) is made up entirely of short interchanges, between the two sisters in the first, and between the chorus and Antigone in the second.

1718–19   [. . .]: we can tell from the matching stanza that a couple of lines are missing here from Ismene's contribution.

1733   [. . .]: two short phrases are missing.

1751 ff.   [*Scene 11*]: the closing lines of the play are, as is usual, in the more dynamic anapaests, whether spoken or chanted.

1766   *our god here*: probably Poseidon, or possibly the hero Colonus.

1779   [SD] *Antigone and Ismene . . . depart in the 'foreign' direction, towards Thebes*: while it is not unthinkable that Sophocles had them all depart in the direction of Athens, with the notion that the girls would go to Thebes in the future, it is much more likely that they head off immediately in the "foreign" direction. The return of the daughters to "home" has already been raised in 1741 ff., and with her last words Antigone refers directly to the imminent battle between her two brothers. This inevitably recalls her agreement to the plea of Polynices that he should be properly buried (see note on 1410). This imparts a rather bitter twist to this closing scene: Theseus, in doing what he supposes will "benefit" Antigone, is actually helping her to the fatal events of her own tragedy, *Antigone*. Oedipus had himself made Theseus promise that he would always do what was best for them (as reported at 1631–7). So even Oedipus, for all the redemptive wonder of his ending, cannot foresee that, through the fallible enactment of this request, he will be sending his beloved Antigone to her death. This final irony casts something of a dark shadow across what might otherwise seem to be a purely silver-lining conclusion to Oedipus' life—see further pp. 216–7.